□
The Context of
Pastoral Counseling

THE CONTEXT OF PASTORAL COUNSELING

Seward Hiltner and Lowell G. Colston

ABINGDON PRESS

NEW YORK • NASHVILLE

THE CONTEXT OF PASTORAL COUNSELING

Copyright © 1961 by Abingdon Press

Library of Congress Catalog Card Number: 61-13193

SET UP, PRINTED, AND BOUND BY THE
PARTHENON PRESS, AT NASHVILLE,
TENNESSEE, UNITED STATES OF AMERICA

☐
This book is appreciatively and
affectionately dedicated to:

RAY FREEMAN JENNEY
Pastor emeritus of Bryn Mawr Community Church, Chicago, Ill.

ELIZABETH MUSSER

JOHN M. MUSSER
Directors of the General Service Foundation, St. Paul, Minn.

CARL R. ROGERS
Professor of psychology and psychiatry, The University of Wisconsin; and formerly professor of psychology and executive secretary of the Counseling Center, The University of Chicago

Foreword

◻ The minister has several functions but only one task. His functions include preaching, counseling, teaching, evangelizing, conducting worship, and leading the social outreach of church into world. His one central task, however, is bringing men into conscious acknowledgment of their dependence upon Jesus Christ as Lord and Savior and aiding them, in that faith, to live still imperfect but Christian lives.

Among the functions, and as a basic part of the central task, counseling has been more and more acknowledged in recent years. Its intent is nothing new in Christian history, but is part of the "shepherding" of the Bible. But our modern psychological and analytical study of *how* to help people when they need and want that help has brought wisdom we did not have before. Our fundamental aims have not changed, but thanks to the study of personality in the modern world, there are rich resources to add to those of our tradition if we know how to use them to Christian ends.

Our book does not advocate counseling as *the* modern method of ministry. Indeed, it hardly advocates counseling at all. If the minister shares our conception of ministry he can hardly avoid doing some counseling, but at the same time he cannot make counseling more than a part of his ministry. If he feels, on the other hand, that counseling is not for him, then our account, while it may lure, is guaranteed not to club him. For our part we do not see how a minister, unless locked in somewhere, can avoid some counseling. We want to help him do it better, not necessarily to do more of it. If counseling is just an American fad it should die. If it is instead, as we believe, a way of approaching one aspect of the traditional work of the minister with new tools and resources, then we believe it deserves new attention.

7

Our book may be rightly considered as one in a long line of ground-breaking modern works on pastoral care and counseling, in the line of John G. McKenzie, Charles T. Holman, Richard C. Cabot and Russell L. Dicks, Anton T. Boisen, Paul E. Johnson, Wayne E. Oates, Carroll A. Wise, and many others.[1] Yet we believe it stands, even in this company, unique, for while it, like its predecessors, is written directly for the practical use of the busy and working pastor, it brings research findings to bear upon this task. No other modern work on pastoral counseling has taken its data entirely from electronically recorded pastoral interviews and from the best psychological personality tests. We are cautious in making claims for what our research findings prove. But they prove at least that systematic research can be done with the best modern techniques and tools without injuring the pastor-parishioner relationship and that study of this kind has immense and even immediate practical value.

The first sentences of our text tell precisely what our book is and is not. It has been written for the pastor, as a working tool.

We have written this volume together, and the use of "we," "our," and "us" should therefore be taken literally. However, there are some points where the references must be individual, to either Hiltner or Colston. There we have chosen the convention of putting the material in the third person.

We want to note here our debt and our gratitude to the four persons to whom the volume is dedicated and to our parishioners and clients who made the data available to us freely in the hope that their experience might help other people. The latter, of course, are anonymous. In our book their names are all fictitious, but their lives, and their counseling, are not. To them we are immensely grateful.

When our study was made, Ray Freeman Jenney was senior minister of the Bryn Mawr Community Church of Chicago. Tribute to some of his wisdom in helping us with this study in his church is contained in the text.

John and Elizabeth Musser, among the directors of the General Service Foundation, had the vision without which our study would never have been conceived. Having recommended that the Foundation make us a grant, administered by the University of Chicago, they demonstrated that most helpful of all characteristics of foundation directors, namely, letting us alone. They received reports, but what we did in study and reports was at all times up to us.

It was the pioneering research of Carl R. Rogers in counseling upon which our study drew unceasingly, and it was his personal encouragement in the planning stage of our project that determined us to go ahead. As we are sure he would like us to say, it was his colleagues too who stood with us in every stage of our study. Yet without his specific help and his imagination that collected the colleagues, nothing reported here would have been possible.

The blessings of our research life would have been much less without the service and help of many other persons. The brevity of our mention is no indication of the warmth of our appreciation. John M. Shlien and Desmond Cartwright, faculty staff members of the counseling center at the time of our study, helped us to develop the research design and to select the testing instruments. Lois Illingworth, then one of the ministers of Bryn Mawr Community Church, also helped with the research design. The tests were administered by Richard Robertson and Mary Lou Bridges, then graduate students in psychology, and were analyzed by Rosalind Dymond Cartwright, then a faculty staff member at the counseling center, and by Harold Boris, then a research associate in the department of Human Development of the University of Chicago. Assignment of clients at the center was done by Hellene Sarett, Charlotte Ellinwood, and Richard Jenney, all of the center's staff. The laborious transcription of the interviews was done by Kathryn Atwater and Frances I. Colston. The psychiatric adviser to the counseling center was Melvin D. Nudelman, M.D.

We are indebted to Dr. Henry K. Shaw, librarian of Christian Theological Seminary; Janet Wiatt; and Janet Farrior for invaluable assistance in the preparation of the index.

Frances Colston is thanked by both authors for her magnificent typing of manuscript as well as interviews, and by one author for the unflagging energy with which she has supported many revisions.

The senior author wishes also to express appreciation to President Arthur R. McKay and the faculty of McCormick Theological Seminary, where part of the material of this book was presented as the Weyerhaeuser Lectures during March, 1961.

SEWARD HILTNER and LOWELL G. COLSTON

9

Contents

11

◻

Chapter 1

THE PASTOR AS COUNSELOR

☐ This book is designed primarily for the working pastor. It contains types of data never available to Hiltner before, and yet it continues the exploration of pastoral care and counseling set forth in his four previous works on this topic.[1] Like the earlier books, it expresses his conviction that what the pastor needs to help him on pastoral care and counseling is, as it was put in *Pastoral Counseling*, both "concrete, practical facts" and "fundamental theory" and a discussion that shows the relationship between the two.[2] What is unprecedented about this book is the precision of the concrete data. Every bit of pastor-parishioner dialogue in this book was taken from electronic recordings, made with the full consent of the parishioners and used with their approval.

The cardinal aim of the volume is, therefore, to help the minister with his daily task of helping other people, under God, to help themselves. At the same time, this is the report of the first comparative study of pastoral counseling in relation to counseling by other counselors. Barring personal limitations, we believe we have reported herein everything that the canons of personality science require of such reports. We are hopeful, as a result, that the findings may be of interest to psychiatrists, clinical psychologists, social workers, vocational counselors, educational counselors, and others who engage in counseling as part of their professional work.

Learning Pastoral Counseling

If the young minister or theological student is going to learn how to counsel in his role as pastor, what is it he should learn? Over and above his general theological education, does he need to put his attention on any matters that may be relatively less important to other counselors? Granted further that he will make discriminating

13

use in counseling, as in all other aspects of his ministry, of the uniquely religious resources that he represents, are there points other than these resources that he must examine in order to be effective as a *pastoral* counselor? Or could he just as well take his theological education in one place, then go have his training in counseling at another place—in a department of psychology, school of education, or school of social work, for example—and be just as well equipped as if his training in counseling had somehow been integrated with his theological study?

Let us consider what might happen with the split method of study, in the case of John Cuddison, who will become in his mid-thirties John Satterthwait Cuddison. Let us suppose that Cuddison, intrigued by the idea of a counseling aspect to his ministry, tries to enroll in a good course on counseling in a department of psychology or education. Suppose further that he is admitted and that the course has excellent instruction and includes eventually Cuddison's doing some counseling under close supervision. Under those conditions, and if sufficient time is allowed, Cuddison learns a good deal about the very principles we shall be enunciating in this and the next two chapters. He learns very crucial things about the counseling process, about his own strengths and blind spots in carrying it out, and about the inner dynamics of people that are revealed in a counseling relationship. All this is to the good. However acquired, such knowledge is needed by every pastor.

Having completed his course on counseling and his theological study, independently, our student becomes the Rev. John Cuddison and goes to his first church. If, during his first month, Mrs. Bridgeton comes to him and says, "I want several counseling sessions with you, to explore my tendency to fly off the handle at my husband," Cuddison should be equipped to help her. But suppose nobody comes with such a request? Pastor Cuddison will be prone to conclude that his people are not ready for counseling—even though he may already have conducted two funerals, married one young couple, called on several sick parishioners at the local hospital, helped a father to have his teen-age son put on probation instead of sent to the reformatory, and so on. What Pastor Cuddison may be most unprepared for is the fact that as much as 90 per cent of his personal and pastoral work will not begin as a formally defined counseling relationship, and that, even when counseling is needed to follow up a relationship begun in more

14

casual ways, a large part of his job is helping the person to come to the point of readiness for the counseling.[3] Of course Pastor Cuddison may be natively shrewd enough to put two and two together for himself. But if his training in counseling has been equivalent to the pure laboratory, even when he makes the transition to the actualities of parish life he may somehow feel that what he is doing is impure, inferior, and mixed. His danger then is of being interested, absorbed, and helpful in the relatively few instances of formal counseling, but frustrated, inattentive, and insecure in the many more situations where the formal counseling conditions do not prevail.

Hiltner's first teaching of pastoral counseling had been with students in clinical pastoral training, the movement that has done so much to stimulate study of this kind.[4] There we had had the students full time for a considerable period. Hiltner's initial attempt to teach pastoral counseling formally in a theological school, without all the time and supporting apparatus available in a clinical setting, came at Union Theological Seminary in New York nearly twenty years ago. Harry Bone, a clinical and consulting psychologist, now a faculty member of the William Alanson White School of Psychiatry, and he had been asked to work out a course on pastoral counseling. Although most of their students were engaged in field work in churches, Hiltner and Bone could not ask them to bring back samples of formal pastoral counseling, because in their youth and inexperience few of them were engaged in such situations. What they did ask was that the students write up reports of any kind of contacts with people in which they engaged in their professional role.[5] To even Hiltner's and Bone's amazement, study of these reports taught far more about pastoral counseling than they had anticipated. They themselves had to examine the great variety of interpersonal relationships in which the pastor normally engages more carefully than before, and they discovered that a combined psychodynamic and pastoral analysis of these was fully as significant as the exploration of formal counseling situations.

Out of this and related experiences came Hiltner's decision, in writing Pastoral Counseling, to use very few "pure" or "laboratory-type" pastoral counseling situations, and instead to use reports of contacts just as they come daily to the local minister. Serious attention was focused on "precounseling pastoral work," as it was called, as well

15

as upon counseling in the formal sense. Above all, what Hiltner wanted to demonstrate was that pastoral counseling, important as it is when fully under way in a formal sense, must pay equal attention to all the types of contacts that precede its initiation and that study of these other relationships is absolutely essential to the understanding of pastoral counseling.

This part of Hiltner's earlier thesis seems to have been generally accepted in the ensuing years. Yet he has been haunted by the crudity and imprecision of the data on which the conviction has rested. Was there some way in which a beginning could be made in testing it out? For instance, could one group of theological students be taught counseling in a pastoral setting, and another group in another setting, and their subsequent performance contrasted? This would still be a valuable study, which it is hoped someone will undertake; but it proved impossible for Hiltner for practical reasons.

During the 1950's Hiltner's thoughts turned more and more to "context" as the best general term to indicate all the types of differences between counseling by the pastor and counseling by other professional persons. Within the limitations of a demanding teaching schedule, could some kind of initial research be done on the context of pastoral counseling? Whether such a project dealt directly with the learning of pastoral counseling or not, its findings would either corroborate or correct our assumptions and hunches about what the young minister ought to pay attention to while he is learning pastoral counseling.

That was the general state of Hiltner's thinking at the time a fortuitous set of circumstances brought together Lowell G. Colston, the University of Chicago Counseling Center, the Bryn Mawr Community Church in Chicago, and the General Service Foundation of St. Paul, Minnesota.

Relevance of the Study

The essence of our research plan was to have the same person act as counselor in two settings and to compare and contrast the processes and results of the counseling. In scientific language, Lowell G. Colston was to be the "independent variable" of our study. That is, he was to be the same person carrying out the same type of counseling in two settings. The "dependent variables" were to begin with the

16

two different settings and extend to whatever should be found consequent upon or related to those settings that affected either process or outcome of the counseling.

The general idea of this basic plank in our design is simple to grasp—same counselor, two settings. Working it out in practice, however, required both good fortune and considerable ingenuity, to say nothing of the help of many people. First, Lowell Colston had to be fully established as a qualified counselor at the University of Chicago Counseling Center. Fortunately this happened to be true, and he was an intern at the center. Second, he had to be fully established in the eyes of the people as a pastor in a local church. Fortunately, this was brought about in extraordinarily able fashion by the senior minister of the Bryn Mawr Community Church, then Ray Freeman Jenney, with the full co-operation of his board.

Third, the actual counseling interviews had to be preserved in as full and natural a form as possible. At the counseling center electronic recording machines were standard practice and there was no problem. We wanted also to use them at the church; but since we were not, at the church, wearing the golden aura of science, we feared they might be an unwelcome and even impossible intrusion into the pastor-parishioner relationship. To our surprise and pleasure, such a fear proved groundless. The majority of the persons counseled at the church responded with as much enthusiasm as at the center to the possibility that their own experience might eventually be of help to pastors counseling other people. Service was at least as important a motive as science in solving this part of our research design.

From the beginning of the planning, it was recognized that the collected, selected, and contrasted case materials would undoubtedly be the most important results of the study, and of clearest relevance to the pastor. But we wanted, fourth, to use whatever scientific tools were available to compare and contrast findings from the two settings. To date the largest amount of research of this kind anywhere in the world has been carried out at the University of Chicago Counseling Center, which was founded by Carl R. Rogers and was still, at the time these data were collected, under his directorship.[6] He and his colleagues gave their full co-operation, without which this aspect of our study would have been wholly impossible, since neither

17

of us is technically equipped to interpret such tests. The interpretation of tests, before and after counseling, was carried out by clinical psychologists, as indicated in detail later on in this volume.

Fifth, funds were needed for the study. These funds were primarily to free Colston for a period of two years to devote full time to the project. Relatively small amounts of money were also needed, however, for the testing services of the clinical psychologists, for recording equipment and transcriptions, and for similar items. All the supervisory, co-operating, and consultative services were rendered free of charge, by Seward Hiltner, Carl R. Rogers and his colleagues, Ray Freeman Jenney and his colleagues, and many outside advisers.

The needed funds were generously supplied by the General Service Foundation. Two of its directors, John and Elizabeth Musser, had long been interested in encouraging some formal study that would begin to test the validity and relevance of pastoral counseling. At their suggestion, the foundation had already supported a pilot study toward this end carried out under the auspices of the National Council of Churches' Department of Pastoral Services.[7] The department and the Mussers, however, both felt that further study could be carried out better in the type of setting we had available in and near the University of Chicago. Accordingly, funds were requested and received. On our request, the amount originally pledged was slightly augmented later on as an opportunity was discovered that had not at first occurred to us. During the latter part of the period of study, the Bryn Mawr Community Church, grateful for what it felt was the service being rendered to the church in connection with the study, made a contribution to the budget.

The counseling, the testing, and, of course, the recording of the interviews began in 1956. Counseling for purposes of the study took place for three or four months beyond the initial year. Most of the remaining time was spent in studying and putting together the data and getting together the outlines of this report and book. Persons who wanted and needed counseling beyond our period of data collection were of course continued. During 1958 Colston wrote the first draft of this volume, which was gone over chapter by chapter by Hiltner. In the intervening years we have worked on the manuscript revisions.

It is especially important for the reader to understand two things about the counseling rendered at the church. First, counseling service was given as requested and as time and circumstance permitted, regardless of whether the person agreed to participate in our research project or not. The majority of the persons did so agree, although not all who agreed could be taken for research. Others who received counseling but demurred on participation in the research—especially men who had come early—almost all expressed later regret that they had not. Second, even though all persons were told that we were prepared to counsel with them according to their conception of its helpfulness, up to twenty interviews without further arrangement (this brought the originally arranged time period equal to that of the project at the counseling center already geared to the same number of hours), we made it clear that it might continue longer as desired and needed.[8]

A follow-up interview, which we tried to space six months after the close of counseling, was held in all the cases where it proved possible. Tests were given before counseling began, although after an exploratory interview in which the person agreed to enter upon counseling, again after the close of the counseling, or after twenty interviews in the cases where counseling exceeded that number, and where possible at the time of the follow-up interview.

Thus, so far as ingenuity and good fortune could provide, the pastoral counseling in which we engaged at the church was as much like that of the ordinary pastor in the ordinary church as could be managed consistent with our research purposes. This is very different from saying that the overall experience was typical of the workday of the ordinary pastor. No pastor has to listen carefully to playbacks of all his counseling sessions, an exercise guaranteed to waver between the induction of humility and boredom. Nor does he have to select, transcribe, collate, and think systematically about what he has been doing—to the tune of at least six hours of follow-up to every hour of counseling.

Nor does the ordinary pastor operate in a church of 2,500 members, with several full-time colleagues who agree to let him devote his time wholly to the counseling, apart from such other activities as are needed to establish him in the eyes of the congregation as one of the ministers of the church. We had toyed with the idea of taking a small church for this project, but realism showed that the time-consuming

19

process of collecting and sifting data would either have wrecked the project or done injustice to the church. We were, then, fully in the role of the pastor within the church setting. It was above all else our schedule, however, that was most radically different from that of most clergy.

The way of the serious researcher, we know now if we did not before, is hard and narrow and mostly alone. Yet only if a beginning can be made, in such fashion as by this study, can we utilize the tools made available by modern personality science to increase our knowledge, our skill, our capacity for self-criticism, and our service through pastoral counseling.

Since Lowell G. Colston was the key counselor and pastor in the study, the reader may wonder what Hiltner had to do with it apart from general supervision and consideration of the findings. At the counseling center he had no specific function. Although he had for some time been accorded the title of a courtesy staff member there, all the needed functions for the study were performed adequately there by Colston, Carl R. Rogers, the clinical psychologists who did our testing, the psychiatric consultant, and other staff members. At the church Hiltner was a kind of "front man." Even before the study began, he was reasonably well known to many members of Bryn Mawr Church through having preached and conducted classes there and from having advised the ministers of the church from time to time on various pastoral problems. Both Colston and Hiltner were named "special ministers" of the church, which seemed satisfactorily to place them before the congregation as genuine ministers but ministers not to be called up to pinch-hit for the speaker who failed to arrive for the young people's meeting.

A considerable number of persons at the church asked to talk personally with Hiltner. In all such instances he did talk at least once with such persons. When further counseling was wanted and needed, virtually all such instances saw successful transfer to Colston. A few of the persons wanted only one session with Hiltner and were not pressed to do anything further. His being known in the church and his having written along these lines may have given an extra aura to the project in the eyes of some of the people. This was considered in advance, and no reason was seen why it would impede the purposes of the study. We do not believe it did so.

20

The Hypothesis

As has been suggested, we felt the most lasting contribution of the study would be reporting, selecting, and presenting in comparative fashion actual data from the counseling itself. And so we conclude in retrospect. In our judgment, every case report or counseling sketch contains at least some useful and practical wisdom not contained in any of the others. The generalizations and inferences and the analysis of the test findings cannot possibly take the place of the reader's examination of the case material.

The practical usefulness of the study, as we see it, depends more on the reader's willingness to take the data—and accept or correct the interpretation of them—than upon our having proved a particular point. Yet we did have such a point from the beginning in the form of a hypothesis. In scientific work a hypothesis is a question but it is also more than a question. It is a tentative and preliminary—but well-informed—hunch about what the answer may turn out to be. The question is then asked in such form that this potential answer to it may be proved correct or incorrect. A hypothesis fosters open-mindedness, but of a pointed kind. It avoids the danger of simply trying to study all about something. In scientific history many important results have been achieved by exploration that showed some hypotheses to be wrong.

The hypothesis in this case was that people seeking counseling help from a pastor, when other conditions are approximately equal, will tend to progress slightly farther and faster in the same amount of time than they will in another setting, like that of a university counseling center. If this were read as a pre-formed conclusion, rather than as a hypothesis, it might indeed sound arrogant. We felt that having this as a hypothesis would help to sharpen our inquiry, since the idea of context, important and useful as we believe it to be, may easily become amorphous.

Our general experience had given us some prior reason to believe that the hypothesis, whether it panned out or not, was legitimate and important as hypothesis. Many persons still look upon the clergy in general as rigid, removed, in the clouds, or authoritarian. When someone finds instead that a particular clergyman is none of these things, but rather is understanding and accepting, then whatever

21

has brought the person to the pastor in the first place combines with the new realization of this pastor's qualities and the result is a kind of double-barrel.

A person knows that a minister stands for something and represents something, whether his perception of what this is turns out to be correct or not. If part of what the minister stands for and represents is a kind of understanding that accepts each person initially just where he is, then the kind of hiatus that so often exists between an ideal and actuality may theoretically be bridged much better with the help of a minister than by many other helpers.

We do not of course mean to imply that other counselors stand for or represent nothing. Indeed, our hunch is that a contextual study of any group of counselors would turn up previously unrecognized assets and liabilities that inhere in what the group is felt to stand for and to represent. This study is about pastors, however, and this hunch and hypothesis are about them.

As the conclusions will suggest in more detail, we ourselves were surprised by the extent to which the data lent support to the hypothesis. This is especially startling in the results of the tests, so surprising indeed that some scientific minds may be inclined to doubt the competence of our psychometrists. On the contrary, we know that better qualified testers would be exceedingly hard to find. We cannot help feeling gratified that our hypothesis, if far from proved, at least gets some support from this study. Anyone from now on who says that counseling is inherently foreign to the minister's task must at least come to terms with our data. On the other hand, the partial support given to our hypothesis by the findings is considerably less important, in our own judgment, than our having secured and presented concrete data of the kind we have, and perhaps even more for having shown how study of this kind can be done without violating the essentials of the pastor-parishioner relationship.

How to Read This Book

This book is designed to maximize the practical usefulness of the material to the active pastor. Following this introduction, it discusses the problem of context in pastoral counseling, what this idea means, why it is important, and how to think usefully about it. We then present our own basic theory of pastoral counseling in summary form, so that the reader may make any allowances he likes if he disagrees with part or all of our assumptions and convictions. After that we present several cases at length: Two that were representative, two that were highly successful in outcome, and two that were failures. The test data and interpretations are then given, followed by an attempt to evaluate all the data of the study, especially the cases themselves, as they shed light on the pastor's understanding of context in counseling.

Appendix A is a brief formal reference guide to all the persons in the study. Appendix B presents, in briefer form than the six cases in the main text, essential data on the other nineteen persons participating in the study.

We believe the pastor will do best to read the book straight through. Since we do not want to give him casuistic indigestion, perhaps he had best leave an interval before reading the additional cases in the appendix. Their inclusion is, we believe, not only evidence of our scientific stewardship but also, in each case, proof of some important discovery bearing upon pastoral counseling.

Chapter 2

THE PROBLEM OF CONTEXT

□ Professional counselors on personal problems may be physicians, psychologists, social workers, educators, vocational specialists, experts on marriage, personnel workers—or they may be clergymen. If they are clergy, what difference does it make to the counseling if any? Does the counseling proceed more or less rapidly? Does it tend to be more or less successful? Does it get more or less deeply into the interior life?

From the time "counseling" began to be used in relation to the work of the pastor, about a generation ago, this question has been close to the forefront of discussion.[1] Any pastor who takes seriously the counseling aspect of his ministry is compelled to speak to it. He may pose the question in various ways. For example, he may ask, What is unique about my counseling as a pastor? Or again, What are my distinctive resources? Or, What do I have that the other fellows do not? All such forms of the question lead eventually to the problem of context in counseling.

Pastoral Counseling Is Still Counseling

Our way of posing this question makes one basic assumption that should be made clear at the outset. This is that, whatever may be different about pastoral counseling, something about it is fundamentally similar to or identical with counseling as done by other professional persons. In a rough and ready way, we assume that the processes involved in counseling, at the level of interpersonal relationships, are the same. In the words used by Hiltner in previous writings, all counseling proceeds through accepting, understanding, and clarifying inner conflicts.[2] All personal counseling involves the process of creating and maintaining a justified sense of trust by the other upon the coun-

24

selor so that he can eventually tell the counselor that which he has not been able to tell himself. The counseling process may be examined from the point of view of the attitude and understanding of the counselor, from that of movement within the other person, and from the perspective of the changing character of the relationship between them. From any of these points of view, we contend, there is an identity in fundamental principles between counseling by the pastor and counseling by other workers.

It was, indeed, an emerging conviction of this kind, a generation ago, that caused "counseling" to enter the pastoral vocabulary. If the pastor, in helping people, had been able to rely wholly and completely upon principles and rules that bore no relationship to the principles and rules used by other professional helpers, then the very idea of "pastoral counseling" would have been an anomaly. Recognition of some basic kinship, therefore, is at the root of the idea of pastoral counseling.[3]

Without attempting at this point to present the full argument for having, in this fashion, a pastoral counseling at all, we may nevertheless note briefly the history of the modern movement for personal counseling, which in itself is a strong argument for our position.

No one of the professions that now attempts to carry out, as a part of its professional work, personal counseling arrived at this after a self-conscious decision to do personal counseling. Every such profession, instead, stumbled upon personal counseling while exploring something else. Look, for example, at the broad outlines by which vocational or occupational counseling developed.[4] As seen at the beginning, the problem was to help a person get the right job. The first approach was hortatory: Some jobs are more socially useful than others; so do one of those if you can. Then came tests of abilities, out of which arose this approach: Do this rather than that because you can do it better. In the third stage tests of interest and personality were added to those of ability, so that the approach became: All things considered, you will probably get along better by doing this kind of thing rather than that.

No one realized more quickly or surely than these testers that their conclusions might be fallible. Even if the test results were certain, which they never are, ability and even interest—as so measured— might overlook deeper aspects of the personality. Whatever validity

25

might lie in the test results, at least their relevance must be established and corrected by reference to the person. This led, in effect, to counseling. So the vocational expert listened. Even if tests showed a young man to have great talent for mathematics and physics, a scientific or engineering career for him might be the road to failure if this symbolized for him an unexamined conformity to or rebellion against his father. So the vocational "guide," while amassing immensely important technical data, nevertheless found that the most crucial and dynamic aspects of his guiding always transcended the purely technical matters. He thus came upon vocational counseling, in which some such statement of principles as we have used—accepting, understanding, clarifying—became central to his work. No matter what his unique technical skills, without the counseling process they could not be fully relevant to highly individualized and complex human beings. Thus his counseling emerged as a by-product of his attempt to perform his vocational guidance function. He did not set out to become a personal counselor.

Although there are variations among the different professions, each of them came to personal counseling in similar and derivative fashion. Each set out to help the human being in some problem area—health, occupation, job, finance, et cetera—and each found eventually that, over and above his technical knowledge in that area, he had to learn and pursue something else as well.[5] Of recent years this something else—the counseling—has become recognized increasingly as similar or identical in its processes. Thus there is a growing conviction that the processes of counseling are a professional village green.

It is the purpose of this volume and of the study upon which it is based to explore the differences that appear in the context in which pastoral counseling takes place. We have not attempted a systematic study of the ways in which pastoral counseling is procedurally similar to other counseling. Yet if we fail to acknowledge, at the beginning, our conviction and assumption about the similarity, the reader might get the impression that everything about pastoral counseling is different from other counseling. It seems clear to us that this is not true. Like other professional persons who do counseling, we pastors also came upon it more by accident than design. Open acknowledgment of these facts seems to us more likely to aid in discovery of the distinctive features than if the similarities are underplayed.

26

As we understand counseling, the term is never properly used for a professional person without the presence of a descriptive adjective. Part of the meaning of this is that counseling as such is not a profession. Instead, counseling is an activity or type of helping relationship carried out by several professions, but always in the context of what is unique or distinctive about each profession. Even if unstated, some realm of expert knowledge beyond the counseling processes themselves is always presupposed of a professional person engaged in counseling.

Thus there are vocational counselors, educational counselors, marriage counselors, health counselors, psychological counselors, and pastoral counselors. Even though not all such terms are precisely co-ordinate with one another, nevertheless the adjectives all indicate: (1) a special area of expertness brought to the relationship, along with knowledge and skill about the "village-green" dimensions of counseling; (2) at least a tacit acknowledgment that the person seeking help is likely to come to the counselor through having a presented problem presumed to relate to the realm of special expertness; (3) the special area of expertness is to be related to the "total-person" needs of him who is seeking help, or else it is to be assumed that another kind of helper or counselor may be better able to give assistance.

Long before our present study, common sense had suggested various ways in which pastoral counseling may be seen as different from other counseling.[6] The pastor represents a concerned religious community and what it stands for.[7] This fact means something in particular to the pastor and something in particular to the person seeking help, even though the two meanings may not be the same. Further, the pastor presumably may call upon uniquely religious resources when they are relevant. All these differences may be an advantage or a disadvantage to him in counseling, depending upon the attitude of the person to what the pastor is felt to represent.

So far as this common sense goes, our study is in full sympathy with it. Yet the statements about it have tended, like the previous paragraph, to be abstract. What does it really mean when we get down to cases? What effect does the difference tend to have upon the course or progress of the counseling? Only a systematic study, however preliminary in character, can offer promise of speaking concretely to this question. It was just this kind of issue that determined us, originally,

27

to make a beginning at such a study. The best comprehensive term we could find to indicate all the orders of significant difference between pastoral and other counseling was "context." We shall return shortly to a more careful definition of context as used in our study.

Counseling and Psychotherapy

It is important, however, that the reader also understand another kind of assumption that underlies our study, namely, what we conceive to be the relationship between counseling—including pastoral counseling—and psychotherapy as carried out by psychiatrists and clinical psychologists.

Between counseling and psychotherapy we see a real but not a categorical difference. Like William C. Perry, we see these two on a continuum with radically different emphases at the two ends but an area in between that cannot easily be compartmentalized.[8] Perry, who first formulated this view of the relationship, saw the psychotherapy end of the continuum as involving problems that are primarily intrapsychic in nature. That is to say, not much else can be done to help the person until he can be aided to deal with his relatively deep inner conflicts. Conversely, Perry saw the counseling end of the continuum as involving problems in which a more or less integrated person—with no deeper inner conflicts than most people have—nevertheless requires special help in dealing with some problem area or areas of life. As a general yardstick, we regard Perry's formulation as correct.

We believe the same point can be made more precisely by using time as the central concept. The person who can respond contemporaneously to contemporaneous events, if he needs help at all, needs some form of counseling. His past experience has thrown minimal chains around his ability now to respond to situations now. In contrast, the person who tends to respond to contemporary situations with recapitulations from past experiences is a candidate for psychotherapy. Relatively speaking, he is governed by unassimilated personal history, impeding his ability to respond to the present as the present. These distinctions plainly belong along a continuum and not in boxes. That is why counseling and psychotherapy are intimately related to each other but why the natural locus of each is observably and significantly different.

Our concern is with pastoral counseling. But the way in which we

28

see the relationship of counseling to psychotherapy is important to our later discussion precisely to show that we do not, by our own definition, at any point trespass upon the psychotherapeutic realm. By taking our type of position, it is clear, for example, that no set number of hours can differentiate arbitrarily between counseling and psychotherapy, as if anything less than twenty hours' consultations were counseling and anything beyond twenty were psychotherapy. Yet psychotherapy, generally speaking, takes a good many more hours than counseling. By the same token we, as counselors, enter into no systematic procedures of dream analysis, free association about childhood, or other systematic techniques that may be used as relevant in psychotherapy. At the same time, it does not mean that we are barred from examining a dream if it appears naturally in the course of the counseling.

That is to say, our definition of the difference between counseling and psychotherapy is one that is seen overall rather than one built up by bits and pieces. The systematic exploration of dreams, for example, certainly belongs to psychotherapy. Examination of a dream is not barred from counseling, however. Thus the distinction is not understood as built up by isolated techniques used by one or the other, but in terms of the overall aims, needs, and limitations placed upon either counseling or psychotherapy. By our own conception, this volume studies counseling and not psychotherapy.

The Four Dimensions of Context

We are now ready to attempt a more precise definition of context in counseling. In terms of context in pastoral counseling, we see it as involving four differentiating factors. We shall state these briefly and then discuss each at some length. The four factors differentiating the context of pastoral counseling are:

1. *Setting.* Even the rudest or most architecturally monstrous church symbolizes something that is not found in a school, library, factory, office, or residence. And whether the pastor's counseling is done at the rear of the church sanctuary, in a study, in an office almost indistinguishable from a business establishment, or in the parishioner's home, the normative setting is still the type of edifice known as church and everything it symbolizes.

2. *Expectation.* Each person who requests counseling of the pas-

29

tor will read into him and his function certain expectations. Some of these expectations may be based upon observation of the pastor individually. The parishioner may have heard him preach, may have consulted him previously, may have sat in meetings or played golf with him. Some of them, however, are likely to be other than personal, that is, they are likely to be based on the parishioner's generalized conception of any pastor's role, function, and convictions. The expectations, personalized or not, may or may not correspond to the pastor's own understanding of function. In any event, they are present, and they are likely to be different in content from the expectations the same person might have of another kind of professional helper.

3. *Shift in Relationship.* In the usual pastoral counseling situation the parishioner does not meet the pastor for the first time in the counseling chamber, nor will this be the final place in which they encounter each other. Thus pastoral counseling is not ordinarily a matter of building a relationship from scratch on the part of two people who have never seen each other before and will not do so again. Instead, it is a matter of creating, out of a previous general pastor-parishioner relationship, a special and temporary helping relationship—and with the recognition that, upon conclusion of the special and temporary relationship, the general relationship will be resumed. Some of the other professions that do counseling have something akin to this—especially teachers and physicians—but none to so marked an extent and so uniformly as the clergy.

4. *Aims and limitations: In the counseling and in other dimensions of relationship.* In terms of the total life course of a parishioner, the pastor cannot finally rest content unless he has done everything within his power to facilitate the "total redemption" of the "total person" whom he sees as sinner and child of God at the same time. If he is wise he will exercise discretion in all phases of his relationship and not try to force or push persons where they are inwardly unable to go. But his professional self-limitation in his counseling must be even more sharp. He is not equipped to do a basic psychotherapeutic job— as we have previously defined that—and even if he were, he would have to neglect other people and other essential duties in order to carry it out. Hence his self-imposed limitation in counseling must be realistic as to time and modest as to skill and training. He sees his counseling as a special and temporary relationship within a larger,

30

continuing, and more general relationship. Counseling by him may or may not be the special assistance required by the parishioner. If it is, he tries, within limitations of time and skill, to give it. If it is not, he does his best to help the parishioner get proper help. In neither event does his ability or inability to give the special help threaten the more general and continuing pastor-parishioner relationship. In summary, his total aim for the person is nothing less than salvation or redemption in the religious sense. His specific aim in pastoral counseling, however, represents self-imposed professional limitations. If he can think of nothing but the first while counseling, he is a poor counselor. If he becomes so intrigued with the second that he forgets the larger aims in which the self-imposed limitation is set, then he is not quite a pastor.

The Meaning of Context

We may illustrate these four aspects of the context of pastoral counseling from the materials of our study, especially the first two. For these, while easy to state, are shown by our study to be very widespread in their significance.

1. *Setting*. The following is reproduced from memory out of the preliminary interview with Mrs. Merz:

MRS. MERZ: I used to drive by this church on the way to work every morning. There was something reassuring about its dignity and beauty. I was going through a very hard time, and I tried to imagine what it would be like to belong to this church. I was looking for peace, and it looked calm and serene.

MR. COLSTON: That is, you were attracted to this church by what it seemed to represent to you.

MRS. MERZ: That's right. Something kept me from coming for quite a while. Finally I got up enough nerve to go to one of the services. The people seemed very friendly. So I decided to become a member. I'm really glad I did.

Mrs. Merz was thus drawn first to the church itself, and later to pastoral counseling in the church. It may not be an accident that, by our criteria applied after her counseling, she was regarded as a "success" case.

Mr. Johnson, also a church member, said in the preliminary interview that the church had played an important part in his life and background and that it seemed "natural to come here with my problems."

Almost any church, and certainly churches in general, have many unique symbols, some of which are even visible from the outside, as shown by Mrs. Merz. For the regular church attender like Mr. Johnson, other symbols are constantly present—art forms, pulpit and Bible, prayer, liturgical music, altar or communion table, and others. Whether a person looks upon this total setting as symbolizing something positive, negative, or ambiguous depends upon him and his total outlook.[9] But they are present in any event and any counseling sought from the pastor is inevitably associated with them in the mind and feelings of the seeker.

It is an understatement to call the setting of the Counseling Center of the University of Chicago different from that of a church. Literally, it is a converted residence made up of plain offices most of which are dominated by highly visible electronic recording machines. Its affiliations being principally with clinical psychology, it has less white paint and fewer awe-inspiring gadgets than a clinic in a medical setting. Located within the larger setting of a university, however, which is not innocent of Gothic buildings, the center, sparse as it is, symbolizes learning and research. The offices may be bare but they have, in the larger physical setting, dignity. Appointments can be made, and at least to this extent the symbol is not separation of town and gown. If office walls are mostly bare, they do afford privacy. Most clients at the center seem to regard it as "neutral ground."

"Neutral ground" carries the connotation of objectivity. As setting, this may be responded to favorably by the person whose usual environment sets off a chain of feelings which he cannot check or the person who feels threatened by what he believes an ecclesiastical—or even a medical—setting stands for. For such people, a setting like the counseling center may, far from being "neutral" in the sense of offering nothing positive, be like the "wilderness" into which many of the great persons of the Bible retreated in order to find new guidelines and strength for their lives. Whatever the church offers as setting, it is not "wilderness" nor emptiness. For some people in some predica-

32

ments, therefore, apparently "neutral ground" may in fact be the necessary retreat out of which advance may eventually emerge. The church can never be neutral in what it stands for. Yet it seemed to us at the outset of our study that the person who needed some degree of neutral ground from which to begin his personal explorations frequently and unnecessarily received short shrift even from well-intentioned pastors. A heavily book-lined study, with a cross and religious pictures displayed prominently, might be good for Mrs. Merz and Mr. Johnson, already positive toward the church setting in general, but might be very bad for someone who could glide ambivalently past the Gothic arches and the sound of the organ but whose need for "retreat" would be hit too hard by many religious symbols in the counseling study at the church. Accordingly, we made this room relatively bare. In this way we hoped to acknowledge the full weight of the larger setting, the church, but offer by visible symbols of relative barrenness something of objectivity at the same time. Our general subsequent experience suggests the wisdom of such a decision where a pastor finds it possible. At least for counseling, every church can profit from a wilderness as well as from stained-glass windows at another place.

Our common sense warned us from the beginning against including in our hypothesis the notion that the church setting for counseling might be better for every one. For many persons another setting or a more neutral setting might be preferable. We were still left with the question, however, of what a "favorable setting" is. Suppose Mrs. Merz feels positively toward the church setting. Does that mean she will progress better, farther, or more rapidly in her counseling? Or does it mean she may use her positive feeling toward the church as setting as a kind of defense against facing her inner problems? Whatever the answer, this was the setting aspect of the problem of context to which we addressed ourselves. As the reader will subsequently see, the evidence from our cases is in favor of more, and more rapid, progress by such people in the church setting, rather than its use as defense. Neither our data nor our common sense permit us to generalize beyond these cases, however. The one dogmatic statement we can make is that attraction of a person to the church as setting does not, automatically, mark him as defensive and regressive in relation to any usual standards of progress in counseling.

33

2. *Expectation*. The second aspect of context is the expectation the person has of the counselor and his function. Just after the fifth session with Mrs. Earle had closed and she was preparing to leave, the following conversation took place:

MRS. EARLE: I've been wanting to say that I find it easy to talk to you.

MR. COLSTON: (*Nods*) Is that so?

MRS. EARLE: Yes—hum—I never would have thought I could talk so freely to a minister. Ministers have always seemed so austere and frightening to me. When I was a teen-ager I tried to talk with a minister about a problem I was having at that time, but he made me feel so ashamed and so worthless that I didn't even go back to church for a while. I guess I really never did get over that. Although I have been active in several churches since, I have never discussed personal problems with any of the ministers. It's good to discover that I can.

The teen-age experience with the minister had given Mrs. Earle ambivalent feelings about the church; yet she had remained a loyal church member. We might say that she was positively affected by the church as setting, but negative in her expectations about the helping function of its representatives. To our shame, this combination of feelings is not rare. There is a pastoral screw loose somewhere when the discovery that a pastor does not shame you comes as a pleasant surprise.

This kind of expectation was revealed many times in our counseling at the church. A small number of persons, believing that the church stood for something, tried to get an immediate answer to their problems in a way that our professional judgment made impossible to render. A few of those, unable to accept our translation of our function away from authoritarian directiveness, left us, no doubt convinced that the church may have points but that these ministers are incompetent. Fortunately, the number of such instances was very small, but even one such shows what expectation may mean.

We had anticipated finding in our counseling at the church some persons who would try dependently to cling to us as rock and refuge and be unable to take, with our help, any initiative in relation to their personal problems. As some of the later cases will show, there were indeed some such tendencies in evidence. But we were, in effect, not encumbered by such attitudes as permanent throughout the counseling. Our own explanation of this fact is twofold. On the one hand, our encouraging permissiveness plus our definition and redefinition— when needed—of the pastoral counseling situation apparently did succeed in energizing capacity for initiative in many people. On the other hand, we presume that the persons not capable of much but sheer dependency—who exist in every church—did not seek our help in counseling. We recognize that the minister always has some such people with whom he must deal as best he can. The offer of counseling, however, far from mobilizing them to use his services, from our experience tends to make them draw back, and those who come, even with strong dependency drives, have also, even if hidden, genuine capacity for personal initiative.

In Colston's work at the Counseling Center of the University of Chicago different expectations were encountered from those at the Bryn Mawr Community Church. As at the church, there tended to be a thread of continuity running through these, and yet there were wide variations among them. For the most part, counselors at the center were viewed by clients as psychologists, concentrating on the study of personality, interested in interpersonal relationships, and doing research on methods of counseling. Thus the general expectation read into Colston by clients at the center was akin to the popular conception of the psychologist who is so much interested in studying you that you are never quite sure that he is genuinely interested in you. Since the general intelligence and educational level of the clients seen at the center was considerably above average, however, the cruder forms of the psychologist-expectation were seldom encountered.

Such a person was Mrs. Frome. She came to the center "to get help on the problem with my son." At the start of the second session the following took place:

Mrs. Frome: I want something. I don't want to just sit and discuss the same subjects. To me, you discuss a subject and it has an answer. I mean, there should be no . . . Maybe I'm wrong, but I feel that if a problem is stated there is a possible answer.

35

There can't always be an exact formula to follow, but there should be an answer.

MR. COLSTON: You get annoyed at just being listened to, I guess, with nothing . . .

MRS. FROME: (*Interrupting*) Very much so. With no—ah—

MR. COLSTON: Nothing being nailed down?

MRS. FROME: Definitely. I can sit, and I could talk to a number of people and get absolutely no answers also. And that is why I came to an outside source, feeling that someone who had no —uh—true concern as to what goes on, an ear that has never heard, it could maybe see what is going wrong and what can be done. And that is what I am looking for, and that is what I want to know.

Mrs. Frome perceived the counselor as one who could offer suggestions about her course of action with her son. In effect, she did not see the situation as providing a counseling opportunity for herself. We were able to work out some understanding of what each of us could legitimately expect of the other; yet her original expectation never quite died and remained to influence both the course and the outcome of the subsequent counseling.

A similar kind of expectation appeared at the center when Colston was cast as a kind of "psychological witch doctor." With intelligent persons, this never appeared directly except in retrospect. The following took place in the sixth session with Miss Troy:

MISS TROY: A couple of things seem very important. One is that I'm not so concerned about what goes on in these sessions, and I think about things beforehand to bring up. But now I don't feel that this is planning the session so much. I feel that there is lots of spontaneity, too.

MR. COLSTON: That although you feel you are planning it, many things are happening which go beyond your plans.

MISS TROY: Exactly. You know, realizing this has removed a lot of the apprehension I had about a lot of things and worry. And that—maybe before I was just exemplifying some of this passivity, which I note quite often in myself. That I came in here and sort of sat down to wait for something to happen (*laughs*).

36

And because it didn't happen, I didn't know just how it should, I was getting sort of upset.

MR. COLSTON: In other words, you see a definite relationship between what you expected from me and what you have often expected in other situations. And now that you realize this, you are feeling better about what this experience is meaning to you.

MISS TROY: Definitely. And—ah—the other thing is that—ah—I just feel more sure of myself all of a sudden. I have a little more control compared to before.

MR. COLSTON: You find it good to discover that you can be in the "driver's seat" and feel you are getting somewhere, not only here, but also in other areas as well, I guess.

MISS TROY: That's right.

Miss Troy's discovery that she could assume responsibility for our sessions and feel that she was doing so effectively had a salutary effect upon her other relationships outside counseling. But she could admit she had seen Colston as a psychological witch doctor only after a different and more realistic appraisal of his role had been experienced and tested out by her. It is quite likely that some of the most egregiously false expectations that people read into us can be genuinely changed only after they have experienced something with us that is manifestly different.

The psychologically sophisticated person might predict that the person coming to the church for counseling would expect authoritarian guidance while he who came to the counseling center would be democratic and expect to work out—with help—his own problems. This was not our finding. Whatever religious or pastoral authority may mean to people these days, with our parishioners it did only rarely carry authoritarian overtones. And whatever the actual objectivity of science and psychology, the prevailing aura over the counseling center, it did not prevent many people from expecting it to produce answers in what they would be shocked to hear called an authoritarian fashion. Religion must continue to work on the problem of authoritarianism, but our experience suggests that science and psychology have it in even larger proportions.

3. *Shift in Relationship.* Ordinarily the parishioner has known

37

the pastor before the special experience of pastoral counseling and will have a general pastoral relationship with him after the counseling is finished. This history and this future are parts of the context of pastoral counseling. Although we were genuinely ministers of Bryn Mawr Community Church, our other duties and our schedules made our relationships with the parishioners with whom we counseled less typical than would be true in the ordinary church. Hence our actual data on this dimension of context were scantier than on any other.

In one of the counseling sessions at the church the following emerged:

Mrs. Williams: Something Dr. Jenney (senior minister) said in his sermon last Sunday got me to thinking. It tied in so well with what we've been talking about that it just kind of hit home to me. Ah—he said—well, I don't remember his exact words, but something like, "If you're just concerned about one or two things most of the time—ah—you're too limited—you cheat yourself; you aren't really giving yourself to the things which will help you to grow." And I realize that's just exactly what I'm doing—I'm sort of playing it safe, not letting myself get involved. But I don't seem to be happy that way.

In the usual situation the minister as preacher and the minister as pastoral counselor would have been the same person. Owing to our special situation, here they were different persons. Yet even in this situation the continuity is evident. Even in the midst of her counseling, Mrs. Williams recalled her past relationships with her minister and anticipated those of the future.

This shift in relationship may affect the pastoral counseling at two points: First when the shift is toward a counseling relationship, and second, when it is back toward the general pastor-parishioner relationship. The nature of our study made it impossible to secure reliable data at either point; so that the comments that follow are from general pastoral experience rather than explicitly from this study.

Hiltner's experience suggests that the shift from the general pastoral relationship to the pastoral-counseling relationship is difficult in proportion as the pastor hesitates to make explicit acknowledgment of the shift and therefore permits the nature of the counseling rela-

38

tionship to remain partially ambiguous. When there are also ties of friendship—they have lunched or golfed or boated together— there may be even more reluctance to declare the nature of the new—although temporary—counseling relationship. Once in the open and articulated, it is our experience that there is little difference from any other counseling.

Against this conclusion might be cited the common practice of psychoanalysts. All psychoanalysts, as part of their professional training, have a personal analysis. In a setting where psychoanalysts are trained, one may be undergoing psychoanalysis from another. Their general rule is to avoid, so far as possible, other relationships while this one is on. This rule, incidentally, makes unusual demands upon the memory of the hostess in a psychoanalytic community. She can not ask Dr. M to dinner with Dr. J, and she is not sure she can ask Dr. M at all because his wife is having therapy with Dr. K and she has already invited Dr. K and his wife. As a sympathetic observer of such a community, Hiltner concluded that the rule is a good rule but that nothing much seems to be set back when, with all good intentions, it is violated.

What of the shift in the other direction—the Mrs. Williams who not only heard a sermon last Sunday but who also anticipates hearing another next Sunday? Here also the psychoanalysts, although marginally, are instructive to us. Although it is not normatively recommended, it has happened that an ex-patient has, at a later time, been chief of service in relation to his former psychoanalyst, and all seem to survive. A similar fate might have its points for bishops.

Is it true that someone who has "confessed all" to another inevitably hides his head in bitter shame when he sees the other outside their confessional framework? It would be folly to deny that this can happen. The Roman Catholic Church knows its human nature when it hides priest-confessor and penitent from each other's physical vision. Granting this wisdom, we would nevertheless argue that the shame-on-later-meeting response is true only to the degree that the special relationship has been cathartic—getting it off the chest— in nature and not also assimilative—accepting, clarifying, and hence making new decision about. In Hiltner's experience, the extent to which ex-parishioners with whom he counseled subsequently avoid him is due in part to his own deficiencies as counselor but more to

39

whether he succeeded in working the problem through or not. If he worked it through, they know his memory of it is much more of resolution than of disclosure. The shame of psychic nudity has been dissolved into the sympathetic understanding of pilgrimage.

By these remarks, going far beyond our research findings, we do not intend to suggest to the pastor that there are no problems about his shift to and from the counseling relationship with his people. We do suggest, however, that psychological honesty, explicit articulation of the new situation, and straightforward dealing fore and aft can usually solve the problem of shift.

4. *Aims and limitations: In the counseling and in other dimensions of relationship.* In our introduction to this aspect of context, we noted that the pastor must have professionally self-imposed limitations of aim concerning his counseling, but that he is concerned in a totalitarian way for the overall healing, salvation, and welfare of the persons.

This is a paradox not a contradiction. The good mother fights to get the doctor to her child when he is sick. She does not struggle to eke out her college biology so as to diagnose and treat her child's illness. Her concern is total. Her self-limitation is obvious.

On this as on the previously mentioned aspect of context, our study throws only indirect light. Its main contribution is to understanding the first two aspects, setting and expectation. Yet the indirect illumination is significant. We can imagine someone asking, "Can a helper be genuinely interested in me if he tells me, in advance, that the time he can give in helping me is limited?" The answer, from our study and elsewhere, is that the question itself alters as genuine concern is evidenced. If someone needs more time and more help than the pastor can give, then referral can be made—not as rejection but as wisdom.

Especially in relation to moral matters, it has sometimes been charged that the minister has such high—i.e., rigid—standards that he cannot genuinely understand the fallibilities and inabilities of ordinary human beings. Mrs. Earle spoke of having consulted a minister when she was an adolescent, with the result that she felt "ashamed" and "worthless." In the absence of other data, let us not be negatively severe upon that minister. Perhaps he was nonunderstanding and read the riot act to the future Mrs. Earle. Or perhaps he was understanding and did not profess, by fiat, to lift the burden of guilt from her until she confessed it. The chances are against the latter, but they are not impossible.

In moral matters the minister cannot possibly go along with the notion that whatever is—or its average incidence—is right. On the other hand, his real temptation is to believe that what is less than what ought to be should be spoken against. Human life always has a tension between what is and what ought to be, moral matters not excepted. As the old distinction in Christian thought between the sin and the sinner tried to make clear, it is not necessary to become angry—nonaccepting and nonunderstanding—with someone in order to try to help him to improve his capacity to behave. Because the minister stands unapologetically for an ideal should make it easier, not more difficult, for him to deal acceptingly with those—all of us—who fail to meet it. Acceptance and understanding are not the same as agreement and concession.

Conclusion

As a counselor the pastor must draw upon the same principles of interpersonal helping relationships as are drawn on by other personal counselors. He has no private electronic connection with heavenly headquarters that enables him to ignore the need for genuineness of interest and concern, acceptance and understanding, wisdom and knowledge, in his attempts to help another human being.

Yet he is not just another counselor. We have chosen to describe what makes him different as "context." Four dimensions or aspects of context have been delineated: Setting, expectation, shift in relationship, and the relation of aims to limitations.

Even while acknowledging the validity of these attempts to define the problem of context descriptively, it may be that some readers will ask why context has not been set exclusively as a matter of the pastor's resources: His administration of the sacraments, his prayer and use of the Bible, and the like.[10] Let there be no mistake that, in our view, these are great resources. But in a Protestantism that believes in the universal priesthood of believers, none of these resources is the exclusive possession of the pastor. True, he is required

41

for the administration of the sacraments, but in most branches of our faith lay helpers must be with him even then. Let us not forget that other counselors may also be Christians! Our task has been to delineate the context of *pastoral*—ordained minister—counseling. The pastor will use the resources of his faith, but others may do so too.

Chapter 3

CONTEXT AND METHOD

◻ Our study was of the work of the same counselor in two settings, the Bryn Mawr Community Church and the Counseling Center of the University of Chicago. We assumed that, at least in some respects, especially setting and expectation as defined in the previous chapter, there would be contextual differences between the work at the two places. And so there tended to be.

In order to study contextual differences while permitting the counselor to be the constant factor, it was also necessary for us to assume that *his* basic approach and method would be the same in both settings. To put the matter in extreme fashion, this would not have been true if at the center he had said, "I understand," and at the church had said, "Here is what God wants you to do." This study would not have been possible unless the researchers believed that the basic approach and method should and would be the same in the two situations, without derogation to either of what was proper to it. What the counselor was trying to do was, we believe in retrospect, the same in both settings so far as basic approach and method were concerned.

If we had held a different theory of counseling or a different theory of pastoral counseling our study might have had to assume a different form and, under some conditions, might not have been possible. Suppose, for example, that a theory of counseling contended that the counselor was automatically disqualified if he inevitably represented anything of the kind the minister has no choice but to represent. That view would have to conclude either that pastoral counseling can never be true counseling, or else that a pastor, when engaged in counseling, has ceased to act as a pastor. This is very close, incidentally, to the view recently set forth by Linn and Schwarz.[1]

Suppose that pastoral counseling were so regarded only when the two parties are explicitly, verbally, and articulately speaking from within the shared community of faith; i.e., that they agree about religion before they start, and the counseling is simply the discovery of the explicit implications for life of the shared religious presuppositions. In that case, most of what would be pastoral counseling to us would not be so to this viewpoint, because in the relative absence of the starting conditions the following procedures would not be pastoral counseling. This is close to the view of "Seelsorge" set forth by Eduard Thurneysen.[2]

Yet except for views of these two types, which seem extreme from our perspective, we hold that the validity of our findings as to context is not dependent upon our having used precisely the approach and method that we followed and in which we believe. That is to say, we believe that another pastor and counselor, holding somewhat different convictions about approach and method in counseling, could have made the same kind of comparative study we did and would have got similar comparative results. Where he would have been different from us, he would have been so consistently in both settings. He would of course have had to share our assumption about the relationship between context and method, namely, that the basic approach, method, and processes are the same, but that the differences, both obvious and nonobvious, may all properly be regarded as contextual in nature. If he had shared this assumption, then he could have differed from us on actual approach and method and still, in our judgment, have done a similar study with the prospect of similar findings.

It is important, nevertheless, that the reader have opportunity to examine our approach and method in counseling. If these make good sense to him then our findings are likely to do so too. If, on the other hand, he finds himself critical of our method, then he deserves all the data he can get in order to see if our findings about context are, in his judgment, nullified by our approach and method.

Getting Inside

In our approach, once counseling is called for or requested of a pastor or of another counselor, our first principle is that we begin

44

by getting as far inside the other person's frame of reference as his readiness, our skill, and the circumstances will permit.

Let it be noted that this was not what always took place chronologically first on the initial encounter. Defining or structuring the counseling situation, discussing what might or might not be expected from it, making a rough initial appraisal about whether the person and his problem might be beyond our powers, trying to evaluate whether there was congruence between what we tried to say and what the person took us to mean—any or all of these might come chronologically before we were permitted to begin to enter the person's point of view. They are, however, all to be regarded as preliminary to the counseling process itself, and we begin for these purposes with the latter. We shall return to the other points.

Psychologists sometimes call this the "phenomenological principle." [3] In our judgment it has three merits. First, it takes seriously individual differences. Three persons reacting to grief, caught in the grip of alcohol, or having spouses they despise may each feel quite different from the other. We cannot assume in advance that external circumstance automatically dictates inner attitude and feeling. This approach not only permits but also compels the counselor to try to capture the individuality of feeling and response.

Second, the phenomenological principle explicitly acknowledges the depth, in the sense of complexity, within the feeling responses of every human being. For instance, a married woman tells us vehemently that, no matter what we clergy think about divorce, she is going to leave her husband. As she proceeds to tick off the multifarious respects in which that gentleman is impossible to live with, it occurs to us that if she meant this *and nothing else* she would be talking with a lawyer rather than a pastor. Yet unvoiced, there must be some other kind of feeling present and active in her as well. Unless, however, we can manifest interest in trying to comprehend her feeling as she is prepared to convey it to us, she may never get to the other feeling at all. Sooner or later, if we can maintain our belief in this phenomenological principle, she is likely to say, "I am going to get a divorce, and yet that is not what I really want." As we pursue that, new complexities are likely to appear on both sides. If they do, then they have been present all along anyhow, and any attempt on our part to push for a quick decision would

45

have simply repressed the more complex factors in the conflict. So depth in the sense of complexity is respected by this phenomenological principle.

The third virtue of the phenomenological principle, at least in the earlier stages of a counseling relationship, is that it encourages the person to assume any degree of initiative in considering his problem and his feelings of which he is capable. Perhaps he can assume much; perhaps, little. In either event, whatever capacity he has is encouraged, and if his capacity be small, he is not penalized within the relationship for what he cannot do.

How do we begin to get inside the other person's frame of reference? Here is one of Colston's attempts. When Mrs. Wright had first come for counseling at the church, she had regarded herself as "liberal minded." Her first perception that this quality was more ambiguous than she had considered it came in the following exchange:

MRS. WRIGHT: The thought came to me—now, I have been open-minded—true. But the reason why I was open-minded hit me like a light. Because I wanted to gain people's approval, that was all. I mean, I was going to be willing to change if I had to so that they would approve of me. I don't know whether I'm making it clear or not.

MR. COLSTON: You mean, not so much that you yourself were convinced of open-mindedness for the sake of being open-minded, but for the sake of gaining approval from people.

MRS. WRIGHT: Well, now, I have always felt you had to be open-minded and I still do. However, the difference that I am trying to make here—ah—is when I have established an ideal and a principle, after having given it as much study and thought as I could possibly do, and then when I didn't stand up for what I believed was right. Then, you see, is where I was seeking approval. Now this is where the conflict is.

MR. COLSTON: Wanting to be open-minded on the one hand, but not liking yourself for relinquishing your hold on your principles, on the other.

MRS. WRIGHT: Yes. This eventually always ended up by my finally standing up for my own principles—but sometimes my route

46

in getting there was pretty crooked (*laughs*). And it was during these periods of giving in when I knew I shouldn't—when I developed these conflicts. If I had held to this firmly, I would never have had the conflict. And now I don't see why it was so important to gain people's approval (*laughs*).

MR. COLSTON: Kind of like part of you selling your own birthright for a mess of pottage, so to speak.

MRS. WRIGHT: Exactly. And the whole trouble with me has been— I'm well aware of this now—that I had to have this approval not for any particular reason—it wasn't that I hoped to even use it—but I had to have it. And of course I always ended up by coming right back to my ideals and principles and then all of this sense of guilt. This is what I built up, because eventually I ended up where I was going to be anyway.

The reader may note that Colston was attempting at each point to concentrate on the central feeling or feelings she was expressing, and to restate them in his own words. In this particular interchange, he mostly got them right, which accounts for the "Yes" and "Exactly." If he had not, they were so put as to invite her correction of them. Her feelings, as is usually true, were mixed; and so the net effect of this exchange was to draw for her into sharp focus the hiatus between her principle of open-mindedness and her unconsciously manipulative use of it as a method of gaining personal advantage.

Most of the responses in the above exchange may be regarded as falling within the category of "reflection of feelings," as enunciated by Carl R. Rogers.[4] When read on paper even the most natural and skillful use of reflection sometimes appears mechanical. But rightly used, reflection is genuinely interpersonal. Perhaps the word is wrong, for it suggests an image bouncing off a mirror. What is involved dynamically is the attempt to understand, to convey that understanding, and to invite correction of any degree of misunderstanding.

To make sure the reader, despite our disclaimers, does not regard us as mere mechanists, let us deal hypothetically with the latter part of the exchange with Mrs. Wright. Let us suppose that, after Colston's statement on the mess of pottage, she had said:

47

Mrs. Wright: Yes, that's what I meant all right. But it seems to me, Mr. Colston, that you are just repeating what I say—in your own words, of course—and that's a nice biblical reference you did it with—but you're not really telling me anything, or giving me anything of yourself and your own views.

Under these conditions he would not say, "Then you feel that I've been withholding something from you." To say that would indeed be mechanical. It would demonstrate that a mere technique had been applied. Here is about what he would say in such a situation:

Mr. Colston: Let me see if I understand what you are saying, Mrs. Wright. You feel let down because I seem simply to have been trying to understand what you have been getting at, instead of contributing something of my own to the solution of your problem. If the premises are right, the conclusion follows. My understanding of our overall situation, however, is that I am trying mainly to help you through helping you, first, to become clearer about just what the forces are that have been at war within you. If you feel that that task has been accomplished and something else is needed, then you do right to tell me so. But that, at any rate, has been my understanding of what we have been trying to do.

This is, technically, a "redefinition" or "restructuring" of the counseling situation, and of that as a general principle we shall speak later. We introduce it hypothetically here to show that we are against any merely mechanical application of the phenomenological principle. Understanding and clarifying the person's feelings is done, if at all, with his at least implicit understanding of what is going on. When he has doubt about the process or antagonism toward it, then we deal with the doubt or antagonism directly. No one has any cards under the table, else the counseling is poor.

Here is another illustration of the phenomenological principle in counseling. Through the first several interviews Mr. Johnson had expressed concern over his feelings of hostility, which he now saw as inappropriate. The idea occurred to him that, in these hostile responses, he might be recapitulating a feeling from some previous situation.

48

MR. JOHNSON: I think my whole problem could possibly stem from holding on to thoughts I should have cleared my mind of. I let things bother me 'way in the back of my mind for a long time, and I feel a lot of resentment. And now I guess I'm trying to take that resentment out on just about everybody that even looks a little cross-eyed at me.

MR. COLSTON: In other words, you feel you may be taking out your resentment on people who haven't deserved it.

MR. JOHNSON: Yeah. There's one thing that dates back to my high-school days when I was either a freshman or a sophomore. And —ah—I had a teacher that was very, very nervous, and I used to unconsciously tap my pencil on the desk, and she'd say to get out—and she would kick me out of class. I never failed an examination of any kind in my whole life—not any kind—but she failed me. And I think that has had a lot to do with my animosity. I still think it bothers me even to this day.

MR. COLSTON: That maybe you still have that in your system, and that it comes out in your dealings with some people now.

MR. JOHNSON: Yeah. I think so.

Mr. Johnson's insight into what was complicating his feelings toward people led the way for him to discover, in actual relationships, that he could make some significant change in this pattern. He was prepared to have Colston move inside both his old problem and his new insight into its meaning. Hence the phenomenological principle was applied with his full consent. Had he not been so ready, Colston would have altered what he was trying to do, very much as in the previous hypothetical interchange with Mrs. Wright.

Every responsible position in counseling—or in psychotherapy for that matter—makes some use of the phenomenological principle. The question is, How far can it go, and to what extent is it adequate in itself? Our own point of view on this question may be stated in two parts. First, when used in conjunction with the other principles we shall shortly name, such as the need to redefine the situation when there is misunderstanding of the task, we believe this principle invariably carries counseling further than the novice believes it will. His first question, when considering counseling, is usually a somewhat less crude form of "When do I get a chance to say something?" With experience and guidance, he learns that the trouble with his question was that he had a wrong impression of what it means to "say something." What is he trying to help, a complex and often misunderstood human being, or his own oral impulses?

The second thing we can say about the adequacy of the phenomenological principle is that, so long as the principle itself is recognized and established within the relationship the hunches of the counselor may ordinarily be trusted later on at least to the extent of doing no harm. If the person has become convinced (1) that the counselor is not superficializing him and his problem, (2) that the counselor can be trusted not to make arbitrary suggestions, (3) that the understanding he has received has enabled him to understand his situation more clearly, (4) that the counselor is genuinely interested in him as a person—then many things may be risked without upset. Once these conditions have been established with a person who is not seriously ill in an emotional sense a counselor may say, "For heaven's sake, Bill, if you really feel as negative about it as all that, why don't you get out of it?" Bill is likely to reply, "O.K., you call my tune. You know blamed well that I am drawn on the other side too." This statement or question by the counselor, coming when it does, means something quite different from what it would had it appeared in a first interview. In words it moves beyond the phenomenological principle, but in spirit it does not. We would hold that the spirit, in this sense, of the phenomenological principle is a permanent accompaniment of all good counseling.

Our shorthand for this principle was "getting inside." Are there occasions when we should limit the degree to which we get inside? May a person tell us things he should not? Or may he tell us more than we can handle? Experts disagree in answering this question. We do concede that the dangers are possible. But our experience suggests them as unlikely and infrequent when the other principles, to which we shall come, are also drawn upon. When people tell too much, it is either because they need a kind of help counselors are not equipped to give anyhow or else because the counselor has not defined the nature and process of the counseling. However, the fact that dangers may exist is one reason why any counselor, pastor included, should have some source where he may "check up" on his counseling.

Appraising and Defining the Situation

The general principle may be put in this way. Throughout a counseling relationship the counselor is alert in appraising the kind and degree of communication that exists between himself and the other in regard to the purposes and processes of the counseling and whenever discrepancies are found, attempts to define or redefine the situation to effect mutual understanding of the task are made. Formal definitions are necessarily complex and abstract, and we shall illustrate the two interrelated aspects of the principle.

An illustration is found in the following bit of dialogue that took place after one of the sessions with Mrs. Wright had been formally concluded but before she had actually left the room:

MRS. WRIGHT: Aren't you going to ask me any questions?

MR. COLSTON: You mean you're rather disappointed that I'm not asking you any questions?

MRS. WRIGHT: Well, I'm not sure if that's what you do or not, but I was wondering if you had any questions.

MR. COLSTON: No, I haven't at the moment, but perhaps I will as time goes on. If I do, I would like to feel that I could ask them.

MRS. WRIGHT: Yes, I really wish you would, but this isn't exactly what I had in mind. I'm not sure I can bring out everything that is needed here, and I thought perhaps you have a series of questions you ask to bring some of these things out.

MR. COLSTON: Well, no. I don't have any formal set of questions. I feel that I really want to know you, and not some facts about you which may satisfy some of my own preconceived ideas. I feel that as you are opening up some of these areas which are concerning you, questions will arise which probably would not occur to us beforehand.

MRS. WRIGHT: Well, that may be. (Pause) I'll have to give this some thought and determine what I'm going to talk about next time.

Later on Mrs. Wright recalled this exchange and said it had been a distressing moment for her. She began to realize, she said, that she was going to have to assume considerable responsibility for the "counseling business," whereas when she had first come—she now

51

saw—she had expected to "dump my problems on you, and walk away feeling better." This particular exchange, she added, "put a different complexion on the whole thing."

On the surface Mrs. Wright had not demonstrated any radically different conception of the counseling situation from that held by the counselor. To use extreme examples, she did not come to the first session and announce that she expected the counselor to get rid of her chilblains by prayer, or that she had understood him to be a miracle man so would he please pass one. Yet down underneath Mrs. Wright acted much as she would if she were requesting a physician to see if her pain were appendicitis. In counseling, however, there is a real difference. Counseling proceeds most effectively when a person assumes all the initiative of which he is capable— although no more than he can handle. As later developments showed, Mrs. Wright was capable of assuming a great deal of responsibility for herself and the course of counseling. What Colston attempted to do was so to redefine the situation as Mrs. Wright had apparently understood it that she could not think of him as simply doing it all for her but would recognize her own part in the process, and yet at the same time he wanted to put this in such fashion that the redefinition would not arouse more anxiety than she could cope with. The less she "leaned," the better. But she had support, and he wanted her to know it. He would not do for her what she could do for herself, but in the task in which they were engaged she was not alone.

The exchange with Mrs. Wright shows what is meant both by appraisal and definition—or redefinition—of the situation. From her first question, "Aren't you going to ask me any questions?" Colston tried to be alert to what she was revealing about her understanding of the counseling situation, and his assessment of this, as she gradually expressed more about it, was what is meant by appraisal. The definition or redefinition—or the attempt to do so— was what he did to try to have her see the basic counseling situation, and our respective responsibilities within it, in the same way. So the appraisal and definition of the situation inevitably go hand in hand.

The reader may ask, "But doesn't that mean that, in reference to understanding the nature of the counseling process, the counselor tries to get the other person to agree with him?" The answer to this is yes. The counselor's expertness lies precisely within the realm of the counseling task and process. He must be faithful to his best understanding of this even if it brings some, although not intolerable, discomfort to the other person. If not, then he is guilty of professional malpractice. If a patient with appendicitis, who requires surgery for cure, requests pills instead, the physician must refuse and tell why. He cannot conscientiously acquiesce in a process that is different from his best knowledge of the process that may help. So it is with the counselor. Let it be noted, however, that his attempt to have the other person agree with him on the task is utterly different from imposing content in regard to the problems under consideration.

Appraising and defining the counseling situation may sometimes involve strong feelings. During her second session Mrs. Frome told something of the frustration she had felt during the initial interview.

MRS. FROME: I feel there is no sense just coming and sitting and talking. I thought maybe if you explained the counseling, I could see. But at no time has anyone discussed any ways of counseling.

MR. COLSTON: You are saying you resent very much not knowing what is expected of you.

MRS. FROME: Exactly. I feel that a person should know somewhat what should be done, what course should be taken, and possible outcomes.

MR. COLSTON: Well, I think that's fair enough, and I am certainly willing to go into it. I would have to say, first of all, that probably we're trying to get at what the effect of what you call your son's "perfectionism" is on you and how this is related to your other feelings. So my feeling is that by simply trying to work out a particular way of handling him we would not fully get at what is involved.

MRS. FROME: In what way do you feel that it would get to the situation?

MR. COLSTON: Well, I feel that counseling gives a person an opportunity to get a perspective on the situation by becoming consciously aware of some of his attitudes and handling them here and now in a specific way.

MRS. FROME: And what would you suggest that the specific way might be?

MR. COLSTON: I mean just what we are doing—going into your feelings at this particular moment.

MRS. FROME: Uh huh, but basically do you feel that just conversation of any type on any subject is going to get this basic problem solved?

MR. COLSTON: No, not if it is just conversation. But if it is conversation that has total meaning to it and involves increasingly your deep feelings, such as I feel this is, it may very well get at it.

MRS. FROME: Well, I am looking for an outsider's opinion, let's put it that way. Not to put it down like that—well, now, he said this and that is the way it is—because I realize nothing goes just that way. I don't want it to be—but I'd like to break it down to find out if I'm going to discuss my son at every counseling session, or just how it is.

MR. COLSTON: Well, no. You may discuss whatever you like, and as I said any or all of what we discuss may help you with that particular problem.

MRS. FROME: Up to now, I don't feel that I am getting any possible answer to what to try with him.

MR. COLSTON: I will suggest some possible courses of action if you wish. Of course it would have to be in regard to some particular matter.

MRS. FROME: All right, that is what I am looking for.

In retrospect, Colston believes he might have clarified his point to Mrs. Frome much more effectively than he did. On the one hand, he stuck to his guns, with the possible danger of his last statement. On the other hand, however, he did not give Mrs. Frome the impression that she had no right to ask these questions. The net effect of this exchange, which had a good deal of feeling in it, was to clear the air, and the counseling improved a bit from this point onward. This case is discussed later on.

We have tried to show how alertness to the possible need for appraisal and definition of the counseling situation is needed when the other person manifests a different understanding of the counseling task and process from that which we believe may help him. Appraisal and definition may, however, become needed through lapses, biases, or other deficiencies of the counselor. In Hiltner's *The Counselor in Counseling* the attempt is made to show how the counselor may, through alertness in his counseling, correct what would otherwise be lapses and biases.[5] As a brief illustration, let us suppose that the person has been droning on for some time and our attention has wandered from time to time; then suddenly we recognize that we are bored and our mind is elsewhere. We at once turn a searchlight on ourselves; our appraisal of the situation is, in this instance, self-appraisal. Suppose further that the person, by this time, has noticed we are not quite with him and pauses. We might then make a direct comment to him. For example, "I seem to be below par today, and I'm afraid I missed the main point of what you were saying. Could you be good enough to try to clarify that?" Or even, "Apparently I'm having difficulty really following you, and I'm not quite sure why. I wonder if anything occurs to you that would shed light on this?" The counselor is neither infallible nor impermeable, and such honesty often moves things ahead.

Appraising Person and Progress

The general principle may be stated thus. Since appraisal of the person psychodynamically and of his progress in counseling is an inevitable part of the counselor's mental processes, he makes this articulate to himself at appropriate times and pursues it as systematically as circumstances warrant.

Even today there is disagreement among counselors about the extent to which counseling includes "diagnosis." The latter term has come into modern speech as a medical idea. Medical progress has come about largely because of growing ability to make differential diagnoses and then to find differential treatments relative to the different causes of disorder. In addition to this principal meaning of "diagnosis" in medicine, however, which is wholly positive, the term has also come to connote a standing outside of, a judgment rendered with a kind of objectivism that makes impossible a genuinely interpersonal

55

relationship. This latter is a danger even in medicine. It could be fatal in counseling.

We use the term "appraisal" rather than "diagnosis" partly because it is more neutral and is less imitative of medicine and partly because it helps us transcend some of the false issues—in our judgment—that have become involved in the controversy about diagnosis in counseling. From our point of view, continuous appraisal—but mostly in post-counseling session reflection, not in the spontaneity of the counseling session itself—is essential in order to make the counseling completely relevant to the complex individuality of the other person. On the other hand, we believe that anything of a detached, impersonal, or objectivistic nature that depersonalizes or dehumanizes the counseling relationship impedes progress. Good appraisal procedures, therefore, work toward individualization, relatedness, and humanization.

We shall not, at this point, take time to give extended illustrations of our own appraisal attempts. For every case discussed in the subsequent chapters is concluded with an appraisal of the type indicated. These "last" appraisals were of course preceded by successive appraisals made between counseling sessions, the final one demonstrating some corrections made possible by later data. As he examines these appraisals in the later chapters, the reader may note especially how often our attempts at being systematic in our assessment altered our view—in both directions—of what the counseling had or had not accomplished for a particular person, granted the kind of person he was and the kind of problem he had. Thus we regard appraisal as essential. We see no reason why it cannot individualize rather than depersonalize. We believe, however, that every counselor must be alert lest he find himself using it for dehumanizing purposes.

Our study contained one kind of appraisal that would not be usual in pastoral counseling. Because of our research aims, our people took certain tests before their counseling began as well as after its completion. Thus we had available at the time the counseling began the results of several tests dealing with certain aspects of personality, character, and deviation from various kinds of norms.[6] We did consult these test results near the start of every counseling case and found them useful in giving us leads or warnings. But they were not infallible, as every clinical psychologist knows even better than the rest of us, and we took great care lest test results obscure our vision of each person's individuality. In this one sense, we had available to us appraisal resources that the ordinary minister would not have. Although we cannot deny the value of such data, rightly and not slavishly used, we found that very few cases, after a few sessions, showed our own appraisals as being at variance with the test results; and our own data were of course richer and more concrete.

It goes almost without saying that the counselor's continuing appraisal includes attention to possible types of response that suggest a kind and degree of disorder that can be better helped by someone other than him. Such danger signals that may indicate the need for referral may include highly inappropriate or extreme emotional expression, genuine depression, dreamy detachment and withdrawal, delusional blaming of other people, and the like.[7] As our case reports show, in very few of our people did such signs appear in form sufficiently extreme to compel our referring them, but there were some. Ordinary pastoral work is likely to find a higher proportion of such people than we did, because our being available for "pastoral counseling" at the church tended to weed out most of the persons who are problems to themselves and others but cannot admit it, whereas ordinary pastoral practice sees many such folk. They are an important responsibility of the ordinary pastor, who will make more referrals proportionately than we did because of the reasons indicated. We can only report that our study could not include investigation of such persons, and we therefore have no new light to shed upon pastoral dealing with them.

We can illustrate, in the case of Miss Verne, our own experience with danger signals in our research. During the initial interview with her Colston noticed that she was very carefully objectivizing all her experiences, as if they were things happening to someone else. As the sessions began, he found himself thinking of her as holding court with herself, she serving as both judge and jury but the accused being someone who was a stranger to her. She exhibited other qualities too. At times she demonstrated both warmth and sensitivity, but for the most part such expressions were immediately followed by a kind of denial in which she treated herself as a big joke. Eventually she required hospital care for a period, but the latest report showed her as improving markedly. We saw the danger signals in her from the be-

57

ginning and should have preferred to refer her at once. But as often happens in practice, at that time she would see us or no one. We believe that our restrained but honest relationship with her made it possible for her to enter later upon the needed hospital treatment, but there is no way to prove this.

Since the point has not been made explicit so far, we may note here that, in all cases representing potential psychotic symptoms as in Miss Verne, we consulted not only between ourselves but also with a psychiatrist serving as psychiatric adviser to the counseling center.

The "danger signal" or "weeding out" function is an important part of appraisal, for the sake both of counselor and the other person. But the more positive aspects of appraisal are even more significant. Potentialities in various persons that, earlier, were concealed by their difficulties, emerged during later sessions, as the releasing power of the counseling began to have its effect. Sensitivity to these is also appraisal.

Religious Understanding in Counseling

The primary task of this chapter has been to show the reader, at least in summary fashion, our basic theory of counseling and of pastoral counseling, so that he might either agree with us that the same person could do counseling in two settings without doing two basically different kinds of things or else so that he might know wherein he disagrees with our assumption. We have stated that, in our judgment, the basic interpersonal processes and principles are the same, and what is different we regard as involving context as defined in the previous chapter.

Common sense suggests that a parishioner seeing a pastor in a church is more likely to talk explicitly about matters he regards as religious. The difference is partly setting and partly the very reason why he came for counseling to the church in the first place. What we need to show here is that, in our opinion, our dealing with the explicitly religious contents, when they were presented, was carried according to the same basic principles we have enunciated above for all aspects and contents of the counseling relationship.

For example, here is a portion of the eighth interview with Mrs. Wright. Previously, Mrs. Wright had examined something of her

58

relationship to her husband's niece—which was poor—in personal and psychological terms. Then she tried to see it also from the point of view of God's forgiveness.

MRS. WRIGHT: I have related it now to—to Betty, for instance, and my problems with her; and I have recognized—ah—I have said and thought, sincerely thought—that I felt this way about her because of what I have done for her. And when I stop to think about it, I think that it was what I had hoped she would do for me. And she failed, and so instead of recognizing that there was error in me, in my relationship with her, I turned against her.

MR. COLSTON: This is something that's opening up to you and you are becoming aware of . . .

MRS. WRIGHT: (Breaking in) You can't do something—you can't just suddenly see something—and be different. Now, of course, in thinking this thing—recognizing that I can't do it alone—I again feel this terrible need for—ah—for a closeness to God which I don't have. I mean, I feel I need to be able to reach out and really—really feel that he is there. And this, again, is where I (pause)

MR. COLSTON: Where you feel frightened, quite separated from God, and feel that somehow this must be bridged before the meaning of all you are saying can come through to you (letting it hang)

MRS. WRIGHT: I find it more difficult—and it's contradictory here too because that statement is true—and yet I find that I cannot forgive myself for my sins at all. I can forgive others for their sins; yet I still can't forgive myself. Even though I realize that God will forgive me, I can't forgive myself because I know better.

MR. COLSTON: In other words, that although you sort of become easier sometimes with others than with yourself, you can't feel easier about it, especially when you know better.

MRS. WRIGHT: Not at all. And of course, because of my feelings and because of my hypocrisy of—of holding up certain standards for myself and for others—and then I have failed. I feel I have been hypocritical. I know it. This makes it hard for me to forgive myself. This is the sort of thing that I feel I'm going to have to

59

find out how to do; and I think, again, the only way I can find this is through—is through my relationship with God. Understanding how he can forgive us and recognize our weakness. I think this we must also be able to do to ourselves, not in condoning what we do or in going on and doing it—repeating it— but in understanding what we are particularly trying to do.

MR. COLSTON: So that you can understand how you can be forgiven in a very personal close way of experiencing this forgiveness from God and what it means, and in this way you may be able to forgive others, now that you see the full range of what this means, and see yourself as forgiven.

From this point on in the counseling Mrs. Wright combined attempts like the above to get at her religious problems or to get at her problems religiously, with discussion of psychological and interpersonal relationships. The "religious" for her was both an area of life and a language of human understanding.

What we have attempted to show through the exchange with Mrs. Wright is the consistency of our approach to religious understanding with that involving any other order of content. For the most part, the phenomenological principle stands out in Colston's work in the portion cited. He should not have hesitated, however, to appraise and redefine the "religious" aspects of the situation just like any other, had this been needed. Since he had come to believe—as a result of appraisal of Mrs. Wright—that her religious struggle was genuine and not a cover-up for something else, he responded to her on that basis in the exchange quoted.

As some of the later case presentations show, the attempt to advance religious understanding and to tie it up in a personal and existential way with one's immediate life situation took place rather often in persons who received counseling at the church. The unique resources of religion were used at times in these situations, much in the fashion Hiltner has previously described.[8] For the most part, however, it was religious clarification and relation of religious understanding to one's immediate life situation that appeared in the sessions.

As the reader examines the cases in the subsequent chapters, he will very likely ask himself, not why religion enters explicitly in many discussions at the church, but why, in a goodly number, it is never mentioned at all. To this question we have no systematic answer. The case reports do show, however, that there was a great variety of reasons why different people sought counseling at the church—sheer availability, feeling at home because of social contacts there, recommendation of a friend, stimulation by a sermon— but not by any means always because the problem was recognized as containing a religious dimension, as in the case of Mrs. Wright. The churchgoer, especially in this day of churchgoing, may take out his religion by attending and have no religious problems left over—or no awareness of them—to consider explicitly in relation to what he regards as his personal or psychological problems.

In Colston's counseling at the counseling center it was exceedingly rare to have anyone mention anything even obliquely about religion. When anyone asked, he of course indicated that he was an ordained minister, but very few asked such a question. The persons seen at the center, therefore, for the most part regarded him as a kind of "psychological counselor." He had the strong impression that the absence of religion from most of these discussions was not always due to a lack of interest, but was much more the result of the assumption that a vaguely psychological kind of counselor obviously would not be interested in that sort of thing. At the same time, the discerning reader of the cases will note that many problems and attitudes which we would regard as religious in nature, because they involved the meaning of life or the evaluation of conscience or attitudes toward loss, were considered during the sessions at the center. Perhaps the fact that these were so seldom identified in any way with the Western religious tradition is an index of the degree to which our society is becoming secularized, even when the fruits of its religious heritage are still present to the trained observer.

Since we hold, as Christian ministers, that the imagination of the human being is such that he must in some way come to terms with ultimates as well as proximates, we believe that the serious consideration of any interior problem through counseling offers new opportunities, at the same time, for relating these proximate concerns to more ultimate ones. It would be going much too far to say that counseling is unsuccessful if it does not touch explicitly upon the religious dimension. We certainly have no intention of implying

61

either that consideration of the ultimate makes it unnecessary to work out the proximate or that the pastor has no concern for the proximate because his focal concern is with the ultimate. Nevertheless, where whatever it is that prompts the counseling also pushes the person on to considering the ultimate, we believe a broader service has been rendered.

For example, Mrs. Merz spent much time wrestling over her feeling of defeat. Nearing the close of childbearing age, she was both unmarried and childless. She examined this feeling both from interpersonal and religious perspectives. What, she asked, was lacking in her faith to leave her feeling so unsustained in this situation, even though she believed in her head that God supported her? Her forthright dealing with prayer as communication with God during the counseling provided her both illumination and correction. Without the articulation of this dimension of her experience, we doubt that the counseling could have turned out so well.

Religiously speaking, an opposite type of case was Miss Verne. She felt cut off from her family. In her sense of isolation, she turned more strenuously to the church, hoping to find there that she "belonged" to a community. She did not, however, take into account that the religious community is a result of people's making active response to God. Miss Verne waited for events to happen or for effective action to be taken for her. Thus her return to religion, so to speak, was of quite a different quality from that of Mrs. Wright or Mrs. Merz.

In our counseling both at the church and the center, we did not raise explicitly religious questions unless they emerged from the stated concerns of the person. In part, this self-limitation expressed our conviction that, if religious discussion were to lead to understanding, there would have to be some clear indication of the desire for it. The limitation was also due to the purposes of our study. We were attempting to make a comparative study of counseling, by one person, in two settings.

We would acknowledge fully that the ordinary pastor can never quite or completely separate his counseling task from that of education, moral guidance, and the like. Hiltner has indicated in *Preface to Pastoral Theology* the theory upon which he believes those alterations in function should rest.[9] He does not regard them as hybrids, but as integral to the work of the minister. But since our study was an attempt to deal with pastoral counseling in as pure a form as possible, we minimized the need to shift gears and functions to the greatest extent possible consistent with rendering service to those who sought our help.

Chapter 4

REPRESENTATIVE CASES

□ Beginning with the present chapter, we take the reader as far inside our counseling with the twenty-five persons participating in our study as space and ingenuity will permit. Six cases are presented at length in this and the two chapters following. In Appendix B six additional cases are presented of intermediate length, that is, less fully than the six in the main text but with enough detail to help the serious reader. The remaining thirteen cases are presented quite briefly, through thumbnail sketches, at the close of Appendix B.

We recognized from the beginning that the main practical value of our study would lie in detailed consideration of the cases themselves. The selection of materials to present, from the fully recorded sessions, has not been easy. The complete report of one case involving twenty interviews would be about the same size as this entire book. We have, therefore, elected to present the case material at three levels: First, six cases with enough detailed material to show the counseling method as well as the personal response; second, six cases to show the dynamics of the persons in the counseling situation; and third, thirteen cases in which minimal information is supplied.

Except for the last five cases, all are presented as "matched pairs." This means only that each member of a "matched pair" tends to correspond with the other in certain formal characteristics—e.g., to be of the same sex, of roughly similar age, or broadly comparable social background and level of educational achievement. In each matched pair the first person presented was seen at the church, while the second received counseling at the counseling center.

In this chapter we present the counseling of two persons, one from the church, Esther Merz, and one from the counseling center, Anne

64

Vick. This pair is presented as representative of our study. We use the term "representative" in two senses. First, what happened to these people is representative of what happened to the people in general through their counseling. Second, what Colston did in the counseling process is representative of his counseling with others as well.

In the two chapters to follow we shall consider two cases that, by our standards, were markedly successful and two that were failures. The two representative cases in the present chapter lean more to success than to failure, which itself seems representative because that was the general direction in the people as a whole.

Since this pair of representative cases is women, a comment is needed here on our counseling with women in comparison with men. In the research report itself, it can be seen at a glance that the overwhelming majority of our research cases were women. This does not indicate, however, that our counseling was so overwhelmingly with women as against men. The ratio was about two women to one man, a fact that does not show up in the research cases. What happened was this: As each person at the church requested counseling we asked him or her if he were willing to participate in the research. Nearly all the women said yes. Some of the men who sought us first said no. When, therefore, at the counseling center we selected clients on the waiting list to match the research cases at the church, their numbers were mostly women since the research cases already accepted at the church were mainly women. After our lists were full for the research, most of the men seeking us at the church were prepared for the project, but we were then unable to take them.

General experience does suggest that more women than men tend to seek out the pastor for counseling, and overall the tendency in our church situation was somewhat in the same direction. What was really radically different, however, was not the number of women at the church who sought counseling, but the reluctance of the first men who sought counseling to participate in the research. We believe the main reason for this difference may be accounted for more on cultural than on individual terms. Men have just as many life problems as women, but our culture regards exploration of the inner life—even in church—as a female rather than a male matter. A man seeking counseling help has to run more against cultural expectation than a woman. If this is found out, therefore, he runs more risks of cultural

65

"exposure"—i.e., as being weak. What the research apparently meant —before counseling began—to the first group of men at the church was the possibility of their "weakness" being known and exhibited. Most of them later expressed regret at not having participated in the research. In accord with our pledge we did not record interviews of, nor give tests to, persons who received counseling but who did not wish to participate in the research. Yet the counseling itself, and its general course, was not overall different with the nonresearch and the research cases.

If we had had more foresight at the opening phases of the study we believe now that we could have had a proportion of men to women in the study itself that would accurately reflect the proportion to whom counseling was given. What we might have done was to give a special kind of description to the men parishioners, noting explicitly to them the greater risk in their helping us in the research and appealing to their potential adventurousness. As it was, it took us some time to realize that the decisions were being made on a trans-individual basis, and by that time our research time was taken up and we could not go back. A future researcher, however, should be able to profit from our experience on this point.

We turn now to the exposition of counseling with the two representative people, beginning with Esther Merz.

Esther Merz (Church)

"I've always wanted to have children of my own," said Esther Merz sadly during her first interview, "but it doesn't look like I ever will." This attractive, dark-complexioned, thirty-seven-year-old widow, who had been childless through two marriages, said she despaired of fulfilling her desire to have a family, and even of now finding "a man I can really respect."

Mrs. Merz said she had come for counseling because of "long periods of depression which come in kind of a cycle." She requested talking with Hiltner, and he had the preliminary interview with her, informing her of his function in the total project and expressing the hope that she would be willing to see Lowell Colston. She agreed and also consented to participate in the study.

In the first regular interview—recorded, as the preliminary interview was not—she told of her frequent periods of depression, adding that

66

she was finding no meaning in her existence. Much of this, she continued, had developed after the sudden death of her second husband. At that time she had begun to develop pains in the heart region, which she found from a physician were only simulated heart attacks. She had also an intense fear of death.

At that time, she went on, she had sought psychiatric treatment, continuing it for some time, "But I kept feeling that the root of my problem was religious and began looking for answers in different churches." The psychiatric work, she said, had helped her, and she had got sufficiently better to be able to function in her job and elsewhere, but she said that many questions had continued to be unanswered and she was still trying to search for meaning in her life. She said, "Sometimes I felt that if I could find something that really gripped me, I would feel like living again." After exploring several churches, she indicated, she had come to Bryn Mawr Community Church, and had joined it because she felt "at home" and liked the total spirit and atmosphere.

Neither of us saw anything in Mrs. Merz that would indicate it as unwise for us to try to help her especially with her question about life's meaning. In her story about the psychiatric treatment, there was nothing to suggest she had run away from it and much to show that she had profited from that and knew it. We felt that if the need for such treatment should become evident again we could take this up directly with Mrs. Merz. Subsequent events proved our judgment correct. Even if a resumption of psychiatric work had been indicated later on, we believe the counseling with us would have made this process easier.

Search for Meaning. At the start of the second session, Mrs. Merz told of the reflections she had had following the first. She wondered whether she could "really do anything to change things much," or if she could hope to get a "different perspective on everything after all that's happened." Then came the following:

MRS. MERZ: Well, religion teaches that—I think, basically—ah—well, maybe all religions, maybe not all—teach that we're controlled by other things besides human powers, and to a certain extent we are to accept what is. We can't change it, and I don't know how true that is, whether it's completely true or not.

67

Whether these things are meant to be and we just sit back and accept them—but I can't believe that—ah—completely. Whether we shape our own destinies—I'm not completely sure. Because I feel powerless to shape mine to suit me the way I think I want it to be.

MR. COLSTON: That is, you can't believe that this is—that while you are not involved in making some decisions which will affect your destiny, you somehow can't believe that just yielding or giving in is the answer to it, either.

MRS. MERZ: No, I can't. I mean, I'm still at the point where I'm fighting. Maybe in another ten years I won't care and I'll say— well—ah—I'll probably reach that point to a certain extent. Because when I see the things that are and the things that happen to people, I realize that many, many of the things that do happen to us—we can't control. Things that happen day after day. But— ah—I'm not sure how much we can control our fate.

MR. COLSTON: You're not sure what your own responsibility is or what decision you can make to effect . . .

MRS. MERZ: (Interrupting) Yes, sometimes I feel—well, I should say more than sometimes because I've always had a deep religious yearning for something and, as I've told you, I have never gone to church before. But—ah—and sometimes when I look back I can say—well, this was for the best. I suppose things worked out for the best but I can't always see it at the time. But it escapes me as to how much we human beings can do about this.

MR. COLSTON: It's difficult to know how much straining against what happens is pointless and where you should exert some effort.

MRS. MERZ: That's very true. Don't most religions teach that our destiny is shaped by something more than human powers? We have to feel that in order to have faith—religious faith—and which I want to have very much. Sometimes I'm bitter within myself—not all the time—but I reach the point where I am bitter. Ah—of course I'm too—I'm thinking I have too much fear of God to rebel. Ah—maybe some day I might reach that point. I don't know—but I think at this stage of the game I still have too much fear, perhaps, to say that I don't believe in God and so on.

MR. COLSTON: You fear any doubts that may arise. You're not sure whether or not you can accept these in you, I guess.

Here Mrs. Merz has been trying to articulate some of the complexities of her two-directional feeling about religion, God, and destiny. On the one side, she has a yearning; she would like to be able to accept many things as they are, and she has had actual experiences in which retrospect showed the benefit that had not been seen at the time. On the other side, not everything that happens is good; men cannot be merely puppets controlled on a string; the allegedly good God must have some queer sides to his nature, and there must be some aspects of one's destiny that he himself can control.

Especially since Mrs. Merz is plainly working here right in the midst of the most crucial religious problem there can be, the reader may wonder why Colston was not more active in trying to help her reconcile these questionings and conflicts. For example, why did he not assure her—for he believes this—that God welcomes confrontation with honest and sincere doubt? There would be situations in which such a question would be put to Colston as teacher and clarifier, in which he would do his best in just that way, but this situation was rather different. This religious problem was existential; it involved Mrs. Merz's attitude toward everything in life, including her daily activities. Besides, since she had attended our church for some time, she had heard effectively expounded, more than once, the general answer to the very question she was posing. As a matter of fact she had, in a Lenten Series, heard us both speak directly to this question. This meant that such an answer could be genuinely meaningful to her only if considered in her way at her pace. This circumstance directed the mode of Colston's counseling at this point.

Thus, even from the point of view of religious education of Mrs. Merz, he had to assume that, since she had already heard the right words, there was some block to her absorbing this answer. If he missed that, he missed her. If the reader asks what he would have said if she had asked the Christian answer to this dilemma, he would probably have given her the briefest possible summary but then added, "But I realize that, in your head, you already know this. Therefore I assume that something going very deep in your experience questions this, is unsure whether it's true or congenial. So my understanding of

69

our task is that we ought to work toward that block. Then later we can come back to the 'right answer.'"

Her central theme was along this line, "I want to have faith, but I find myself doubting, and I become frightened by my own doubts, even those doubts about the values of faith." The following also came in the second session:

MRS. MERZ: Yes, I mean (pauses)

MR. COLSTON: You ask the question, "Don't most religions teach that you should accept the action or purpose of a greater power?"

MRS. MERZ: Yes. So are we to just sit back and say—well, if that's it there is nothing I can do about it?

MR. COLSTON: Do I have any responsibility or any freedom really to . . .

MRS. MERZ: (Cutting in) Yes, that's true. You wonder and you say that you feel that certain things are mapped out from the beginning. You see young people die and old people live on in suffering. And you think that there must be some reason for it. It doesn't make sense to us human beings but you (pauses.) And the older you get, I think, the more you fear that type of thing, and you feel that there must be some reason for it.

MR. COLSTON: That these things all seem so irrational to you but there must be some design that you can't quite see.

MRS. MERZ: Yes, but sometimes you doubt whether these things should be or why these should happen, and then you have a fear that you have no right to doubt these things. I think I told you that I quite often have dreams about religion. Did I tell you about the one that—I think I probably told Dr. Hiltner about it. But I have had similar dreams. Ten years ago I had this dream— that it was a very moonlight night, and I was standing someplace and all of a sudden this fear came over me, and there were clouds —like on a moonlight night—and as I looked up into the sky I saw this light that got brighter around the clouds, you know, around the edges. And as I stood there the cross floated down from the cloud, and on the cross was the figure of Christ.

And in this dream I thought to myself that this must be what it's like to die. And I was sitting someplace, and it seems like

70

I just relaxed and just became numb all over—thinking that I must be dying. And I had—not exactly the same dream—but I had recurrent types of dreams about this vision in the sky. I attribute it probably to the fact that I was kind of searching for a religion and a place for myself in some religion.

MR. COLSTON: In other words, you are searching for a religion which will mean fulfillment for you in the face of your thoughts about death.

MRS. MERZ: I think so. I mean, I know that I was. I know that I have been, probably since I've been old enough to think about it. And probably a lot of it was subconscious. It was about ten years ago that I had that dream, and I've had similar dreams since, and I think it's probably that yearning for a religion or something. I certainly think it's a very sad thing for any individual to grow up without any religious background. My mother was Roman Catholic and my father was Jewish. I was actually baptized but we weren't brought up in any religion. I think—it seems—that I, more than any of the others, felt a need for it. I don't know why.

MR. COLSTON: So that somehow, you're saying, you miss this.

MRS. MERZ: Very definitely. It's a very definite part of my life that I felt I didn't have.

Mrs. Merz really wonders if she and all people are not perhaps trapped by a capricious deity. But, shocked by having articulated this presumption, she retreats to regarding this as a deficiency in her understanding. Her yearnings for a meaningful religious faith, which she believes well up from deep within her for reasons she does not understand, she has nevertheless accepted as real expressions of herelf. Her lack of religious training in childhood she now sees as having deprived her of a resource.

Mrs. Merz's dream of ten years before, along with the general report of similar dreams since, is fascinating from every point of view. Whatever else one might say about the dream, it bears primarily the marks of just that experience of "*mysterium tremendum et fascinans*" about which Rudolph Otto wrote so brilliantly nearly two generations ago.[1] Although it might indeed have also other levels of meaning—such as a desire to integrate her own experience of divi-

71

sion in early family experience—there is no reason not to take it seriously in the form in which it is presented, as Mrs. Merz herself had taken it.

Mrs. Merz's perception and interpretation of her dream as a message from her own subconscious dimensions telling her she longed for a meaningful religion seemed to make good sense. She had, after all, over a period of years begun to heed this message which was, indeed, connected with her coming to the pastor for counseling. There seemed to be no reason to stop her with the dream and insist that it be interpreted in detail, since it was obviously simply a part of the larger situation she was attempting to get hold of and convey.

Plainly, Colston's main attempt in this interview, of which we have given so much, was to express acceptance of her dilemma as she saw it, and thus to suggest that he could understand how she felt pulled and divided as she did. Although he was not always equally effective, he believes he did accomplish this main purpose at this stage of the counseling.

Only toward the very end of this second interview, after having discussed the religious dilemma so forthrightly, did Mrs. Merz disclose that she had been immensely reluctant to discuss her religious views with anyone since she was painfully conscious of being naïve in the way she saw them. The fact that Colston had diverged, in this interview, almost not at all from reflecting feeling did prove, therefore, at this stage to have been a wise decision.

Attitudes to People. In the third session Mrs. Merz reflected on her attitudes toward other people, especially those with whom she was associated in her job. She found it puzzling that "I find myself identifying with the 'underdog' all the time." This was particularly true of the way in which Negro employees were treated. But why, she asked, did she not have similar feelings of empathy for Jewish people, since she herself was half Jewish in ancestry?

MRS. MERZ: Mr. Gedler said to me, "I can't understand why you can't adjust. You're a person who is understanding, sympathetic, and you're warm in your attitude toward other people. Why can't you be sympathetic toward these Jewish patrons?" And I told him that I didn't know. I can't be. That's what I didn't understand about myself. Why do I have a block against these

72

people? I'm sympathetic toward Negroes and minority groups, I'm sympathetic toward anybody who I feel has problems—yet I can't be sympathetic toward this one isolated group. Why not? If I were basically an intolerant person who was very self-centered and wasn't sympathetic toward anybody, then it would be very easy to see why I couldn't be tolerant or sympathetic to anybody. But I'm not.

MR. COLSTON: Your feelings toward this group don't coincide with the way you view yourself, basically.

MRS. MERZ: Not at all, and I do have guilt feelings about it. Because I know in my heart that I—I mean, I don't have these feelings toward other groups, and why should I—I should be sympathizing with them because they're a minority group.

MR. COLSTON: "Why should I pick on them?"

MRS. MERZ: That's right. I seem to lean toward other people who are in minority groups as far as being understanding of them and sympathetic. But this is one group that I should—but I somehow can't seem to—ah—change my feeling about. It isn't something that preys on my mind constantly or anything like that, but it's something that I think about. Occasionally when—on my job—I come in contact with these very demanding people, it seems that they're really never satisfied no matter what you do for them.

MR. COLSTON: You resent this kind of treatment?

MRS. MERZ: Yes, very definitely. Yes, I do.

Colston felt that what Mrs. Merz was trying to get at was that these people (Jews) aroused strong feelings of resentment in her because they violated her conception of how one should feel about other people. Of course it occurred to him that there was probably a ghost of her father's Jewishness lurking in the background, and that she felt she had conquered these inconsiderate feelings so why did they not conquer theirs? Throughout there was the touch of "tolerance except to the intolerant!" Mrs. Merz went on.

MRS. MERZ: I wonder what's wrong with me that I do have these resentments, if it's not a normal thing to have them? (Pauses)

73

I'm battling with myself all the time, it seems (*laughs*). I get tired of it sometimes.

MR. COLSTON: It's really tough to have to take everything you do and pull it apart and analyze it.

MRS. MERZ: Yes, it is. Very hard. I think sometimes if I could just black out certain areas in my mind that I wouldn't have to think about or be so conscientious—conscientiousness or guilt or whatever it is—I'd be a much happier person, believe me. I've seen people who just don't seem to give a darn about anything or anybody and they seem to be happy. I don't know, maybe they aren't.

MR. COLSTON: To have to carry this weight around and be constantly confused about what's acceptable here or there, and analyzing it all the time, really gets pretty hard?

MRS. MERZ: It does. I've always been that type of person ever since I can remember—always. I've always thought that everything I did or said—I wondered and thought about it and mulled it over and made mountains out of mole hills many, many times. And I know it, I'm aware of it. Outwardly, I suppose I think most people are well-adjusted. Maybe I am; I don't know (*laughs*). Maybe this is being—well—adjusted, I don't know, but it seems to me it could be a little less painful.

MR. COLSTON: You're saying, "Am I so different from other people? And yet I seem to have more of these problems. But, maybe they're not something . . ."

MRS. MERZ: And I apparently shouldn't be because other people— well, I should say all other people—but it seems—I don't know —unless I don't know other people. You can't tell what their inner thoughts are.

MR. COLSTON: You're not sure you are seeing other people as they really are . . .

MRS. MERZ: No, I'm not, and this bothers me.

What Mrs. Merz has been trying to convey here is that she feels trapped in her own brand of personality, which she regards as in some ways inferior to that of others. She feels she may get her own problems out of proportion and wonders if other people secretly do so too. As we went on, Mrs. Merz questioned whether she was ever genuinely aware of the feelings of other people. This made her feel cut off.

MRS. MERZ: Today I don't feel that way. The other night I did. This reaction or whatever you call it. Today I don't feel that way.

MR. COLSTON: It's very strange.

MRS. MERZ: (*Pauses then begins to weep*) Last night I was upset this way (*weeping continues*)

MR. COLSTON: Hurts pretty deeply?

MRS. MERZ: (*Weeping goes on*) It's such a terrifying experience. People don't care. I don't mean that people don't care, I don't mean it that way, but . . .

MR. COLSTON: But you're so cut off. You feel quite alone.

MRS. MERZ: (*After long pause*) It's so terrifying—you feel that no one can reach you or do anything for you.

MR. COLSTON: Like trying to yell out of a well—ah—to reach somebody?

At this point Kierkegaard's abyss was not far away.[2] Mrs. Merz was, in the counseling session, recalling her feeling of terror and despair of being almost completely alone and estranged on many occasions. This was not her first mention of feelings of isolation. But here she was re-experiencing and confronting them, and the torrent of emotion choked her up. Colston was trying to give her support, but not in such fashion that would make her question the acceptability of what she was doing. His support has still to help her face the complexity of her problem through acknowledging the intensity of her feelings. Stark isolation can be faced only when the context manifests something else as well.

What Mrs. Merz was doing throughout this interchange was bringing into awareness various levels of her picture of herself and of her relationships to other people, all of which she knew before but which she ordinarily kept in separate compartments so they did not encounter one another. She saw herself as sympathetic and understanding; yet Jews irritated her. She felt she was warm toward people; yet she did not really see things from their point of view. She got along well with all kinds of people except Jews; yet she really felt isolated from everybody. These contain contradictions. The previous

75

compartmentalized division of them was breaking down through the very articulation, and she felt suspended in a no man's land.

A small sidelight is that later on Mrs. Merz revealed that she had been considering plastic surgery to remove the traces of Jewish appearance she had felt she had. As she came later to accept this part of her background, this notion simply disappeared.

Sister. Mrs. Merz felt inadequate in relation to her older sister, who "is my idea of a person who functions well." She said she despaired of ever having her sister's poise and serenity. Then came the following:

MRS. MERZ: I really sound very morbid, I know that.

MR. COLSTON: You're worried about how I'm taking what you are saying?

MRS. MERZ: Like this girl friend of mine that I saw today, she asked me if anything exciting had happened. And my sister spoke up and said, "Yes, she's been misbehaving." (*After long pause*) If all your people are like this you must have an awfully, terribly gloomy time.

MR. COLSTON: You mean that you must be pretty hard for me to have to take?

MRS. MERZ: Well, yes, if everybody carries on like this (*long pause*). I think you must have to be a certain kind of a person to have to listen day after day to people's problems and be objective about them. I mean, I realize that this is one of the things that I realize is a fault of mine. I get involved in other people's problems. This girl that is working for me—I know that that is very much on my mind, and I get very upset about it. And I just don't think that I should get so upset about things like that.

MR. COLSTON: That you really get caught in it.

MRS. MERZ: Well, no—except that these things have an effect on me. I have a lot of sympathy for her but too much, because they take hold of me.

MR. COLSTON: In other words, you feel really that you identify with her too much?

MRS. MERZ: Yes, they take something out of me every time I get involved in these situations. I don't mean that in the sense that I don't want to, that I don't want to be sympathetic to them—because I do—I just can't help myself though.

MR. COLSTON: It's pretty tough to care about them?

Colston's last response was intended to lift up the strength she had in being sympathetic toward people and yet also to acknowledge the pain this caused her. She interpreted the pain as weakness. She was really saying she ought to be able to care for people without suffering with them, and her reflections on his having to listen to—or suffer with—her came out of that frame of reference. Their exchange continued in this way:

MRS. MERZ: Yes, it is. But besides your difficulties you feel all that they are feeling.

MR. COLSTON: So that you're saying, "I can't help myself."

MRS. MERZ: No, I can't seem to. I just can't pass these situations off. Like this fellow that I've been seeing—he's younger than I am. I don't know exactly what my feelings are with him, but I know that I have a great deal of empathy for him because he went through something similar to this—having these same types of feelings—and so that of course made kind of a bond between us. And I feel sorry for him and think that he's lonely, and it bothers me very much because I can understand it.

MR. COLSTON: You feel for him and understand how he feels?

MRS. MERZ: Yes, because I know what it is to be lonely myself. Maybe he doesn't feel nearly as bad as I think he feels (laughs). Maybe it doesn't bother him as much as I think it does.

MR. COLSTON: In other words, "Maybe I'm seeing him too much through my eyes?"

MRS. MERZ: Yes, that's right. For instance with my sister. A couple of times when she's had a battle with her husband, my heart just aches. After it was over, she had forgotten about it—and here my heart was just aching for her something terrible because I was putting myself in her place.

Mrs. Merz contrasted her inability to "shrug off the hurts" with the marked ability of her sister. Her sister seemed "to take things pretty much in stride." She said she realized that she depended on her

77

sister to buoy her up when she became depressed, to reassure her, and to give her a sense of confidence when she had to face a task that seemed beyond her.

MRS. MERZ: And my sister is so different—I always compare myself with her. Well, I have a certain amount of drive, but I don't have anywhere near the drive that she has. She gets up at five in the morning and does some work, goes to work at seven and works until four, and then she goes over to her husband's offices and works from six to nine or ten (*laughs*) and goes to bed probably about midnight. Well, she claims she is much happier than I am—but I don't think physically I could stand it.

MR. COLSTON: You just don't feel you can be like your sister?

MRS. MERZ: Well, no. I don't seem to be able to. I don't know.

From our point of view it is doubtful whether the sister is the paragon she seems to Mrs. Merz. Whether she is just compulsive, finds this schedule a way to control her husband, or is genuinely absorbed in something she believes important, we do not know. What is clear is that the sister is an active person who always acts "strong," whatever she may be under the surface. Mrs. Merz has begun to realize how ambivalent are her feelings toward this activistic Juno. She has not yet realized how deeply divided her feelings are. By the fourth session, however, Mrs. Merz had begun to realize how strong was her emotional dependence on her sister.

MRS. MERZ: I finally went back over to the office about five o'clock to try to do some work and ease my mind. I haven't had a spell like that for quite some time; so I felt a little bit (*pauses*). Then last night I—ah—my sister called and she really bawled me out. And—ah—I went out to dinner with them, and my brother-in-law gave me something, and I slept last night and I was all right. But it's a terrible thing. They can't find anything wrong with me. But it's a terrible thing.

My sister says I'm trying to find something wrong with me. I'm not really. These things may not be particularly significant, but I do know that I have these feelings. Maybe other people don't have as much fear as I have. I can't understand my sister's attitude toward this. That just makes me worse. And I can't understand why she feels that way. When this happened before, my sister talked me out of it.

MR. COLSTON: So that you really feel ashamed of your behavior, and fearful . . .

MRS. MERZ: Well, yes, and my sister just can't understand. She says she never gets depressed. Well, perhaps she doesn't but I—ah— I wish I could develop that talent. She never thinks about the past; she never allows herself to get depressed; she never lets people hurt her—I wish I could be that way but I'm not.

MR. COLSTON: Sort of—you admire your sister's ability to . . .

MRS. MERZ: In a way, yes. I mean—she means a great deal to me, and she probably worries about me, but she thinks that I'm just being silly and misbehaving (pauses).

MR. COLSTON: You hate to be a problem to her.

MRS. MERZ: Well, yes (long pause). Maybe I felt that I would die, I don't know. They don't understand what a terrible, horrifying thing it is. I just seem to be slipping away. I just can't (pause)

MR. COLSTON: You mean it's hard to tell me . . .

MRS. MERZ: (Breaking in) Because it's so terrifying. Maybe you would understand, but some people don't. They just can't understand. They say there's nothing wrong with you, and it's ridiculous. And you know that there's nothing wrong with you. I know that's true, but nevertheless, I have this feeling, "You're going to die."

Mrs. Merz's sense of isolation had been increased because she had been unable to communicate how she felt even to her closest relative, her sister. Since her second husband's death she had had a fear of dying, but really being afraid of this seemed nonsensical to a compulsive and aggressive woman like her sister. Every time she contrasted herself with her sister, Mrs. Merz felt thwarted, weak, unacceptable, dependent, and incapable of acting on her own. No doubt with the best conscious intent, the sister had made use of this deference by Mrs. Merz to try to mold her into the aggressive-compulsive pattern. What Mrs. Merz began to realize in the above exchange was the depth of her attachment to and dependence upon her sister and her sister's standards. In character, she is utterly unlike the sister—

79

sensitive where her sister is a bulldozer, reflective where her sister simply gets more work done, imaginative where her sister deals with "plain facts," emotional where her sister at least gives the appearance of calmness and no-bother. Yet she has allowed herself to regard her sister's as the proper standards. She has begun to realize the true state of affairs.

Plateau. The four interviews that followed—fourth through seventh—were focused around Mrs. Merz's despair about remarrying or, at her age, of ever having children. Some aspects of her job that she did not like also came into the discussion. With the last she had been trying to improve things by some rearrangements but felt frustrated over the prospects.

In the ninth session Mrs. Merz expressed appreciation for the opportunity her counseling had afforded to experience directly some of the feelings she had had and to open up areas she knew had been bothering her but that she had not felt free to discuss with anyone else.

MRS. MERZ: I haven't had any more of those spells like I had before. I seem to be getting along much better. I seem to be just kind of going along neither happy nor unhappy—kind of on an even keel.

MR. COLSTON: You feel that at least if you can keep some equilibrium you feel O.K. about it?

MRS. MERZ: Yes, at least I'm not desperately unhappy because—at least not to the point where I feel so depressed. In other words, I don't think that there is anything that I am particularly happy about, and yet I'm not depressed. I haven't been for the past couple of days. I get exhausted with these inner conflicts sometimes and want to shut them out altogether. I just get tired of thinking about them. I should get tired of thinking about them more often—I'd probably be better off.

The "even keel" was not Mrs. Merz's real solution, but it was a plateau, a point of equilibrium, on which she was resting, as it turned out, "marking time" until she gathered her resources for a new climb.

Person or Sexual Object? Through the tenth and eleventh sessions Mrs. Merz remained, in general, on her plateau. She did not feel that she was as desperate as she had been nor as prone to be self-accusatory. She talked in these sessions about having had dates with some men friends. She said she now felt more like "going out" than she had before.

When Mrs. Merz appeared for the twelfth interview, she was extremely agitated, more so than in any previous session. Her feeling, however, was of irritation rather than despair.

MRS. MERZ: And I've sort of reached the point where I'm trying to find someone that interests me. I mean, I meet new people, and I meet many men and I have talks with them. All the men I meet are interested in just one thing. They're not interested in me as a person, and I get fed up even going out with them when they have to argue, and so forth. And I just don't even want to go out with them.

MR. COLSTON: You sort of feel like you're regarded as just an object?

MRS. MERZ: Yes, and I just don't understand. I don't know if it's my attitude. Because I would—ah—I don't know whether I meet the wrong kind of people or what.

MR. COLSTON: It's awfully discouraging not to be able to find someone that you really click with.

MRS. MERZ: That's right. There is surely a great deal more to me than just sex. I mean, it bothers me that I can't seem to find anyone who—who—who can see these other things. And believe me, I'm not the type of girl that most of these men are. And as I said, I don't want to meet anybody any more. It's the same thing over and over again. And it's not flattering to me. It might be to some, but it isn't to me.

MR. COLSTON: It's really discouraging because somehow sex seems to be the only interest, and you just can't seem to get through to them in any other sense.

MRS. MERZ: People don't seem to be thinking of anything else. And I consider that I have a half a brain and that I have understanding—and why can't people find these things in me? And it makes me very angry.

MR. COLSTON: It makes you angry to have other very important aspects of you neglected?

81

MRS. MERZ: That's right. Many's the time when I've been dating, and I go out with somebody and just face them and say, "Well, gee, can't you see that there's more to me than this? Can't you see I have half a brain or something like this?" This has happened many times. Sometimes I reach the point where I just explode over it and can't contain myself any longer about it. I've reached the point where I don't want to go out any more. I can't be bothered with this all the time.

The issue in the foreground was obvious. Colston felt that, in the background, Mrs. Merz was also wondering whether the insights she had gained in counseling were really of much value, for they did not seem to alter this dimension of her life. On the other hand, her anger was a different and more openly constructive reaction than had been her previous despair.

A Critical Period. The thirteenth through the fifteenth sessions were devoted largely to discussion of Mrs. Merz's job and of her desire to find a better one. During this time she visited another city about a job of the same kind she was then doing, was offended by the kind of offer she received, and returned "glad to get back to my old job, as soon as possible."

She telephoned to cancel several subsequent appointments she had made, and Colston feared she was on the verge of terminating the counseling. She did, however, finally come for the sixteenth interview, in which the following took place:

MRS. MERZ: In the first place, I haven't been feeling completely well. Sometimes just the thought of driving all the way down here and back—a couple of times—it's really been too much for me. Sometimes I think it's just neurotic and nothing very wrong; but I really just haven't felt like making this trip. And even today I really didn't feel like coming down.

Maybe it's partially a—ah—I suppose in a way I feel that I have problems, that I have probably talked and discussed so many things with you that I feel probably that I have run out of discussion to a certain extent. Ordinarily this trip down here doesn't bother me. I don't know whether it's psychological or not.

A couple of times I've just gone home and gone to sleep. I

just didn't feel up to coming down. I get up at 5:30 in the morning. And—ah—ordinarily the thought of driving down here and driving back have been a little more burdensome than I had felt before. It has nothing to do with you; it's just one of those things.

She was giving herself and Colston plenty of excuses. Later in the same interview she said she had felt that for the time being she did not need to have further counseling.

MRS. MERZ: About two weeks ago I thought—for no reason at all—well, perhaps I've gone as far with the counseling thing as I can and that maybe I should discontinue it. I thought that on the one hand, and then I thought—well, actually I haven't solved all of my problems—and so would it be just a matter of temporarily feeling better and feeling a little bit more at ease—and then would this come back again?

Of course you can develop too much of a dependence on another person as far as depending on them to solve or help you with your problems too. I realize that. Sometimes that happens in psychiatry. But in a way I thought perhaps I had accomplished as much as I could. And then again I thought—well, really I haven't done anything definite that I can say that I have accomplished in terms of changing any of these things. Do you find this in any of the other people you counsel with? Have any of them tapered off?

MR. COLSTON: Yes, some do. But I'd really like to see if I am understanding what is . . .

Here Colston was trying to see what this possibility of termination really meant to Mrs. Merz, but she went on in this fashion:

MRS. MERZ: Of course it could indicate another thing too. Which wouldn't be good. And that would be turning your back on your problems—because that isn't good either, in the strict sense of the word. You can't shut them all out and pretend they don't exist. I mean, again you would be . . .

MR. COLSTON: Turning your head?

MRS. MERZ: That's right. I don't know. I think some of my thinking has changed a little bit. I don't know whether it's a subtle thing

83

because of some of the things that have happened. I seemed to have changed my thinking a little bit. Some things that happened about a week or so ago made me wonder about some of the things that I think I want most in life. And—ah—I'm beginning to think or wonder whether these are the things I really want after all. Such as marriage and children. All of a sudden—ah—it seems like for some reason this is becoming not so important all at once. I don't want—I don't know where this all started, but I'm not—ah . . .

MR. COLSTON: You mean, it's not really nagging at you?

MRS. MERZ: Yes, that's right. And it seems that some of the things that have happened—ah—perhaps things that in the past I have blamed myself for—now it appears that I'm either wrong in blaming myself or I wasn't at fault. And that is perhaps (*trails off*). If someone should ask me what I wanted most, or what I was unhappiest about—of course I would say that I wasn't married and I didn't have children. But—ah—so many things have happened that have put me in a position where I just can't, and I turn my back on it.

During these thirteenth through sixteenth interviews it seemed to Colston that Mrs. Merz was resisting the idea of further counseling sessions without coming out and saying so. She seemed more resigned than acceptant toward herself and her own situation. Yet she said she was feeling better and getting along more effectively. One constructive insight did emerge during these sessions, that she tended to blame herself in exaggerated fashion whenever anything went wrong. Colston kept wondering during these sessions if he were letting her down, if there were more he could do to help her through this critical period of assimilation combined with resistance to going further. When he made a half stab at it once, Mrs. Merz herself saw its folly and cut him off quickly.

Becoming a Self. From the sixteenth interview onward Mrs. Merz moved ahead. She said she was generally feeling "more confident and secure," even though she added that she was unsure if she could trust this feeling. She was discovering, however, she continued, that she could act on her own without fearing how other people would take it. The following came in the seventeenth session:

84

MRS. MERZ: I don't know, I just made up my mind that I wasn't going to get upset and I didn't. I don't know. The last couple of weeks I just seem to have adopted an "I don't care" attitude. That doesn't seem to suit people either (*laughs*). I said that I didn't have any definite plans (*said this to her sister*), and she said, "Why don't you?" And I said that I just didn't have any interest in doing it. Well, she just blew up. And I said that frankly I just don't care. She said, "Well, this isn't you." So, you see, you can't please people (*laughs*). You get upset about something and she doesn't like that, and now that I don't care she doesn't like that (*laughs again*). And I said that I really mean it, I don't care frankly; so now she's upset because I don't care. I can see that I can't win one way or the other.

MR. COLSTON: So that you can't please her one way or the other?

It seemed clear that Mrs. Merz was experiencing a different kind of capacity in dealing with her sister, was enjoying this, and yet was still not really prepared for her sister's response to this change. The sister faces the prospect, if nothing else, of losing the effectiveness of her righteous indignation. Mrs. Merz continued:

MRS. MERZ: No, apparently I can't. If I get upset she's very displeased about it. And she said, "Well, this *is* a new you." I really mean it. It's darn if you do and darn if you don't (*laughs*).

MR. COLSTON: I don't know whether or not you're saying, "Am I becoming an insensitive person?"

MRS. MERZ: Well, I don't particularly care if I do become insensitive. I think I'd be better off if I did become more insensitive, frankly. I mean, from all the times that I have tortured myself, it's just no good to be like that. I mean, I'm really not concerned about it. I think to myself, so what? If I am becoming insensitive, I am. At least I'll keep myself from being hurt. Maybe I'll start to hurt other people, I don't know. I never have. Maybe I should hurt other people for a change instead of myself. But I'm not concerned right now. Although if you would ask me if I would deliberately hurt anybody I would say no. I don't really want to. I don't really want to. I don't really think that. As I told you once before, anything that I have done that I have

85

considered wrong has always been to hurt myself and, as I know of, I have never hurt anyone else.

MR. COLSTON: So you're saying that, although you're not really just bending over backwards to have regard for "how I affect somebody, I really am still very sensitive to other people."

MRS. MERZ: Yes, up to now I am. Maybe I'll change. It appears that maybe I'd be better off. I don't know. Maybe this is what people mean when they say people (words lost)—I don't feel any bitterness. How long that will last, I don't know. Maybe tomorrow I'll be 'way out here again (laughs).

She is not on the verge of becoming immorally insensitive to other people, but of recognizing the difference between a constant vulnerability to blaming herself and accepting blame from others and, on the other hand, taking some things in stride. Colston's putting the question about insensitivity seems, in retrospect, to have been off the beam. Fortunately she was now able to show that this was not quite what she meant. She was warning him, especially from this point, against trying to balance everything up. Truly enough, she would have to experience the new feeling in itself before she could balance it with something else.

Her Mother. In the latter interviews Mrs. Merz said she was noticing more and more, in reflection, how much in the past she had failed to act on the basis of her own genuine feelings. She said she had been mulling this over concerning her parents. The following came in the eighteenth session:

MRS. MERZ: I know that my mother would have done anything in the world for her children. But as far as outward show of affection, there never has been any. And I think I inherited that temperament that my father had. He was kind of a warm person and I feel—ah—(clears her throat), as I said, today if my mother goes away some place I may kiss her on the cheek and that's it. I feel a little uncomfortable even doing that.

MR. COLSTON: Now, here, you're saying several things. One is that you regret that somehow you just didn't express your affection toward your father, because now there's no opportunity. You say, "It kind of depresses me."

86

Mrs. Merz: Yes, and—ah—although I never thought about it until after my father died, and then it was very strong—because I wasn't even living at home when he died of coronary. I was living in B—— at the time and I had been rather sickly for about a year, and for all that time I didn't see him. And I felt for a long time afterwards, you know, the feeling of guilt afterwards. And not that I mistreated him, because I never did, nothing really serious . . .

Mr. Colston: So that you just regret that you didn't take the opportunity before he died, really to let him know how you felt about him.

Mrs. Merz: That's right. In a way, I feel sometimes like that about my mother. Even though I know that she doesn't receive affection or apparently doesn't welcome it. Ah—yet many times I think—when she's been here for a visit—and after she's gone I think to myself maybe I didn't treat her just as nicely as I should, although I don't mistreat her.

Mr. Colston: You mean you feel that maybe you should go ahead and embrace her and show affection for her, even though you cannot be sure she will accept it?

Mrs. Merz: Yes. I usually am involved in some of my own problems and perhaps I'm not completely—giving her complete attention, you see. When she goes, then I realize it.

Colston believes this exchange not only helped her to go over the old regret in relation to her father but also to consider her course of action in relation to her mother. What the mother seemed to want or not to want had apparently been the guidepost of past relationship, and yet perhaps Mrs. Merz's own preoccupations had got in the way. In any event, why could she not treat her mother as *she* wanted to treat her, instead of just as the mother seemed to want to be treated? She worked more on this in the latter half of this interview.

Prayer. In the nineteenth session Mrs. Merz came back to the religious issues with which her counseling had begun, taken especially from the point of view of prayer.

Mrs. Merz: My sister thinks that I appear to be better. My attitude is better, and I look better, and I guess my general outlook

87

seems to be improved. I still haven't been able to get back to prayer, though. It disturbs me that I have abandoned it. I don't know why.

MR. COLSTON: You don't feel right about it?

MRS. MERZ: You know, in a way—and this doesn't make sense—it isn't right, and yet it seems like I feel as though—and this isn't in the sense of being—ah—of changing my belief in God—it seems in a way that I feel as though all of the times that I've said prayers, that they were never answered. That while I haven't had any prayers answered it seems that things haven't been any worse than they were when I didn't. And sometimes it seemed as though they were worse. Of course, as I told you last week, I feel that the help that I have gotten has been something that has come from—ah—from above. I mean, I feel that and I know it in a way, and yet I can't somehow (pauses)—it seems that when I would say a prayer that really nothing ever came of it. Of course I apparently was asking for things I shouldn't be asking for, I suppose. I realize that.

MR. COLSTON: But what you're saying as you reflect upon it is that prayer didn't make a difference. In fact . . .

MRS. MERZ: (Interrupting) It didn't seem to. It doesn't seem to. It sounds—it sounds—ah—what word do I want to use?

MR. COLSTON: You mean sacrilegious?

MRS. MERZ: Sacrilegious, yes. It sounds sacrilegious to say that—it really bothers me to say that, but I'm trying to analyze it. Ah— in the particular times when I was really in terrific desperation perhaps, and I felt that prayers weren't answered—perhaps the prayers are really answered but they may be answered in a de- layed reaction, in other words (laughs), I mean, perhaps that's true, but for some reason I don't know, I can't seem to explain it. I just can't seem to.

MR. COLSTON: You mean maybe your prayers are being answered but in a different way than you had anticipated?

She seemed to be saying that the counseling experience had been a form of answer to her prayer, but that she had not so understood it until she began to say it. From a theological point of view she was certainly showing evidence of a deeper understanding of prayer.

MRS. MERZ: Well, I suppose, later on than I expected it to be anyway. I was taught—ah—I wasn't taught—when I was living in T—— and when my husband disappeared I went through a really tough time. And I was living with a—I was living in a rooming house, had a room there, and this woman was a very understanding person and she knew what I was going through. She taught me the prayer, "Guide me in thy wisdom; give me strength to pray."

I mean, she taught me this and—it seems to me the type of prayers that I have said—ah—seem to be—I mean, that was one that has become kind of a part of me rather than just a petition for something in particular. I don't mean that there haven't been times when I have prayed this, but this has been kind of a prayer that has stuck with me and—ah—I can't—I mean, I don't feel that I was asking for anything in the sense of—it is asking in a way, but not for something definite. But doesn't our religion think that you should ask sometimes? Isn't that true? Does our religion think that you should?

MR. COLSTON: Make specific requests?

MRS. MERZ: Yes. Or do you say—I mean, you just say we also teach whatever is the will of God, which I suppose is probably the most important thing. But I think Roman Catholics have different—they have prayers of petition and prayers of thanksgiving. Do we have different types of prayers?

MR. COLSTON: Well, I think it depends pretty largely on what group is offering and viewing the prayer. Some groups within the Protestant churches, especially the higher church groups, have definite categories for prayer, and this ranges all the way from free groups who believe that the most sincere prayer is the spontaneous prayer that has no particular order to it. But I guess I feel that any form which expresses or speaks to your own soul's concern is the proper kind of prayer.

Summary on Esther Merz. We understand the general course of Mrs. Merz's counseling to have gone this way. She began with intensity, spurred by recurrent depressions and fear of them, but also lured by the prospect of getting a religious faith she had never had before but toward which she had been working. She began genuinely to think reflectively about religion. She then moved to her attitudes toward other people, starting with the discrepancy between her usual sympathy and her negative feeling about Jews. As she moved to consider her attitudes toward herself, she found these complex but the conviction about her constant blaming of herself grew. She began to see the deeper ambivalence of feeling toward her sister than she had previously realized. All this made possible some improvement in actual living.

Then came a bit of an explosion about the way men tried to use her. This was followed, however, by a plateau on which she was consolidating her gains. First circumstance, and then hesitant feeling, caused her to cancel several appointments. Even when they were resumed, it was not clear whether she was going to try to settle for what she had gained so far or would attempt to move ahead. She did make some further moves ahead, not radical ones, but especially in reconsidering her attitudes toward her deceased father and still-living mother and in her understanding of religion. However, the basic level at which she considered her problems was really achieved about half way through. Up to that point there was steady deepening. Even though there were, thereafter, important consolidations of her gains, some new insights, and some explorations into new areas, the fundamental level of consideration changed little. We interpret this to mean that, short of a depth procedure like psychoanalysis, this is the level to which Mrs. Merz was prepared to go in re-examining herself and her problems.

What happened to her certainly seems to lean toward the side of success rather than failure, in our subjective estimate, a judgment supported by her test scores. Yet hers is not a story of constant onward and upward movement. She is especially representative because the counseling enabled her to reach a certain new level in considering herself, her relationships, and her whole situation, but did not force her to go beneath that. As it turned out, this new level will probably have enormous meaning in the rest of her life. The content—including the recognition of her intrapunitive (self-blaming) tendencies, her recognition that her self-respect does not need to depend upon another marriage or upon having children, et cetera—has all been given in the running account and need not be repeated here. Why could Mrs. Merz go so far—and yet go no farther? Our interpretation of her is as a quite intelligent person, torn early in life between a cold mother and a warm father and by their religious differences, early accepting her older sister's self-estimate and always thereafter weighing herself on her sister's scales to her own detriment, having two marriages, one unsuccessful and one quite successful, but which left her a widow. On the second occasion her anxiety was so extreme that she, recognizing it, had psychiatric treatment. Stimulated for a long time by yearnings for a religious faith that would be meaningful, she began actively to search for this, joined Bryn Mawr Church, and through this came into the counseling.

She was, at the time of her counseling, both more captive than she knew and also more desirous of freedom than she realized. She was captive to her sister's standards and expectations, to the notion that a woman's life was empty without children, to expectations that almost anyone might have of her, and to much else. On the other side, she wanted more than she knew to be a person—with her sister, at her work, with men, even with God. The early religious discussion was apparently valuable in its own right, but it also seems to have served as a bridge by which she could get at these various aspects of her conflict, the captivities and the desires for freedom. Seen in the light of her bondages, her progress is very considerable during the counseling. Yet looking at some of the evidences of her deep desire for liberation, one wonders why she could not go further. The outcome seems to show about the proper point of adaptation between the strength of the two forces at the present time. If she lives more or less successfuly with her new insights she may be able to go further.

Anne Vick (Center)

Anne Vick came to the counseling center torn between a strong desire to keep her family together and an equally strong feeling of futility about working out a satisfactory relationship with her husband. The center had been suggested to her by a social agency to which she had first gone.

Mrs. Vick was in her late thirties and the mother of a small son. At the time her counseling began she was living in the city with her

91

invalid sister, having left the suburban home she and her husband had built. At this time she was not working outside the home, nor had she done so regularly since her boy was born, but she had previously worked as a seamstress.

Our matching of Mrs. Vick with Mrs. Merz was partly in terms of the usual formal characteristics but also because the first round of tests showed them to be very similar types of people. We thought that this fact would help us to see with clarity what difference the setting made, and so we believe it does. The reader has already seen that Mrs. Merz was explicitly seeking meaning in her life at a religious as well as at other levels. Mrs. Vick, on the other hand, dealt entirely in the realm of personal and sociocultural values, as we shall see. Both persons, while not our most outstanding successes, nevertheless made marked progress in their counseling as shown both by our judgment and by the tests.

Stature. Mrs. Vick was fat and very tall at the same time. Her height was more than six feet, and she said she had always been self-conscious about her obesity. Even as a young child, she said, "More was expected of me because I was larger than the other children." In those days, she added, "If anything happened to me, I didn't get much sympathy because, I guess, I was expected to be big enough to take care of myself." The following came in the first interview:

MRS. VICK: I never thought that I was quite what I was supposed to be, you know—ah—my parents, they never had any money or anything and I never had a social life like—ah—you know. I mean, I have been in business at one time, and you hear people talk about what they do and places they've been and the things they've done—and it just seemed like I never did any of those things. Yet I feel that it has affected me in some way anyway.

MR. COLSTON: That somehow you've missed out on interesting things?

MRS. VICK: Well, not interesting things but—ah—things that other people have done and—ah—places they've gone and things like that. It seems like I've always been—I've always had more responsibilities than I think I was capable of carrying, because I was always big and strong looking.

MR. COLSTON: People always expected more of you?

92

MRS. VICK: Yes, all the time.

MR. COLSTON: And I guess that what you're saying there is that on the one hand you haven't felt inside quite as capable of doing what people assumed you could do.

MRS. VICK: Well, people just seemed to think—to expect—that I go ahead and do it. And ever since I was young I was always a big child. When I was born I was thirteen pounds, and when I was two years old I was like a three- or four-year-old.

MR. COLSTON: So that it's always been kind of a handicap to you.

MRS. VICK: Actually I've done things. Don't get me wrong that I haven't done a lot of things. I graduated from grammar school when I was eleven years old. I was the youngest in the class, but I was also the biggest, the tallest and the heaviest. And it was the same through high school. It seemed that I was always with people who were older, and I had to act like them.

In retrospect, it becomes clear that Mrs. Vick was expressing here two interrelated types of feeling: In direct fashion, that other people had expected more of her because of her stature, and that she had usually been able to meet the expectations; in indirect fashion, that all this had isolated her. Colston was a bit too much struck with the former to be properly sensitive to the latter, and so, for example, she rejected his final remark in the above exchange.

Mrs. Vick then turned to consider her husband's rejection of her. His feeling ashamed of her, his making her look ridiculous in the eyes of her friends—these emerged just after her talk about her school years. Since being separated recently from her husband, she said she had attended some dances because she said she felt the need for some social contacts.

MRS. VICK: I had gotten to the point where I was afraid to express an opinion. And yet with anybody else I could talk and feel very much at home. In fact, since I've been separated from him now, I seem to have a lot of company and I go—I don't go to parties or anything—but I've been going to dances, and I've been meeting people. And yet for some reason or other he seems to feel that I'm doing this for another purpose except to make myself

93

feel better. He thinks there's another motive behind why I'm going to dances.

MR. COLSTON: In other words, you're doing this because you feel it really is an outlet for you?

MRS. VICK: That's right. I meet people and actually I'm not going out to meet anybody, and yet I like the feeling of having someone think that I'm attractive enough to ask me. Because my husband told me that he was ashamed of me. And I think in a way I'm trying to prove that he was wrong. I like to feel that there's somebody else who's not ashamed of me anyway (*long pause*). And that's something I don't like (*weeps*). Oh, yes, he's nice looking and everything, but if he had gotten bald, would that have been an excuse for me to say—well, I'm ashamed of you? I mean, everybody has done—everybody has some things that they may not even like about themselves (*pause*). I don't know. Maybe I tried too hard to please him.

MR. COLSTON: So that you're saying, "Well, now, is this really fair? I took *him* for better or worse."

MRS. VICK: That's right.

Mrs. Vick expressed a great deal of emotion during this first interview and wept frequently. She began with the discussion of her stature in early years implying a feeling of isolation as a result, then went on to her husband's being ashamed of her, and finally to her conviction that she was accepted by people other than her husband.

Estrangement from Husband. After having received much physical and mental abuse from her husband, Mrs. Vick said, she had resolved "not to take it any longer." So she had left their suburban home and taken her child to live with her sister in the city. Yet, she continued, she often felt she ought to consider returning to her husband for the sake of the child. She continued to feel confused about what the right decision was, she added. Toward the very end of the first session the following emerged:

MRS. VICK: I'm still living from boxes. I mean, I still have stuff packed in boxes, and that's what I have to live with. It's still not a house. I still feel like I'm in back of a store or something, and I might as well be.

94

MR. COLSTON: You feel that you just don't have any real roots, I guess.

MRS. VICK: Yes, that's the way I feel. I'm just floating around from here to there, and I'm afraid for my child. I wouldn't want him to have that insecure feeling that I have given to him. He seems to be a very happy baby and everything. I mean—oh, I guess he cries as much as the next baby, but nothing unusual.

MR. COLSTON: That is, you worry about whether or not this unsettled situation is affecting him, and yet . . .

MRS. VICK: Yes, that's what I'm afraid of. And the thing is—I have made up my mind that I was going back to my husband; and yet when it comes to doing it, I can't do it. I can't. I just can't bring myself to do it. I don't know why. I can't explain it.

MR. COLSTON: You mean you're caught between wanting to go back and resisting the idea at the same time?

MRS. VICK: I mean, when you live with someone for as long as I have—ah—I'm afraid I can't respect him as much as I should because as far as I'm concerned—ah—striking a person, whether it's a female striking a male or a male striking a female, doesn't settle anything. As far as I'm concerned, that person feels something that they can't explain and they're only expressing it in violence. And I can't see violence. I never could.

MR. COLSTON: In other words, you resent his treatment of you, especially violence which you just can't accept.

MRS. VICK: That's right. I never believed in it. Even when I was a youngster I would see children fighting one another, and I would rather break it up. Believe me, that's true. There's been a good many of times when I've been hurt breaking something up rather than going in and fighting.

MR. COLSTON: You regard yourself as fundamentally a peacemaker?

MRS. VICK: Yes (pauses). And yet my husband has very good qualities. The man is intelligent. It isn't that he's—mentally, I have to keep on my toes to even live with him, because I wouldn't dare contradict myself in any way because right away he would spot it because he's very good at spotting mistakes. At work, if

95

somebody's made a mistake, he—whether he knows what the job is or not—he knows what the mistakes are.

And he had gotten to the point where he was continually telling me what was wrong. And I would say, "Well, don't you ever find anything good about me?" And he'd say that he was telling me those things so I could make myself perfect. But yet, if I told him that—the things that I didn't like—he wouldn't talk to me for two, three, or four days—sometimes weeks. There's been times when he hasn't talked to me for three weeks.

Mrs. Vick felt grossly sinned against. Yet also she kept examining her relationships with other people to find reassurance that her husband's nagging at her was not justified. The extreme complexity of her feelings about her husband is suggested in the following, also in the first interview.

MRS. VICK: When I'm living with him, I don't seem to have that—I don't know whether you call it gumption or not—something.

MR. COLSTON: I guess you're saying, "Well, this isn't like me. Why don't I stand up for myself?"

MRS. VICK: Yes. Am I afraid of him? My husband is a very big man. I mean, he's a very strong man, and is it because I'm afraid of his brute strength?

MR. COLSTON: So you're wondering if just outright physical fear . . .

MRS. VICK: Because my lawyer even has said to me, "Why did you leave your house?" Well, I wouldn't have stayed there under no circumstances. When I saw the look on his face. He even admitted it to me. He says that morning he felt like killing me. And I'm wondering—is that why I'm afraid to go back. I know I was actually afraid of him when I left.

MR. COLSTON: And maybe you still fear him?

MRS. VICK: I just don't understand it at all. Actually I don't know if I fear him or not. Is it something underneath that I fear? I know this one time when I was at my sister's and he brought the baby back—and I dreamed that he had kicked the baby in the head and the baby's head rolled under the bed. I woke up terrified. I actually saw that head just roll right under the bed like a ball. And I was thinking, "Well, is that what I'm afraid of?"

96

Because of her stature, courage has been attributed to Mrs. Vick all her life; yet she has often felt uncourageous, especially in relation to her husband. She is genuinely puzzled about the nature of her compliance to him. Certainly her feelings about him are complex.

During the second session Mrs. Vick considered mostly childhood experiences with special reference to her mother. Strangely enough, however, what she said about her mother was put in prosaic factual fashion, almost devoid of either positive or negative tones of feeling. She never did return, in subsequent counseling sessions, to her childhood. From this it may probably be inferred that the blocks to recovering her actual feelings of childhood were considerable, but her complete preoccupation with the relationship to her husband in the present was surely also a factor.

Toward the end of the second interview she began to deal with her own possible complicity in the alienation from her husband. She did recognize at times, she said, that she was "nagging" him. She always tried, she added, to make amends, while her husband steadily refused to accept these gestures. It was on such occasions, after refusing her apologies, she continued, that he would chide her publicly in front of her friends.

MRS. VICK: Sometimes I think he's said these things hoping that he would hurt me. He has. I admit it, of course. I've never showed him, but they have.

MR. COLSTON: Fundamentally, I guess you're asking, "Should I tolerate this behavior toward me?"

MRS. VICK: I've wondered about that a lot. He says—well, he didn't love me. But yet he seems to have forgotten that maybe I didn't have the love for him that I had six or seven years ago, because I had to take a lot of things that I didn't understand. I tried to take them, but I got tired of it.

MR. COLSTON: You have made an effort but feel it isn't being reciprocated, and you are weary of carrying what you feel is the full load . . .

MRS. VICK: That's right.

The first two sessions not only laid out the problem, so to speak, but contained a lot of sheer ventilation of feelings on Mrs. Vick's part. Little seemed required of Colston other than accepting and try-

97

ing to understand what she was saying. She moved ahead in high gear and made no requests of the counselor he could not fulfill; hence no explicit definition or redefinition of the counseling situation was required.

Relative Calm. During the third session, and those immediately following, Mrs. Vick described herself as feeling comparatively calm, an unusual experience for her of late.

MRS. VICK: I've been rather calm for some reason or other.

MR. COLSTON: You're not particularly bothered or pushed, or concerned too much?

MRS. VICK: No. I won't say calm because you can't be calm when you have a baby running around climbing up on chairs and climbing up on the table. But I've felt rather confident for some reason or other. The quiet before the storm or something like that (*laughs*).

She had even felt a bit sorry for her husband's missing these antics of their son. Yet this feeling about her husband was tied up with another.

MRS. VICK: But then I think that if he were a lot more interested and had made a bigger effort—because for a while there he wouldn't even take the baby overnight. He didn't pick the baby up for nine weeks.

After this interval her husband had called to say he was taking the baby for overnight, but Mrs. Vick had flatly refused. Yet she feared the child would forget his father and felt a bit guilty over such a prospect. Children, she said, all seemed to be fond of her husband.

MR. COLSTON: When you see how children like him and seem sometimes to prefer him to you, you wonder if this isn't some indication that something is lacking in you . . .

MRS. VICK: (*Weeping*) That's right. I just don't know what to think about it.

As the full recordings have been replayed in retrospect, this exchange seemed to mark a real change in the counseling process. Before this, there had been much expression or catharsis of feelings. But the feelings had been so weighty that expressing them and re-

98

flecting on them could not take place at the same time. This present exchange seems to be where more reflectiveness about herself in a new way began in Mrs. Vick.

Something of this same kind continued in the next several sessions. Although she expressed emotion, it was not in such degree as to prevent self-reflection. She said in several different ways that she recognized herself as being "on the defensive" much of the time, especially in relation to her husband. She said she saw also that his being on the defensive was hanging herself on a hook already prepared by her husband, and yet she continued to do it. She then suggested she was seeing that her constant need to be reassured was what made her vulnerable to these hooks, which in turn made her defensive. The following came in the sixth interview:

MR. COLSTON: You feel like you just don't count with him?

MRS. VICK: That's right. I mean, a person can't feel that way and still be perfectly happy; so I gained weight because whenever he does that I start eating. And—ah—when he was in the Marines for that year, there was times when he didn't talk to me for three weeks. He'd be in the apartment and there was no talking at all. But he wasn't like that when I first married him. I mean, I kept saying that it was because he had been overseas and he'd been through all this bombing and stuff like that. But I can't make that excuse all my life.

MR. COLSTON: You just can't go on making excuses to yourself to cover up how you feel toward him?

MRS. VICK: No, I can't. And when I tell him about these things, he tells me—I'm neurotic (weeps). That's all he tells me—I'm neurotic. But I don't feel that I'm neurotic. I'm away from him now and I'm fine. Sometimes he wants to go back, but I think it's because of the baby. Because he loves the baby. I can see that and it just breaks my heart, you know, but yet I can't hurt my baby's health. So I get real emotional over it and that's it.

MR. COLSTON: You're really caught between a desire to go back to him and a fear of what that all means to you. So you feel pulled in both directions and you are just thrashing it out inside.

MRS. VICK: That's right.

99

The third through the sixth interviews showed this relative calm, in contrast to the first two. Yet the above excerpt shows that Mrs. Vick tended to worry at precisely the same problem—whether or not to return to her husband—all the way. By this time she was able to be more reflective over it. As she became reflective, however, she tried spontaneously to examine previous experiences with her husband in order to try to get at the factors underlying the relational difficulty. The following came in the seventh session:

MRS. VICK: I was always larger and appeared older, but yet I married a man that was my age. He also had a handicap. Actually it is a handicap because I could never feel as free and at ease and my husband had the same trouble because he was real tall. He was six feet five, and everybody always took him for being older too. In fact, that was one reason that he couldn't finish school—because they made fun of him because he was tall and slender. And so he had the same trouble. He always felt more comfortable with older people too.

MR. COLSTON: So that you're saying that you had in common sort of being different and shut out, and feeling more accepted in older groups?

MRS. VICK: Yes. It's not that they laugh at you. They never laughed at me. He never did either. It was that we were unusual, and if there was any pairing off to do, we always were the ones that were left alone.

She denied that their relationship had grown out of these circumstantial factors alone, but said that the circumstances did tend to keep them both isolated from other people of their own age, and that this in turn had put extra strains on their relationship from the beginning. She added that she thought each of them—her husband also—had therefore looked to the other for emotional support to an unusual degree. She said her husband often boasted to other people that he could read his wife like a book, but that she felt this was false or how could he do so many of the things he did? "If he understood me, then he should be able to talk to me; shouldn't he?" As she continued in this vein she certainly was implying that she understood her husband but that he did not understand her. Colston

1 6 6 5 4

replied to this, "But you're saying that you understand him pretty well." Although she was not quite prepared to take this, put so directly, she took no offence, probably indicating that by this time she felt some trust in him.

Mrs. Vick's reflection in this same seventh session asserted that she could get along financially without her husband, if necessary, and raise her son giving him "maybe not everything he wanted but everything he needed." But "I wouldn't want the child to ever think that I didn't do the most to make the marriage go, you know." The possible future criticism by the baby is, she feels, an added factor on her to try to do "everything that I could" to make the marriage work. And yet, in the very next sentence, Mrs. Vick said, "There's no sense in my going back if he's going to be digging me an early grave." If only there were some sign on her husband's part, she continued, that he might be willing to make some change, she felt it might be different. But on the one occasion when this had been discussed, she reported him as having said, "You want to change me." What she did want was for her husband to become again what he had been after their marriage.

A good deal of the content of this session was repetitive of what had gone before, and all in relation to her husband. Yet the tone throughout was calm and even had some confidence in it. The self-pity and near-hysterical emotionality were gone. This seemed to mark a movement toward a level at which she could move and make decisions. On the whole, this level did not significantly alter through the remainder of the counseling.

Consolidation and Action. In a general sense the interviews after the seventh—through the fifteenth, when she terminated—represented consolidations of what she felt she had gained and trying out her capacities in decision and action. It was not of course all smooth going. For example, she came to the tenth interview disturbed over her own response to the fact that her husband had been late in sending the support money.

MRS. VICK: I seem to be at a loss for words when I'm talking to him. I don't know, he doesn't say anything to me much. I knew if I said anything it would probably be the wrong thing and probably sound real harsh. There doesn't seem to be any softness about that man at all. And it may not be that at all. He may just be one of those people who are quiet. A lot of people give him credit for knowing a lot more than he really does because he just doesn't say anything. But I don't know why he should affect me like he does. I don't know if it's because of the baby or what.

She continued in the same vein, wondering on the one hand what kind of person her husband really was and on the other why her reaction to him still threatened to get out of control. She said she could never please him. At breakfast the coffee was either too strong or too weak, never right. "Any way I do it it's wrong." In this tenth interview she did come close to acknowledging the hostility she felt for her husband.

MRS. VICK: You want to know something? (Weeps) I'd like to hurt that man as much as he's hurt me, but I don't think he's capable of feeling anything that deep—I've never seen that man excited about anything. I have never seen him enthusiastic about anything. The only thing I've ever seen is to see him lose his temper. Then he'd strike me.

By the time of the eleventh interview Mrs. Vick reported that the practical arrangements of support money, baby visiting husband, and so on, had considerably improved. Apparently her husband was accepting the *status quo*. Mrs. Vick said she thought she had learned how to assert herself about things like this without any longer feeling blocked or breaking down.

The same theme was elaborated, at about the same level, during the following three interviews, that is, through the fourteenth.

At the start of the fifteenth session Mrs. Vick said she had decided to terminate her counseling. She felt she was "getting along well," and, so long as this was true, she saw no purpose in spending her time, and that of the counselor, in going further.

MRS. VICK: I mean, I'm at a point now where I'm pretty good as long as I don't get in any situations with him. I haven't seen him now in three weeks, so I feel like I've . . . (pause)

MR. COLSTON: In other words, you just wish to stop for a while?

MRS. VICK: Yes. Because if I happen to get into any emotional difficulties with him—ah—as I am now I'm fine. It's funny—I mean, I don't fear to meet him and yet—ah—I'm all right as long as— it's not when I talk to him but it's afterwards. Why does he keep me off balance like that? I mean—it's hard to understand. I can talk to him. For a while there I couldn't but it seems like I never get any satisfaction in talking to him because he just doesn't talk back.

MR. COLSTON: You don't feel that you're getting anywhere really?

MRS. VICK: I get that frustrated feeling afterwards that I actually haven't penetrated or something. I don't know if I'm explaining it or not. I talk to him very calmly and everything else, but actually (pauses) can somebody be so emotionally involved with somebody that they can be affected like that for a long time?

MR. COLSTON: You wonder if you really are so bound up with him . . .

MRS. VICK: (Cutting in) Yes. I don't know (trailing off).

MR. COLSTON: That you hardly realize it.

MRS. VICK: Do I expect too much of myself and him? Or—I don't know—I just have these doubts, you know what I mean?

She concluded by saying that she still did not know, in relation to her husband and her tie to him, where she stood.

In leaving, Mrs. Vick said she would like to be able to have some further counseling later on if she should need it. She asked if Colston would telephone her at the end of the summer, this being the beginning. He agreed to do so and later did. When he called, she reported that she had just completed proceedings for a divorce, that she had continued to get along well and felt she did not at this point need further counseling. She said she had been surprised and pleased at her ability to carry through the divorce proceedings with some self-assurance despite the pain attached to it. She said, "Not that I was so eager to get the divorce, but I just couldn't take it any more. I was just pleased that I could face him and not be afraid . . . it was a big step for me to get up enough courage even to face him."

Mrs. Vick took both the post-counseling and the follow-up tests.

Summary on Anne Vick. Less of the direct dialogue material about Anne Vick has been presented than in relation to her matched partner, Esther Merz. This is because much more of the content of Mrs.

103

Vick's counseling was repetitive than was true of Mrs. Merz. The course of Mrs. Vick's counseling may be summarized roughly as follows:

During the first two sessions her emotion and its expression were at their height. Despite small ups and downs from the third interview onward, the general course of Mrs. Vick's expressions from then on was greater calmness, increased confidence, and finally greater ability to decide and act about those things where she felt she must. There was never a digging to a deeper level of feeling. Indeed, depth and intensity of feeling seemed to Mrs. Vick to be the same thing, and, having got away from what she exhibited in the first sessions, she tried to keep away from similar strong feelings, which to her meant weakness. That there can be another kind of depth of feeling, of course we know, but Mrs. Vick did not move in that direction.

From beginning to end of her counseling, Mrs. Vick talked about her husband—what he did and felt and thought and attempted, and how and perhaps why she felt and reacted and did this or that—but always about her husband. Her early life relationships emerged only in the earliest cathartic interviews, and even her baby was discussed only in relation to her husband. She did not actually work to analyze actual relationships with any specific people other than her husband. Thus, the content focus of her counseling was a narrow-gauge track from start to finish.

There was of course something logical about her constant preoccupation over her relationship to her husband. This was her obvious and realistic life problem about which something had to be done. Yet, by keeping her focus so narrow, she never gave herself opportunity to get a fresh insight into herself from some less emotion-laden perspective which might, in turn, shed light upon the husband relationship. She was like a football team that tries to make its touchdown by one center rush after another. Some end runs, passes, and punts are very much more likely to achieve even the narrowly conceived goal. Such lines Mrs. Vick avoided.

In retrospect, the big question about Colston's counseling with Mrs. Vick has been this: Was he correct in letting her remain with such single-minded preoccupation on the problem of her husband throughout the sessions? Or could he have suggested somewhere along that trying to examine some other relationships of hers might be of value? Once the pattern had been established in which she talked almost solely of her husband, it was then natural for her to think only of this when she came to one of the sessions. Did he acquiesce too easily in this?

His first inclination is to deny such a criticism. Mrs. Vick did stick with her central problem and this was the one some decision had to be made about. Anything else would have appeared to her as diversion. She went as far as she could with this leading problem. A strong case could be made for this line of argument.

Yet retrospect—and his colleague—have compelled him to think that in allowing the counseling to concentrate exclusively on the husband he probably did fail to redefine the counseling situation and process in such a way that larger benefits might have come to Mrs. Vick. She fell finally into an assumption that what was to be discussed was her husband. By letting this stand without comment, Colston was probably allowing her to hold, uncorrected, a view of the counseling situation which he did not share. However, such comments are of necessity speculative.

In retrospect, how may we best understand the psychodynamic factors evident in Mrs. Vick? It would seem that much of the situation could be accounted for by Alfred Adler's early theory of compensation for "organ inferiority." Mrs. Vick should be seen as a handicapped person. The way she had felt inside as a child and what had been expected of her from outside were often radically at variance. Responsive to the need to try to meet the expectations in order to have acceptance at all she had outdone herself and usually seemed to make it as when she completed grammar school at the age of eleven. Yet inside there was discrepancy from such external achievements and, in all probability, much hidden resentment at having too much expected. At least in terms of the material that emerged during the counseling, there is no evidence that there were grossly distorted relationships in Mrs. Vick's life other than with her husband. She had, so to speak, resigned herself to a certain distance from most people brought on initially by her handicap, and her ordinary relationships, therefore, while not intimate, seem not to have been unsatisfactory.

The one person with whom she became intimate, however, and with whom came all the overt trouble, was one who had a handicap like hers. Logic would suggest that the opposite should be true. Two

105

people having been partly isolated from their peers by a common type of handicap, having apparently also found certain mutual interests and concerns, might be expected to be unusually warm toward each other. What *could* account for the opposite's being true, granted that we have not the data to answer the question surely? Our suggestion is that each of these people tended, daily and hourly, but unconsciously, to remind the other of his own handicap and, to the extent that the handicap had not been assimilated, was therefore steadily threatened by the other.

We have only Mrs. Vick's comments about her husband and must be cautious in saying anything about him that professes objectivity. Yet common sense suggests that a height of six feet five inches in a man, which may bring him cries of "Slats" and make it impossible for him to play smooth baseball at the age of seventeen, may at the age of thirty or forty become just a part of the general background —not at all the same kind of continuing social handicap that he would have if he were five feet one inch instead of six feet five inches. Mrs. Vick's situation is different, for height to a woman continues to be a handicap at any age. When it is joined to obesity, the problem becomes still more evident. Whatever the individual causes of the increasing difficulty between the two, we do suggest these more general factors as having also been involved.

Suppose the counselor who dealt with Mrs. Vick had manifested the greatest skill possible, might he, in the allotted time, have helped her in such a way that return to her husband, without destroying her as a person, could have been possible? We cannot know. Mrs. Vick did succeed in developing certain areas of lessened sensitivity to the assaults of her husband. Confronted by real threat, this was like the development of a callus or some other kind of compensation. Granted the threat, she had previously tended to be too open to be able to withstand it without crumbling. In a definite sense, then, the counseling allowed her to build defenses against this threat.

The potential tragedy—not necessarily actual—we see, on reflection, is that this new system of defenses—the new "callus," so to speak—may work not only in relation to her husband but also with her other relationships. The violinist needs his calluses for playing, but he might thereby find it difficult to read Braille. In helping Mrs.

Vick to deal with her immediate and overriding problem, we may, however against our intentions, have narrowed her potentialities for sensitive response through the remainder of her life. We hope not, but honesty compels us to set forth this self-questioning.

Esther Merz and Anne Vick

Since we have not yet explained and described the several tests used, we shall refer to their findings here only in a general way in order to check up on the subjective judgments that have been expressed. The full scores are contained in a later chapter.

Mrs. Merz's scores on the tests moved steadily upward from pre-counseling to post-counseling to follow-up periods. On the test that we regard as most crucial, however, Mrs. Vick's scores moved steadily downward. The meaning of this difference, however, must be considered cautiously. The actual numerical values of the scores on Mrs. Vick's tests were higher than those of Mrs. Merz, showing at least that she had certain kinds of personal potentialities considerably in excess of those of Mrs. Merz. Why the downward movement in Mrs. Vick on the most crucial of the tests?

The principal aspect of the test that accounted for this downward movement in scoring may be put, in layman's terms, as relative ability to tolerate range and complexity of feeling in oneself. As demonstrated in her first two interviews and in her precounseling test, Mrs. Vick had this ability in high degree. Confronted, as she was, however, with a situation in which just this capacity was what made her most vulnerable in relation to her husband, she moved to extend her defenses against him by narrowing her range of emotional sensitivity. Under more fortunate circumstances her capacity for feeling might have brought her unusual richness and complexity of experience. Right now, the charging elephant had to be dealt with.

Although Mrs. Merz did not show, through the tests, the same degree of capacity for experiencing a range of feelings, she did manifest steady growth in this at every period. The direction of her subsequent movement, in this regard, is therefore reasonably predictable, barring some catastrophe. With Mrs. Vick, of great capacity as a human being, our prediction must be quite ambiguous. As her separation from her husband continues and she ceases to feel daily

107

the threats coming out of her capacity for feeling, will her calluses subside and other relationships become richer? Or will she, burned by one kind of fire and grateful to relieving ointment, eschew all types of fires and spend the remainder of her life keeping on the grease? We can only hope.

Chapter 5

SUCCESS CASES

Helen Wright (Church)

◻ Having considered two persons from the respective contexts who were regarded as "representative," we turn now to persons judged to be "successful" in the outcome of their counseling. Success in this instance was based upon several considerations: The person's own evaluation and rating of himself after the counseling was over; our judgment based upon clues from the interview material; our general assessment of the person's movement toward genuine self-acceptance; and the ratings emerging from the testing.

Mrs. Wright ranked high in all these respects at the close of her counseling. By the time of the follow-up interview a bit later on, it is true that there had come to be some tapering off in her gains. Her over-all advance, however, seemed clearly to indicate that she had made many constructive changes and that she was operating at a much more productive level than before her counseling. She is, therefore, presented here as one of the "success" cases at the church. We shall examine the dynamics of the counseling relationship with her in order to try to assess the factors that contributed to her success.

A petite, blond, and attractive woman in her early forties, Mrs. Wright flashed a wide smile as she talked during the first interview with a good deal of vitality. Her facial expressions were pleasantly and appropriately animated, giving correct evidence of her intelligence and her energy. It soon appeared that she was the mother of a mentally retarded boy, at that time in his late adolescence. Tragedy though this continued to be in her life and that of her husband; she had lived with it for many years, and it was clear that this was not the immediate occasion for seeking counseling.

The immediate problem, as Mrs. Wright put it, was that she was

109

"finding it difficult to get along" with Betty, her husband's seventeen-year-old niece who now lived in their home. Having come to stay with the Wrights following the death of her own mother, Betty stayed on because her father felt she would get better care there and because the Wrights wished to be helpful. The longer Betty stayed, however, said Mrs. Wright, the less Betty seemed to respect her and the less she accepted any efforts at discipline. By this time, Mrs. Wright went on, she found herself quite anxious over Betty and her attitude. In fact, she had concluded that it was impossible for Betty to act as she should in the Wright home and as a result had written a letter to Betty's father asking him to take Betty back with him. But before sending the letter, she continued, she wanted Colston to read and comment on it.

As it turned out, it was not necessary for Colston to make a direct comment on the letter. As the first interview continued, Mrs. Wright perceived that the letter and the niece were involved in a complex network of conflicts within her and that she needed to explore the whole works in order to get perspective on the initial problem. By the third interview she had moved still further to see the interrelationship among various kinds of inner conflicts. Here is a sample of that interview:

MRS. WRIGHT: Well, I never quite know where to start, but it seems like once I start, I go from there. But—ah—I suppose the thing to stay with is the scope of confusion and doubt more than anything else, and see if I can eliminate some of it.

I know one thing that has confused me a great deal in trying to think about it and analyze it. This has been true over a long period of time and I think I have become more conscious of it just recently, and that's in regard to the things that I read in the Bible, and of course, the things I have been taught as a youngster in Sunday school. And probably what—ah—my interpretation of them has been—not so much when I was young as when I have grown older and probably have taken various portions at school and at the university, and then I think in terms of, "Well, that wasn't what I was taught when I was a child."

So, one thing that I think of in particular, which has confused me in terms of the Ten Commandments—ah—of course, this would apply to a lot of Christ's teachings, because in the various prophets in the Bible (pause). Now, I have had the feeling that what we were taught was basic to our form of life. What I mean is, the way that we are taught—that we must live —the way that we are taught that we must live is because we emphasize the family, and family structure in our society, and to live in that manner we must have God.

Now the thing that confuses me about this is, I was told that all of these teachings are divine, and this had—I remember it even confused me as a child because I thought, "Well, now, people live too who live good lives who are not good Christians." They have—at that time I did not know about societies which are perfectly adequate and certainly less fraught with emotion and tension and frustration than we are. And so this about the Bible confuses me because I feel that to be a Christian I'm supposed to believe that this is divine, that this comes straight from God. And it bothers me that I seem to see that there is a life that can be just as good without it, provided we would know how to structure it and use it.

Mr. Colston: The fact that somehow this doesn't coincide at every point with your experience of what life is like is confusing because on the one hand this is supposed to be the church on which you can depend, only now you discover that your experience opens up questions about it and it gets you pretty confused to realize that there is this kind of contradiction.

Mrs. Wright: It's this feeling, again, in everything that seems to confront me, that although I had believed this to be the absolute truth—and I think that we are taught, as a child I was taught— that this is the absolute, this is it. There is no deviation. And then to discover that this is not true, that there are other ways that are equally as good and could be better.

Mr. Colston: Sort of shattering?

Mrs. Wright: Yes (laughs nervously).

Here we see Mrs. Wright wrestling not only with her growing awareness of internal complexity in general but also with the specific complexities of her rather legalistic religious background. She shows

111

herself to be perplexed about the apparent contradiction between what had been her normative understanding of the Christian faith and what she is now experiencing through her counseling and her contemporary experience in general including her adult observation of other societies and patterns. She is saying that the more she had confronted the relativity of values the more disturbed she became about her doubts, fearing that she was laying herself open to entertaining agnostic views.

Colston's main effort here was to try to help her proceed with clarification of the inner conflicting feelings, the primary focus of which was to aid her to accept the feeling reality of the doubts themselves. Since she was bringing out the fact of these doubts to him, a minister, it seemed likely that she was, internally, maintaining a potentially constructive tension between her doubts and her faith and was probably not easily disposed to give way to an easy solution of throwing the whole religious business out the window. If she had been completely disillusioned with Christian faith, or her understanding of it at that time, it is likely that she would not have come to talk with Colston at all. Yet if she had not seriously questioned her own understanding of Christian faith, it is equally doubtful that she would have come.

In the light of what he took her to be conveying to him, in the very act of coming as well as in her words and manner, Colston interpreted his task at that point as helping her to carry on the dialogue between her understanding of her faith and her understanding of her doubts. During several of the early interviews, although not in the verbatim conversation given above, Mrs. Wright said she wanted him to point out the places where she was wrong. Whether such pointing out is ever justified or necessary in general is one question. In this instance it seemed clear that anything of the kind would be, to say the least, premature, for that would make it appear that Colston was operating in precisely the kind of legalistic framework which some part of her was trying creatively to cast off. Even at this early stage, furthermore, it appeared that her dependency needs were fairly strong. If he had then given her a normative answer about how she ought to feel concerning faith, it would have been but a step to her requesting that he tell her how she ought to feel about other things. Attempts to wring normative views out of him might then easily have replaced

112

struggle with the specific factors in her own conflicts. So at this point at least his course of action seems still, in retrospect, to have been correct.

The Break-Through. During the first four interviews Mrs. Wright covered an increasing expanse of ground, but her way of doing so was substantially at the same level. One might say that she was reconnoitering, examining the area, before digging in at any point. Or it could be said that she was examining the extent of her defenses before really yielding any of them. Form often follows function immediately; and it was significant that when, in the fifth interview, she first began to break through her defenses, she spoke of some of her attitudes in the past tense.

MRS. WRIGHT: Yes, I mean I can look at myself and see the things that I do and say to other people—ah—the quick anger, the quick resentment—and recognize that the only reason that I have done it was because I was emotionally immature and didn't care. I have always, apparently, felt very insecure, and it seems to be my defense against insecurity to build up all these walls of forcing people to my will. And I definitely think I have always tried to force people to my will. I've been aware of that, and maybe that's why I needed to feel that I was right. Because I insisted on forcing people to do what I wanted.

MR. COLSTON: You mean that somehow this is more in keeping with this feeling of needing to have other people fit into your notions. That maybe basically it was a feeling of needing to be sure that you were right.

MRS. WRIGHT: Well, I think—ah—that I have always sincerely felt that what I wanted people to do was for their own good. And I think as I examine mostly what I want people to do, I think that probably fundamentally that isn't true, even though maybe I was motivated by it to show my power, but I think that what I mean is, I had to have the self-confidence of knowing that what I wanted other people to do was for their own good, otherwise I was undermined.

MR. COLSTON: You weren't sure of that, you were trying to make sure.

113

There is some confusion all through this, but this last response of Colston's seems, in retrospect, to be only on the edge of what she was trying to communicate. There is in her a real beginning at breaking through the old defenses. She does see that she has tried to force or dominate other people, but at once she goes on to deny that her domination has been motivated by selfish reasons. Even though a first step has been made, it would still violate her picture of herself to see herself as getting satisfaction out of the manipulation of other people. Such action could be justified only if she could view it as having benevolent intentions. These subtleties were missed at the time and Colston came forth with something rather vague. The fact that this did not divert her is probably due in part to the fact that by this time rapport was good and in part to the fact that, if Colston failed to say the right thing, at least he did not lead her to a wrong one.

While still in the fifth interview, Mrs. Wright came soon to a further consideration of her faith and her doubts. Although a first reading of the following dialogue may make it sound abstract, it seems to Colston now that this is the first occasion in which Mrs. Wright moved far enough out of the particular content of her faith and doubt to ask about the level at which she was seeing them. She was like the philosopher who has wrestled with what is "being" and who suddenly stops to ask himself why there is anything at all. The apparent retreat to abstraction is actually an attempt to look at the data from a new perspective.

MRS. WRIGHT: It may have been where all of this terrific doubt has arisen in me. Because I have insisted on this and have suddenly come to realize, "Well, now why am I right, why more than anybody else." It's interesting—it has so many facets, I could go off in several different tangents and examine it and probably will have to before I'll have any security at all.

MR. COLSTON: That as you begin to question your own attitudes toward other people in terms of this rightness, you begin to say, "Why should I assume that I can decide." And I guess you're saying, "Heretofore, this has been a kind of threatening thing for me," because to question this would leave you without any idea of yourself, or respect for yourself.

MRS. WRIGHT: I think I was attacking it about half way up the line instead of going down to the bottom. I was attacking the wrong thing. I mean, I recognized that I had all these doubts and I was trying to find out actually what was right and what was wrong. Instead of going down here to find out why I have all these doubts.

MR. COLSTON: In a way saying, "Instead of trying to make the thing fit into the notions that I already had, and trying to find out what *is* right and wrong, I am going beyond or beneath that to find out why I was holding this view in the first place."

MRS. WRIGHT: Or, why I felt it was necessary to define things as black or white. I can see many, many things. I don't think at the time I could have done any different, because I didn't know any better. I was so mixed up emotionally, but I think now, perhaps, I could do better (*laughs*).

Mrs. Wright here is trying to say that a new thrust of "learning" about herself has begun to appear as a result of her counseling. Previously, the counseling had moved horizontally, with subjects touched over a broader surface. When this had happened, she now sees, she had been trying to force new areas and modes of experience into old patterns of interpretation. Now something new has been added, not one more thing but another dimension.

The break-through came initially in her attempt to work at her religious problem of faith and doubt, as she then conceived it. As the interchange above demonstrates, however, she immediately began to explore its significance for her at an intrapersonal level. Beginning to see how strongly she had previously been attached to religion as a thing of certainty, she now gets a glimmer that a similar attachment has heretofore been operating in regard to her feeling about herself. She had had to be right, but her conscience made her writhe every time she went on a binge of self-justification. She had then been tempted to deal with the conscience by denying its validity or relevance. Hence the nature of the conflict began first to become intelligible to her in terms of religious faith and doubt, but at once showed itself also in terms of attitudes toward herself.

One may see this movement in Mrs. Wright correctly as the emergence of something genuinely new, ultimately to be constructive, but its immediate effect upon her was by no means without ambiguity.

115

In seeing at least something of the inadequacy of previous struggles, both religiously and generally, she could no longer rely on the old automatic defense system. Consequently in the exchange presented above Mrs. Wright was in effect asking for Colston's support while she was erecting new "underpinnings" that could sustain her.

Colston did seek to demonstrate to her his support in the sense of being with that in her which was new while at the same time not shouting hallelujah as if the old had been completely left behind. The temptation was, in view of the emergence of something authentically new, to rush it, to give a push to her crumbling "system." He was particularly tempted to do this religiously and theologically. What she was moving toward was of course closer to his own religious and theological understanding. That was precisely the danger. If he had said in effect, "Wonderful, you are now joining me," she could easily have been shifted over to trying to deal with him and his views instead of continuing to work at her own.

In this emergence of something new, we have seen that it began at the religious level as she understood that, and then moved to her attitudes toward herself. In the same interview she then moved on to consider some of the implications for her interpersonal relationships.

She felt, she noted, very inadequate in the attempts she had made to interpret values to Betty, her niece, and she now saw that this was because of the confusion in her own values. Yet the pressure of the situation following upon her responsibility for Betty had pushed her in the direction of facing the inconsistencies within herself. So far as her relationship with Betty was concerned, she continued, the net effect was to make her feel quite uncomfortable over the attempts she had been making to impose her idealized values on Betty. Now, she said, she had begun to recognize that she had not actually been seeing Betty at all but instead had been projecting her own conflicts into Betty. She had not, as a matter of fact, actually been listening to the real Betty. Before this interview ended, she said she had now resolved that, whatever might come of it, she would give explicit attention to what Betty might try to say to her.

When Mrs. Wright appeared for the sixth interview, she began about her relationship with Betty. She was both surprised and greatly pleased, she said, at what had almost instantly happened between them when she had resolved genuinely to listen to whatever Betty was trying to say. Then came the following interchange:

MR. COLSTON: . . . the feeling as though the end you were seeking is a secondary thing. You're saying, "Now I've tried seeing things through Betty's eyes and lo, I'm discovering that the other thing that I have wanted is occurring, that is—an improved relationship with Betty."

MRS. WRIGHT: It seems to me that at last, certainly we have been on a much better plane of communication than we have ever been before. Of course, there are several other contributing factors, too, of which I am aware. But, nonetheless, it's there. Ah—I have come to know—she has told me things in the last few times that we have talked about her childhood and the years before she came to us which she never would have told me before. And, of course, it has led to an understanding of her and what has created her to be as she is, so that I'm very glad to have her want to talk to me.

MR. COLSTON: You feel much better to discover that she can turn to you with some feeling of confidence and share her significant concerns.

MRS. WRIGHT: Yes, even if I don't approve of what she thinks or how she acted at certain times. To me this is not important because we, many of us, do things at a certain time influenced by our life experience.

MR. COLSTON: Although you see things differently, you really don't stand in judgment of her.

MRS. WRIGHT: No, she—ah—as I say, these last few weeks have been very interesting because she has said a number of things to me that she would never have said before that has cemented our relationship. Of course, here again—ah—I found myself—last night, now we were talking—she was telling me some of the things that had happened in her childhood and, of course, I got that real warm feeling, you know, of just having her talk to me, and then I immediately find myself thinking, "Now, wait a minute, don't get too soft (laughs), you're heading for a downfall," because if I let myself get all entangled again—if she does again to me what she's done in the past, I just wonder (laughs),

117

I wonder if I'll be able to take it. So, actually, in a way, although I am warmed by this, I still am quite guarded because I am—ah—not sure how the future is.

MR. COLSTON: Even aware of holding back a little bit when you find this feeling of warmth coming up, because you fear that it may have the same kind of consequence as it has had in the past.

Here Mrs. Wright was showing that, despite the gain and the new kind of "warm feeling," she nevertheless still could not wholly trust herself in that relationship. At first glance this looks like a step backward. Now that she has experienced a new level of relationship with Betty, precisely what she has previously wanted but been unable to achieve, why does she not simply rejoice in it? The answer is of course that patterns that have been deeply imbedded for years do not vanish overnight. To experience the satisfaction of something that makes them unnecessary is the necessary start toward change, but in itself it is not a substitute for a long-term "working out" of the implications. Thus the new order of self-doubt that appeared in Mrs. Wright at this point is less regression than realism. If she had not had it, Colston should have been suspicious of the authenticity of what had emerged constructively. His own last response to her, as indicated above, suffered from vagueness although its direction was correct. At least the self-doubt was not censured. She immediately sliced through the diffusion and this emerged:

MRS. WRIGHT: I don't want to be hurt again. I mean—I get so hurt that I suppose I'm just building up a defense again. Of course, I think that—I don't know whether all people do that or not, I mean—I've never talked closely enough with them, but I find in my own mind that I am inclined to build up a defense against someone dear, you know, such as—I think in terms of the tragedy we had to bear with our son. Now, this was something that I would never want to happen to me again. And I have found myself—well, now among friends of ours—I will not let myself become closely entangled with a child. I don't want to get to where I love him too much.

Here was human defensive prudence quite suspicious about the superiority of having loved and lost over never having loved at all. It

118

referred to the whole long-continued tragic feeling she and her husband had had over their son, which had come to a poignant head when they were trying to decide about putting him in an institution for the mentally retarded. The decision had been in this instance clearly the correct one for the sake of all concerned, but it had been heart-rending and guilt-ridden nevertheless.

MRS. WRIGHT: It's again, another case of just not getting into a position where I can be hurt. Now, is that a normal thing for most people? I know my husband has done it, because we were thinking of adopting a child a number of years ago and—ah—in fact, we did apply for one child and then something went wrong. When the child was born it was born with a defect and and we couldn't get it. And then we had a second opportunity and my husband finally said, "I don't believe I want to adopt a child, I couldn't stand to have anything like this happen to us again." So he has had some of the same feelings, too, and I suppose the fact that when we did bring Betty into our home to fill this gap for us, we let all bars down, you see, and it's hard to realize that . . . (pause).

MR. COLSTON: The question you raise is, "Well, should I really be protecting myself in this way, or is this the way other people do, or has my experience been such that I'm pretty unique in this?" That is, "Has this experience with our child made us a little more sensitive than a lot of people would be?" This means—this seems almost automatically watching that you don't get involved because of the pain in the past. That you're not sure really whether you could trust yourself to get into that kind of warmth and closeness with all the potential for a deeper hurting.

MRS. WRIGHT: Yes, I think that is true. I do think, as I said, when Betty came I was willing to do it with her, and, of course, that failed too—which didn't help any. But, now—well, I have had some of my friends say to me—ah—why don't you like children and, of course, I'm very fond of children but I will admit I don't let them get too close to me. I won't take care of them and do the things that are necessary to do without their . . . (pause)

119

MR. COLSTON: Not that you don't like them, but you fear you might like them too much.

MRS. WRIGHT: I'm a little inclined that way and I think that is very difficult for others to understand. And, of course, through this I recognize that I am denying myself a lot of joy.

MR. COLSTON: That you may be missing some things—some joys and warmth—that in a way you ought not to be denying yourself.

Her current reworking of her relationship with Betty has moved her to re-examine other aspects of her interpersonal relationships, beginning with her son and then extending to the almost-adopted baby and to children in general. The prospect of any closeness thus, she begins to see, has ambiguous meaning for her. That which she loved most was torn away with the pain of guilt as well as that of separation. Yet, as she now pursues this line, she sees that a "no-involvement-beyond-a-certain-point" kind of attitude, while offering protection against immediate pain, nevertheless has cheated her of the enrichment and joy that might become possible if she opened herself.

The strong opposite pulls within Mrs. Wright are at this point revealed openly and explicitly. Colston could not have expressed understanding had he ridden one side at the expense of the other. She wished to accept her own feelings of warmth toward children and express them, and yet she feared that she could not stand the possible rejection to which such openness would expose her. In his responses he attempted to convey not only that her communication was getting through to him but also that he left her free to explore further in any direction she chose.

The entire interchange of the fifth and sixth interviews was especially interesting in that movement to a new level came first in the religious area, then next in terms of relationship to herself, and finally at the point of interpersonal relationships.

Accepting God's Forgiveness. Especially by working at the inconsistencies in her attitude toward Betty, Mrs. Wright went on to consolidate her new understandings in several areas of life and relationship. In the eighth interview she swung back to the religious issues and finally noted that she had previously been "unwilling to

120

accept God's forgiveness" because she had not felt worthy of receiving it. She put it this way:

MRS. WRIGHT: I have related it now to—to Betty, for instance, and my problems with her and I have recognized—ah—I have said that—and thought—sincerely thought, that I felt this way about her because of what I have done for her, and when I stop to think about it, I think that it was what I had hoped she would do for me. And she failed, and so instead of recognizing that there was error in me in my relationship with her, I turned against her and it—ah—I really think—now, this isn't something that happened overnight—I think you can't suddenly change an entire attitude and an entire approach, because I've been this way for forty-two years and I can't—ah—suddenly be completely changed.

MR. COLSTON: It isn't that you're just turning completely around— it's something that's happened—something that's opening up to you in a way and you're saying, "I may have to work with this and live with this. . . ."

MRS. WRIGHT: I think that I will come to—I will have to work hard because of the fact that it is so deeply embedded and it must have been embedded for me not to have been aware of it. Probably more so than for others who realize it. And for that reason, I'll probably have more trouble than they would (laughs).

MR. COLSTON: The fact that you haven't been aware of it . . .

Here she is recognizing that her pattern of having judged other people entirely from her own internal and uncriticized point of view had become firmly entrenched, and even though now she sees in principle what she has been doing, she must give the working out of it special attention and effort. We may note that this realism emerged following the insight that she had not felt worthy to receive forgiveness from God. Colston might of course have pointed out to her that the reception of forgiveness is not based on a conviction of one's worthiness to receive it but upon faith and trust in a forgiving God. But the fact was that she had come very close to realizing this herself and proved it by the way she moved on to its implication for her interpersonal relationships. The reality of the new kind of "faith" is proved by her turning, in consequence, to a new kind of "work," that is,

121

a working with effort and attention at making the new thing stick and not regressing the minute the new insight failed to carry itself through automatically. Mrs. Wright then continued:

MRS. WRIGHT: Well, the thing that I mean—I'm going to have to take out each—each motivation that I have and examine it, and say, "Now, what is the reason behind why I think this and why I do this." I know why. I mean you can't do something—you just can't suddenly see something and be different. It's impossible. You have to have help and, of course, in this particular article (she had referred earlier to an article on the meaning of the love of God) it naturally refers to channeling God's love and this I interpret to mean first loving God and then letting him love us, and then channeling this love out into the world in a—in an objective and unselfish manner without ever any thought of return. It's an entirely different concept.

Now, of course, in thinking this thing—recognizing that I can't do it alone, I again feel this terrible need for—ah—for a closeness to God which I don't have. I mean, I feel I need to—to be able to reach out and really—really feel that he is there and that he will come and help me. And this, again, is where I . . . (pause).

MR. COLSTON: Where you feel frightened, quite separated from God and feel that somehow that this must be bridged before the meaning of all of what you're saying here can come through to you?

MRS. WRIGHT: Yes, because I don't think that I am, as a human being, as capable of doing this alone or even of understanding it, or knowing what I'm supposed to do, or—somehow—it has been said that if you open up yourself you will be directed. And this may be true, this may be why I'm not directed, because I don't feel that it's possible to just sort of hold yourself blank and then something fills in. That may be where my fault lies, I don't know. Maybe I think too hard to understand or something. Do you suppose that's it?

MR. COLSTON: You mean, maybe you're struggling too hard to find answers to things, et cetera. Maybe this kind of relaxing and opening up will enable you to find them?

122

At this point Mrs. Wright was wrestling with the basic religious question of the relationship of faith to works. Having begun her exploration in the religious dimension, she had moved to the same problem in its interpersonal aspects, and now has returned to consider it again religiously. Theologically speaking, she has still not reached the goal, but there is a whole new quality in her thinking and feeling about it.

Colston's attempt was to respond not so much to the details as to the total feeling tone she was trying to convey. Her gestures as well as her words showed him that she was tense and anxious, that although she was closer to the truth she nevertheless was still trying to "force" answers rather than to be receptive to them. Yet at the same time she recognized in part that such answers could not be forced. Her own partial understanding of the subtleties of self-deception in this complex were revealed in what followed.

MRS. WRIGHT: Yes, I've wondered about that because I have known people who claim that it can be done. Of course, there, again, my doubt comes into it because I think then in terms of—well, then if you say you're sitting and letting somebody guide you, no matter what you do then you can blame on someone else. And —ah . . . (pause).

MR. COLSTON: Sort of, "What's my own responsibility in this?"

MRS. WRIGHT: Yes. . . .

MR. COLSTON: "How much of it must I take on myself?"

MRS. WRIGHT: I find it more difficult—and it's contradictory here, too, because that statement is true and yet I find that I cannot forgive myself for my sins at all, and I can't forgive myself. And I can't forgive others for their sins—and I can't forgive myself. Even though I realize that God will forgive me, I can't forgive myself because I knew better.

MR. COLSTON: In other words, although sometimes you sort of become easier with others than with yourself, you can't feel easier about it—especially when you know better.

MRS. WRIGHT: Not at all. And, of course, because of my feelings and because of my hypocrisy of—of holding up certain standards for myself and for others and then I have failed. I feel I have been

123

hypocritical, I know it. This makes it hard for me to forgive myself. This is the sort of thing that I feel I'm going to have to find how to do, and I think, again, the only way I can find this is through—is through my relationship with God. Understanding how he can forgive us and recognize our weakness. I think this we must also be able to do to ourselves, not in condoning what we do or in going on and doing it—repeating it—but in understanding what we are particularly trying to do.

MR. COLSTON: So that you can understand how you can be forgiven in a very personal close way of experiencing this forgiveness from God and what it means, and in this way you may be able to forgive others if you see the full range of what this means—and see yourself as forgiven.

This represents further wrestling with faith and works with forgiveness as something out there offered by God and forgiveness in here as something received. Some of the subtlety of what is going on in Mrs. Wright is shown in that some of her references to God's forgiveness were in the future tense, "God will forgive me." That is, God's forgiveness is a potential that may happen under certain conditions. Colston's last response in the exchange above went somewhat beyond what Mrs. Wright had said. For good or for ill, he was "nudging" her toward bringing forgiveness into the present tense. She did not pick up the "extra" that he had added. This seems to mean that she was not ready to go beyond this point at this time. At the same time, their relationship was such that she did not feel threatened by his "nudge."

Anticipating the Termination of Counseling. Mrs. Wright's feelings about the prospective termination of her counseling are shown in this exchange from the twentieth interview.

MRS. WRIGHT: I know, when you told me a few weeks ago that there was going to be an end to this, it came as quite a shock because (*laughs*) I thought this was going to go on forever. And I realized, too, then how much I really was leaning on you and drawing from your strength and I think the realization that this was going to end, there for a moment I was a little frightened. I thought—well, how am I going to handle it alone without this support that I had been getting. And—ah—for a few seconds I really thought I—I can't even think like it's going—it's going to be an empty world.

MR. COLSTON: A real threat to you.

MRS. WRIGHT: It frightened me, momentarily, and, however, I think —I—in fact, I've gotten over that. I realized that what I had gained is going to be intensely helpful.

She was accepting the idea of the termination, and yet she still found it threatening. As Colston had already done at the very beginning, he told her again that this termination point was arbitrary and was set for purposes of this study and that he would be willing to see her further if she so wished. At this point she seemed visibly to relax, saying she would return if it seemed wise. It was not the idea of planning a specific return, but the notion that she could plan it, which had the relaxing effect. This kind of response was fairly typical of a number of the persons counseled in the church context.

New Vitality in Religious Faith. From the eighth interview onward, Mrs. Wright made progress in "working out" and working through the implications of the new understandings that had emerged by that time. There were movements up and down, back and forth, but the general line was clearly forward. As has been demonstrated in the sixth and the eighth interviews, the religious material alternated with the personal and interpersonal. There seemed always to be a dynamic connection among the three types of material, so that she did not leave one as an escape in order to get to the other.

In evaluating the material that emerged in the eighth interview, Colston interpreted this as involving the emergence of a new order of depth in considering all dimensions of her life, nascent rather than finished, but real nonetheless. Did she, in the subsequent interviews, take still another plunge toward yet a deeper level? In the sense of depth as the psychoanalyst thinks of it, the answer is no. The remaining interviews were, in effect, attempts to consolidate the new understandings that emerged about the eighth interview. In this instance there was no particular difficulty in having the counseling remain at the level proper to counseling, without threatening to go more deeply into material that would have required extensive psychotherapy. To what extent this fact was due to Mrs. Wright, her degree of need and readiness, and to what extent it was due to the way

125

Colston proceeded with her is not wholly clear even from a full review of all the interviews. His conclusion is that a bit of both are involved.

Near the end of the twentieth or final interview, Mrs. Wright brought out rather forcibly that she felt she was experiencing renewed vitality in her religious faith. But she added, "Something's strange, though, because now I can't talk about my religious awakening to other people, for fear of appearing hypocritical." She wondered, in view of this, whether she was genuinely committed to the new understandings that had appeared. Nevertheless, she went on, the "rebirth" she felt she had experienced was very real. She put it this way:

MRS. WRIGHT: I really feel as though I—I am on the square with God. I somehow don't have any sense of—I mean, I figure that if he knows what I am trying to do and understands—but then why would I have that feeling? Do you suppose, again, it's what other people are thinking? I mean, you know I operated on what other people think for so long. . . .

MR. COLSTON: That maybe you're not so sure that other people really understand your . . .

MRS. WRIGHT: Well, for instance—ah—I know the thought had come to me, in fact I have hesitated in a couple of instances in talking to people about these revelations—these new revelations that I have had because I recognize that they would say, "Well, look who's getting religious," you know, and scorn me. And so for that reason I have hesitated to reveal that this is the way I feel. Of course, now that is not good either. Because if I am sincere about this thing I can't care what other people think, can I?

MR. COLSTON: You mean, it shouldn't make any difference. . . .

MRS. WRIGHT: No, it shouldn't. I mean—they know me—they knew me as a sinner and, of course, they may not realize that I am trying to repent. But this shouldn't make any difference, what they think, should it? Do you suppose that's it?

MR. COLSTON: If I'm really satisfied with myself and all of this, or that, "O. K., I know it—so it doesn't matter—so they do doubt it—they'll see eventually," or something like that.

126

Mrs. Wright: That's exactly the feeling that I have had, exactly. Well, then why would there be a sort of a latent sense of guilt with me in having that feeling?

Mr. Colston: Why the doubts arise at all—why should there be any doubts? "Am I so sure that I do feel this way?"

Mrs. Wright: No, I don't have any doubt in that area. I mean, I really feel that this—as far as I'm concerned—is it. I could almost say—I think I feel, just like Paul felt when he saw those lights. That may sound facetious—I don't intend it that way, but (words lost) this is actually a conversion. Now there are many times I have thought that people didn't experience things like this, that it was all "tommy-rot." Now—to me, I have no doubt in that area.

Mr. Colston: It has all the force of a conversion experience.

Mrs. Wright: Yes, it really has. And I don't want anything different. I want it that way. I like it. It's a good feeling.

It seems clear that the net effect of what happened to her religiously is quite positive and that there is something constructive even in the new order of self-doubt. To be sure, the hesitation in talking to other people has its ambiguities, but so long as she recognizes that fact the genuineness of her experience is saved. In the notion that talking of this to other people should come naturally in its own good time, she is probably dealing in the best fashion with the reality of her "conversion."

In Colston's own part in this last exchange, he acknowledged principally the continuing negative aspect of her feelings. The result was that she herself affirmed their positive aspect.

In the follow-up interview held some time later, Mrs. Wright said she had been doing some "leveling off." That is, the close of counseling had found her a bit too high in her "mountaintop" experience. She was now doing some of the ordinary work in the valley. But she said she was fascinated to realize that her development was continuing without the counseling. She had enrolled for some responsible graduate study and was, she said, daily being challenged to "become a person."

Summary on Helen Wright. Mrs. Wright and her matched partner, Mrs. Reede from the counseling center, had striking resemblances

127

in their respective high degrees of self-awareness before the counseling began. Thus the process of self-reflection was with both of them advanced before the counseling. Both had strong motivation to move quickly into areas that were troubling them, and both showed themselves prepared to move at least one level deeper in their consideration. This prior readiness was undoubtedly a factor in the relative success of the counseling with both of them.

The most striking thing in the counseling with Mrs. Wright, as has been noted in the running analysis, was the way in which her discussion of religion, as she saw it, was intertwined throughout with her discussion of attitudes toward herself and other people. Very often the emergence in her of some new understanding began at the point of religion, and then the implications were pursued in terms of interpersonal relationships and attitudes toward herself and her own inner defenses. She would then return to the religious arena with more clarity. Such a sequence might of course have occurred elsewhere than in the church context, but undoubtedly it was this context that made it most likely. In the later interviews, and especially on religious matters, Mrs. Wright and Colston were more free in their exchange of interpretative ideas than the quoted protocols show.

Looking at the counseling relationship with Mrs. Wright as a whole, Colston feels that a relationship or a communion was established between them that usually enabled him to understand her communications as she was wrestling with them. She in turn seemed to accept his understanding of her as an intention even when at times he had to be corrected in practice. The longer they continued, the greater seemed her sense of freedom to bring forth the various aspects of her total view of the world, God, values, and everything else of importance.

The reader may wonder, especially in reading the selected protocols, whether we ever dealt directly with "bread and butter" matters in the valley. It is true that there is a certain abstraction and rarified atmosphere in very many of Mrs. Wright's communications, and such lingering on the mountain may of course itself be a defensive maneuver. Looked at as a whole, we do not believe this was so with Mrs. Wright. The kind of communication she was trying to make to the pastor—and thus to herself—was that which was most important to her. Others may dispute this interpretation, and we cannot prove it, but it was Colston's impression throughout, even at those times when he knew it would be easier for him if she were a bit more prosaic. Even if it be adjudged that there were defensive elements in the mode of communication Mrs. Wright used, we would still argue that the helping process would have been impeded if she had been pushed to communicate in a different mode before she was prepared to do so.

Early in the relationship, when she was leaving Colston's office at the close of the third interview, Mrs. Wright gave voice to an eleventh-hour concern. She asked him if he were not going to evaluate her and "tell me what to do." At that moment he was torn between the desire to rush to her side with verbal support, accepting the "expertness" and authority she was bestowing on him, and on the other hand to try to convey to her his respect for her and her capacity to come through this counseling process. Actually, it was not necessary for him to carry out either course explicitly, for the very asking of the question, followed by a moment of concerned but not detached hesitation on his part, gave her enough answer so that she could bid him farewell and speak of their next meeting.

One way to see the chief characteristic of her progress is to put it in terms of her ability abstractly to symbolize previously unexamined aspects of her experience and to recognize the emerging tensions in doing so. It was the latter point that made us conclude that the mode of her communication was thrusting forward and was not in itself a defense. Her awareness of her own one-sided search for closure at all costs steadily grew and was slowly and critically rejected. This opened her to ask new orders of questions about her own potentialities and creative powers. In the follow-up interview, some time after the counseling had been concluded, she said, "It is amazing to discover how, for all these years, I have wasted my capacities, and how much I have been learning during the past two years. I had not dreamed that this was possible for me." Nor was this sheer romanticism. The course of action on which she had launched made real sense by objective standards, and she was happy in its pursuit.

She had, we believe, moved in the direction of genuine self-discovery and did not seem wrongly dismayed at the new order of obligation as well as release given by these possibilities. We believe she had made progress in accepting the ambiguities of her particular existence and was especially more willing to risk encounter with other people.

She had relaxed her demands that the world be seen as she saw it and was more ready to acknowledge herself as other than the center of her universe. She said, in the follow-up interview, that she thought she could continue to try to understand the process of being related to God, without demanding that some authority line this out for her. We regard all these as very positive and constructive steps, in which religion and life are dynamically and constructively interrelated.

Margaret Reede (Center)

There were two striking similarities in the content of material presented during the counseling sessions by Helen Wright of the church, who has just been described, and her matching partner at the center, Margaret Reede. Each was wrestling, as modern jargon has it, in an existential fashion with the meaning and possible fulfillment of her life, and each was trying to develop the undoubted intellectual capacities that she possessed. More than with most of our matched pairs, these two had many similarities in terms of social status, background conditions, and vocational interests. In terms of formal characteristics these two were as nearly matched as is ever possible in a study of this kind.

In the account just presented of Helen Wright, we have seen how religious factors, religious interest, and a religious mode of discourse, played a prominent part in her counseling. The situation was radically different with Mrs. Reede, who dealt throughout with interpersonal processes and a psychological mode of discourse. Yet as can be seen from the data that follow, the fundamental problem with which Mrs. Reede was struggling was very similar to that of Mrs. Wright. We adjudge the outcome in both cases as unusually successful. Careful attention by the reader, therefore, to these two stories may be unusually valuable in suggesting some of the differences made by context in all its senses.

Margaret Reede was a slender woman of dignity, in her early forties, who exuded an aura of intensity. Married but without children, she was temporarily separated from her husband. Her time was being devoted to the pursuit of a career in social work.

Marriage. Most of the material in the early interviews concerned her relationship to her husband, but there was some also about her sister. Toward her husband her feelings were deeply mixed. They

130

shared many interests and values and communicated well with each other, said Mrs. Reede, but she had always felt a revulsion over her husband's attitude toward sex. He had frequently become involved in sexual relationships with other women, she continued, and on one occasion even brought such a woman to their home, "as though he were flaunting his infidelity before me."

She said she found herself constantly "blocked" by regrets, resentments, self-pity and frustration, and she found herself physically wracked by frequent weeping.

MRS. REEDE: (Weeping) I tried to think about it. I tried to think of some feasible thing that I could work on.

MR. COLSTON: Even more imperative now that you get at the basic . . .

MRS. REEDE: (Breaking in) Well, I don't know. I think maybe what I need is to straighten out one of my real conflicts which is very important and which I have to do something about pretty soon. And the other is to try to get over this present block which is interfering with my work. I think it's very threatening to me —this whole situation—because—ah . . .

MR. COLSTON: Really frightens you?

MRS. REEDE: Well, I don't want to fail, you know. And—ah—yet I somehow can't seem to get the strength or energy to do it. I'm just thoroughly blocked. I remember a few years ago I was ill and in the hospital for a month, and one of the doctors who was there said to me and my sister and my husband, "For a long time you have been doing a lot of things you don't really want to do." I thought about that a lot and it's true, although I probably felt I wanted to enough to push myself to do it. But now I'm more aware of when I'm doing something that I don't really want to do.

MR. COLSTON: That the things you do are somehow things you feel you ought to do or should do, but you are not really committed to them?

MRS. REEDE: Or that—ah—not that I don't really like what I'm doing. I like the work I'm doing. I could have taken off in any number of directions. So the choice really lay between teaching and social work. I tried a little of both until I could see how it

131

went. The psychologist who tested me at that time suggested social work and—ah—and so I started back. Again I started somehow with this feeling of pressure. I don't think I started in completely the right emotional frame of mind, but there was something I really wanted to do and I went gladly into it.

MR. COLSTON: So that you felt that this was something that you really had to do, for some reason or another.

She had begun this discussion about her marriage, but had then moved to its results in terms of her deep frustration, which was affecting her present work. She was plainly moving in the direction of revealing more of her underlying conflict, but by this point had a good distance to go. Helping her to move in that direction at her own proper pace seemed Colston's task at that time.

Mrs. Reede repeated her "feeling of pressure," to which Colston responded. Then came the following:

MRS. REEDE: Well, it was a very—there was a good reason for it. I married when I was quite young and—ah . . . (pauses). My husband had—had a number of affairs, and finally at that time I asked him for a divorce. I couldn't somehow get him to accept the fact, and he just wouldn't do anything. And I felt he was quite sick himself. He had met this girl and had known her about three years and came home believing that she was pregnant.

And I don't think—ah—that was the situation. And he wouldn't take any kind of responsibility for it. He left it entirely up to me.

He seemed to expect that I was going to somehow make it easy for him and I would just disappear somehow. He wasn't quite clear about the details. He was quite surprised when I told him I would get a divorce, but I wanted to get a legal divorce and on grounds that were just, and he couldn't accept this. And he made a lot of suggestions—and then when I suggested that all he had to do to get a divorce was to get the papers, et cetera, he said, "Well, I don't intend to leave." And so I felt that if he couldn't be inconvenienced to that extent, he couldn't want it very much. It didn't really mean very much to him and why should I upset my whole life?

132

Mr. Colston: "Why should I make it easy?"

The main thing she was saying was that, having been treated unfairly, she was not willing to forfeit her legal rights or to let the implication stand that she was solely responsible for the trouble between them. She felt strengthened in this course because her husband seemed to have no deep feelings for the girl, pregnant or otherwise. Schematically, she might have put it like this: "Although I feel most rejected, I'm not ready to change the whole pattern of my life at least until I see some evidence that my husband is acting on the basis of strong feelings."

Colston's response barely caught an edge of what she had been saying, and missed the deeper implications. She rejected it and continued this way:

Mrs. Reede: Well, it wasn't why should I make it easy, but why should I (pauses) why should I be so inconvenienced and have my whole life upset and my security threatened and everything for the sake of something that apparently meant so little to him? I think I really wanted him to show me that he could be strong about it, and if he had been strong about it I don't think . . . (pauses).

Mr. Colston: "That this is what I really wanted him to do?"

Mrs. Reede: Yes. But he was very sick. And I think that's what he wanted—he just wanted me to go off and leave a sick man and then all his friends could pity him.

Mr. Colston: And make you feel guilty about leaving him?

Mrs. Reede: Yes. And then the next year he could go and bring back this lovely girl, and everyone would say, "Well, isn't it nice that he has found somebody now?" I don't think that's fair.

Mr. Colston: You don't intend to take this kind of treatment.

Mrs. Reede: No.

Mrs. Reede resented being maneuvered into a position where the decisions made would seem to reflect guilt primarily upon her. She was suggesting that she had remained in an otherwise intolerable marriage because it might be even worse to break it up but take the guilt. Colston's responses in the above exchange seem a good deal closer to the mark than did the one previous.

133

Why Unproductive? As the interviews proceeded, Mrs. Reede acknowledged more openly the depth of her feelings of resentment toward her husband. But she began seriously to question the assumption that the sole or even main cause of the unproductivity in her work was this frustration about her marriage. The following emerged in the eighth interview:

MRS. REEDE: Yeah, I really want to. There's an awful lot of—sort of aggression, you know, that's—ah—very close to the surface . . . (*pauses*). And I—I don't want to express this against people, and I think I could sort of put it to some good use if I just sort of attack my research and attack my problem that I have to do, you see, instead of letting it come out in that—fruitless way. And I know it would irritate me to have to consider these problems that I'm not interested in at the moment . . . (*pauses*).

MR. COLSTON: You feel like attacking something—really—throwing your energy into something . . .

MRS. REEDE: (*Cutting in*) Well, I do, mentally I feel—ah—sort of creative and alive at this time and—ah—people have been coming to me. And I have been helping them with their ideas for their papers. I don't know why, but all this abundance is there for other people and not available to me somehow.

MR. COLSTON: Surprised at the—readiness of your . . .

MRS. REEDE: There's a lot there.

MR. COLSTON: Of your potential in some instances?

Colston felt that this was movement ahead on the part of Mrs. Reede. She was facing the evidence that she possessed a potential for productive work. At the same time she was considering what blocked her as something in her, over which she might have some control, and not merely as something happening to her from outside. Both types of responses are in the direction of realism and concreteness.

By the time of the eleventh session, Mrs. Reede saw that she had earlier been excusing her unproductivity in work on the basis of her feelings of frustration about her marriage.

MRS. REEDE: I feel that even with these mistakes and these handicaps, if I had really got down to work in the kind of high-powered con-

134

centrated way that I know I'm capable of, I could have done it any way.

MR. COLSTON: Then you really can't excuse yourself. You know you can do it.

MRS. REEDE: I could have done it. It might have been harder, but I —I don't know whether this is grandiose or not, but I just do have that feeling within myself, you know, that if I would really get down to it, I can do certain things and that's a problem I haven't met before. I've always been in one way or another fairly highly motivated. But maybe in all this . . . (*hesitating*)

MR. COLSTON: It's a different experience for you . . .

MRS. REEDE: It's an important kind of transition. We talked once before about the motivation, and I think that I have been in the past motivated a lot by fear, which for some reason or other I don't particularly feel now. I don't feel any external pressure, and there doesn't seem to be enough internal push, you know, to compensate for that, but it might be—I hope it might be—that I will develop this and I can substitute the internal—ambition for this kind of external anxiety and fear pressure, you know. But I guess I don't know how to operate without it—in the interim. It's just like having a habit, you know—or working under that kind of stimulus. When that isn't present, you don't quite know how to—you don't know quite how to act.

Not only does she recognize her complicity in past unproductivity. She also recognizes that something novel is now happening to her thinking about her work. Before a great deal of that had been done under compulsion when done at all. Now she sees the possibility of its being done through her own initiative. This is a further step toward responsibility, in our judgment.

Between the eighth and the eleventh sessions, she said she had recognized how much previously she had been "motivated by external pressures." Now, she continued, she wanted to be more inner-directed. Yet she said she still found it difficult to "operate" without the external stimuli. She described herself as in a period of transition. She had a new freedom and initiative, but the ability to use it was still ambiguous. From the point of view of honest acknowledg-

135

ment of feelings, recognizing the ambiguity of growing freedom is realism.

Colston's statements in the above exchange were unusually brief. This was because she was keeping the ball rolling and his main business in this interview seemed to be to keep from stopping it.

The Marriage from a New Perspective. After the eleventh session, Mrs. Reede talked by telephone with her husband. During the call, as she reported at the twelfth interview, her husband had urged her to return to live with him. She said she found herself pulled strongly in that direction but feared that she was simply being gullible. Yet, since she was experiencing positive changes in other areas of life, she found herself curious as to what difference her new capacities might have if she were living with her husband. The following came in this twelfth session.

MRS. REEDE: He wants me to come back and begin life over again, but I don't know.

MR. COLSTON: You're not sure you can trust this?

MRS. REEDE: (*Pausing*) I don't know what this means, you know. It's happened before, and I got so I'm kind of immune to these declarations of loyalty, because it's happened both times that he's written me glowing letters about what a wonderful relationship we have and nothing can come between us and all this sort of thing. Then very—almost within a week or ten days almost literally—he's got into some trap with a woman. It almost seems as though this is his expression of his own resistance to the idea, you see, of doing this. It isn't something that—that he expresses as a conviction. It's almost as though he's trying to convince himself. I'm uneasy about these—and saying . . .

MR. COLSTON: And saying, "Well, I'm really—caught between how far I want to go along with this, and how much I really know is a repetition of the same old story." Is that it?

MRS. REEDE: Well, I would like very much to maintain the marriage, I think, and if I felt that there was some possibility of making something out of it . . . (*sobs*). But there just isn't anything in what he says when he talks about it. It's just, "Well, come on down and we'll have a lot of fun." I think—well, having fun is a kind of shallow goal. It's a kind of a shallow thing to express

136

about a relationship like this (*pause*). Guess I've kind of passed the point where I can just go and have fun.

MR. COLSTON: You feel rather hopeless about your relationship coming to mean what you'd like to see it mean.

MRS. REEDE: Well, I know that we could have fun together. I know that, I mean, it's a—frustrating and so forth, but it's all so frustrating. There's nothing deeper behind it. (*Pauses.*) Perhaps I want the wrong thing. Perhaps it's not meant to be like this.

MR. COLSTON: But you feel so cheated somehow and wonder if you should really expect it to . . .

MRS. REEDE: (*Breaking in*) Yeah, I'm kind of puzzled, you know. Because it's certainly true that in spite of everything, he's been very good to me (*blows nose*). And he's been a very sort of constant friend. He is a deep person. I don't know why I feel this way really.

MR. COLSTON: He has many qualities which you do appreciate.

By this point in her reflections, Mrs. Reede had been able to acknowledge more forthrightly than ever before the depth of her alienation from her husband. Then, however, in the exchange above, even though her conclusion about the potentiality of the marriage still leans toward the negative side, she was able to begin to deal openly with her attractions to her husband for reasons other than guilt and habit. Previously she had gone to some lengths to avoid any acknowledgment of positive feeling toward a man who kept her shamed if she did and shamed if she did not. Recognition then of her attraction would automatically have meant denying the fact of alienation. Now she is becoming able to consider the two feelings as coexistent—not a peaceful inner world, to be sure, with its overtones of cold war, but a mere honest and deeper acknowledgment of her true inner feelings with all their ambivalence and diversity. She went on immediately as follows:

MRS. REEDE: Yes, and through everything he's been—at least verbally and in his attitude—in his dealings with me—not considerate, but he's kept a kind of regard and respect for me, you know. It's kind of hard to say, exactly, when I say this, because I feel this and at the same time I feel that he's done really outrageous

137

things that show he's a real paradox. Well, things are just not simple, that's all.

MR. COLSTON: And the complexity of it is . . .

MRS. REEDE: (*Picking it up*) I mean, it's true that you can feel respect and admiration and closeness and sympathy to a person, even while you do—you act in quite an outrageous way, you know. And it's true that I can see how he's acted in ways that have angered me and at times I have felt quite contemptuous about him, not simply for the way he's treated me but the way he's treated the other girls in some ways too. And yet, somehow, it doesn't seem to affect the fact that I see many things in him that I admire (*weeps*) and respect.

MR. COLSTON: Seems strange to you that you are caught in this . . .

MRS. REEDE: Yeah, and I think that I trust him more than anyone I've ever known. I don't think if he ever had any choice—any conscious choice—about anything that he would be really mean or dishonorable with me (*blows nose*). And I guess in the long run I depend on him emotionally (*pauses*). And there is no one I've ever met—and I think I can say that honestly—there have been men I was more emotionally attached to in some ways— but there's no one I've ever met that I had a better time with or could more easily share ideas or—share a whole life with, you know, and get along with an—over a long period of time.

MR. COLSTON: So that you do feel—quite close to him in many regards.

MRS. REEDE: (*After a pause*) In most regards.

Most of this came in a flood from Mrs. Reede. Having once begun to confess to herself and to Colston not only that she had deep positive feelings for her husband but also that there was good reason for these, she plunged right on. This session proved to be a turning point in the counseling. In the thirteenth interview that followed, she decided to return to live with her husband. Still acknowledging how divided her feelings were, she nevertheless concluded that she felt ready to "try to make the marriage work" because "I know now that's what I really want."

What had really happened here? One way to put it is that she had moved beyond the usual defensive bookkeeping mentality which the great majority of quite normal people use in considering matters of this kind. Someone has done us dirt, so much dirt—let us say 70 per cent dirt. Except for the dirt-splattering occasions, of course, the person has brought us much joy or peace or interest or something else positive—let us say 80 per cent plus except for the occasions. What we tend to do is to make our totals like a jittery bookkeeper and to cloud and alter the items while we are doing so because no bookkeeper can draw up a sum with 80 plus and 70 minus. The underlying assumption is that if one is true the other cannot be true in anything like equal proportions. Sometimes in real life that is exactly the actual situation, however. Any attempt at a bookkeeping balance is bound to distort. It seems to us it was just this kind of assumption that Mrs. Reede was transcending. She was acknowledging that she could hold deeply divided feelings in a situation where it might not be possible to have one drive out the other. Either she could learn to live with the range of feelings, or she was stuck whatever her decision.

Sister and Husband. Having made a basic decision in relation to her husband, Mrs. Reede turned in the next two sessions—thirteen and fourteen—to explore why she found it difficult to maintain relationships of intimacy with other people. She talked about her relationships with various members of her original family, and especially with her older sister who had always appeared to reject her.

MRS. REEDE: If I thought I was telling them in confidence, then they'd get emotionally indignant about it and then—they wouldn't realize that breaking confidence—that what I needed more was emotional support and understanding than any action —any drastic action that they could take to prevent it, but—ah —so I just—probably grew up with this feeling.

MR. COLSTON: That it's been a long pattern for you of never really daring to experience your own feelings?

MRS. REEDE: No. And I couldn't talk later, you know, with my sister about any of these things, because this still goes on. If I discuss my problem with her, she'll say—well, she's a very direct person who seems to be able to take action and doesn't understand why I can't. Then she'll say, "Well, what is it you want to do?" And I really don't know, you see, in the situation. Then she'll

139

say, "Well, you're a coward," or something like this. And she'll say it with such—and this again brings up another issue. She'll say it as though, "Well, you don't belong to our breed," you know, or "You're not like anyone else in this family," or something like this. And—ah—rejecting me . . .

MR. COLSTON: In such a way that you feel completely shut out?

MRS. REEDE: She's ashamed of me, and she's rejecting me. I don't belong, I'm not like them, and she doesn't know what to do for me. If I can't make up my mind, well, there's nothing she can do. And then, "Please don't talk about it. You're upsetting me." She'll tell me this. And so I get hostility from her and rejection if I try to let her know how I really feel.

Whatever his faults, which were very real, she continued, she had turned from reflection on her relationship to her sister with a new appreciation of the fact that she could "be myself" with her husband in a way "I was never permitted to be at home." The following came in the fourteenth interview:

MRS. REEDE: I think probably that one of the deepest ties I have to my husband is that (weeps) I've been more able with him, throughout a long life really, to be myself—to say what I thought and even be unpleasant if I felt it. And he has been very accepting. Only I think I fell into the trap when this sexual business arose— again seeing his problem and his need and, you know, falling into this family pattern of reaction, and I shouldn't have.

MR. COLSTON: You mean blaming yourself for falling into a pattern of catering to him and trying to deny your own feelings?

MRS. REEDE: And accepting something that I shouldn't have accepted. Well, if I wanted to accept it then it's all right, but I shouldn't have participated in it—really—and it's hard getting it straightened out.

MR. COLSTON: Then I get from you . . .

MRS. REEDE: (Breaking in) I think it's confused him.

MR. COLSTON: You are saying, "Here is a relationship in which I am able, as nearly as I know, to be myself, and really be spontaneous, really come to the point of expressing negative feelings; and although the sexual area is frustrating to me, I find that in very important ways he means more to me than I have realized."

Mrs. Reede. Yeah (*weeps*).

Mrs. Reede's sister is a present reality, but more significantly she is representative of the criticism, judgment, and rejection that Mrs. Reede experienced from her family during earlier years. Her feelings about her sister are set by Mrs. Reede dialectically against her feelings toward her husband. Whatever the latter's deficiencies, he has given her a kind of acceptance her family did not. Mrs. Reede is now understanding the fact that, in her own attraction to her husband, there may have been, as she thought for a long time, neurotic factors, but that very deep aspects of her attraction are constructive.

Mrs. Reede remained in counseling for the entire twenty interviews. Following the fourteenth reported above, she spent the remaining sessions consolidating the insights gained up to this point especially: Her research work and her creative potentialities along these lines, her decision to pay more attention to her own genuine feelings in her dealings with other people, and the implications of her decision to return to her husband.

Summary on Margaret Reede. Our own subjective judgment of Mrs. Reede's relative success through her counseling was confirmed by the test results. Follow-up interview and tests, however, did not prove possible with her because her counseling came close to the end of our research period.

Margaret Reede came for counseling to the center and not to the church. Although it was never brought up by her for discussion, she did discover that Colston was a minister. It is interesting to speculate on how the counseling might have been different had Mrs. Reede seen him at the church.

A great deal of the problem on which Mrs. Reede wanted help concerned her relationship to her husband. As she reported it, he had been sexually unfaithful to her all through their marriage. If she had been talking to Colston at the church, would she have been more tempted simply to get moral reinforcement on staying away from her husband? Of course we can only guess, but in view of the way clergy are usually seen the answer might well have been yes. In that case, it would have been harder, but not impossible, for the

141

counselor, to establish his desire to see the whole matter from inside the complex feelings of Mrs. Reede without making a prejudgment about what she ought to do. If he had been able to do this as a clergyman, however, it is possible that the later sessions of the counseling would have been able to deal with certain moral factors which, in the actual situation, never were articulated. That is, if the initial disadvantage of being a clergyman in such a situation can be overcome, the final advantage may be greater.

This, however, is speculative. What Mrs. Reede did in fact was to learn gradually to consider more of the range and complexity of her own feelings—especially about her husband, but also about her sister and other people and about her own creative abilities in her work. Once she had articulated more strongly than ever before the depth of negative feelings she had toward her husband, she was then and only then able to come to terms with her very deep positive feeling—and to see that the one did not wipe out the other. The old approach to the problem by a kind of bookkeeping became impossible. A decision had to be made about whether or not she would go to live with her husband. If she should decide yes, it was desirable that she not open herself romantically to a disillusionment based on repressing some of her genuine feelings about him. If she should decide no, it was important that she not repress the understanding of the needs in her that her husband satisfied. That is, in whatever direction her decision was made, it seems to us that her chances of self-respecting and genuine living seem increased by what she discovered through her counseling.

The reader may ask, however, "Why did you not try to do something about Mr. Reede? If he would not come for counseling anyhow or lived in another city and all that, we can see why you might not have been able to work directly with him. But we never did find out whether he is out and out immoral or not. Isn't it possible that he has sought these other women because his wife did not take the trouble to be attractive to him, or more likely because she mothered him too much and did not stand up for her own rights? Why did you pursue nothing of this kind in your sessions with Mrs. Reede?"

Such questions are much to the point. Our answer is along two lines. First, we believe we went as far in the direction of strengthening Mrs. Reede to face and deal with her husband—whatever her deci-

142

sion about living with him—as she was prepared to go at that time. Second we believe we helped her to see that the part of the problem— in this instance, relationship with husband—over which she had control was her own feelings about it, that attempted manipulation either of herself—which she had done before—or of her husband would both work against the best possible long-range solution. In these two senses we believe the questions asked above are pertinent, but that the answers to them were better approached indirectly than directly.

It is of course difficult to make any attempt at objective assessment of Mr. Reede through what his wife has told us. The probabilities are that her statements tend to err in both directions so far as outside observers are concerned—that he is not quite such a paragon as part of her believes and not quite so callous and detached as the other part thinks. What he does sound like is an intelligent, pleasant, and interesting man who, although married, still thinks and feels like a happy-go-lucky bachelor, and who was able to find a woman to perform for him the combined roles of mother and companion while he could continue a kind of unassimilated romantic and sexual life elsewhere. If there is any truth in this guess, then he is Mr. Oedipus Complex to the teeth—dressed up, to be sure, with culture, good conversation, and a minimum of nay-saying to anyone, including his wife. His own defenses against life then center around not taking the serious things of life seriously. His wife, who tends to take them all so seriously that she is inhibited at every turn, finds relief and release in this atmosphere. She too, we might say, has in her some "unlived adolescence" despite her serious-mindedness. "Having fun" cloys with her, but she finds it hard to think of life without this.

Suppose, then, we put the worst possible construction upon Mr. Reede and his motivations. In that case, his sexual escapades, offensive as they might be, would be symptoms of his refusal to accept his wife or any other woman as a human person to be taken seriously across the gamut of interpersonal relationships; so would his expecting to be mothered. So long as we look at this situation, then, from a point of view involving self-respect in the abstract, we are bound to ask how it could be any improvement for Mrs. Reede to return to live with him.

That decision, after all, is not ours. Concerned with her, however, we cannot avoid recognizing that what we do or fail to do in counseling may affect it. Yet here, as in so many similar cases, we see the crucial factor—even the factor that, in the long run, can make for genuine morality in a situation—in terms of the attitudes the person brings, and the depth of his understanding of his own needs and feelings. Whether Mrs. Reede returns to live with her husband or not, she will, after so many years of marriage, always be mentally bound to him, for good or for ill, in the organic terms the Bible describes as "one-flesh." If she leaves him, with her feelings about him unassimilated, she may be more disastrously bound to him than if she returned. If she returns, however, with no new insight that may cushion her disillusionment about the parts of his character and action she cannot stand, she risks new and not remedial suffering. Hence the most important thing is not the decision itself but the basis upon which it is made. We believe that Mrs. Reede now has more chance of being a genuine person in living with her husband than before. If he can take this, then even his side of the marriage may improve. If he cannot, Mrs. Reede will find it more possible either to live with an unreconstructed husband, or to leave him, conscious that such a decision by her will lose something as well as gain something. Personal freedom of this responsible kind is, we believe, the essence of personal morality, and we believe the counseling increased it.

Comparison of Helen Wright and Margaret Reede. At the beginning of the account of Mrs. Reede's counseling, it was noted that there were remarkable similarities between what she did and what Mrs. Wright did, but that one did it through explicitly religious reflection and the other without articulate reference to matters beyond interpersonal relationships. The external problems confronted by the two women were of course different, Mrs. Reede's centering around relationship to an interesting and perennially unfaithful husband and Mrs. Wright's around relationship to her niece. Yet the kind of accretion in self-discovery toward which both persons moved was remarkably similar.

Both these women were imaginative. Neither approached either life or counseling in prosaic, matter-of-fact terms. Perhaps this is a quality more often found in women than in men, but in any event it was strong in both these persons. It has dangers, which are most evident in Mrs. Wright. She may talk, think, and reflect with such

144

high abstractions about her feelings that the concreteness that lies behind them may be lost. We have already indicated that we believe Mrs. Wright to have avoided that danger, but we acknowledge it was ever present.

The really great difference between the women was Mrs. Reede's complete avoidance of anything at the religious or philosophic level in her counseling, even though the issues with which she was dealing clearly trespassed upon that realm. Mrs. Wright wrestled with the problem of forgiveness and reconciliation as Christian faith has understood it; from a theological point of view, Mrs. Reede had the same problem to deal with, but never did so in those terms. Suppose she had added this perspective to her consideration of the basic problem? Would her counseling have been more effective? Of course we do not know, but we believe its net effect would have had wider range, for the reason that she was always on the verge of this dimension of her experience but never quite ready to begin articulating it. Yet much of her actual progress in counseling involved coming to terms with wider ranges of feeling, both positive and negative, than she had done before. Hence a coming to terms with religious perspectives might simply have gone a further step in the direction she had already taken. But we cannot prove this.

Mrs. Reede knew that Colston was a pastor, but she never mentioned anything of this, nor talked about religion. On one occasion, when it seemed she wanted to move into this realm and needed only a bit of help to begin, he gave her a lead, but she refused to take it. His tentative conclusion is that she has, all her life, associated religion with just the kind of attitude she described in her early family life and especially in her older sister. Since Colston did not talk like that, she was willing to see him as all right rather than as religious—like her sister. She may well have had a deep fear, however, that if an issue were opened at a religious level he would forget to be a counselor and would become like her sister. In the church context it would have been much more likely to have the discussion move in such a direction. At the center it was easier for her to keep this matter at arm's length.

Yet it seems to us that the actual content of Mrs. Reede's feelings and attitudes is deeply religious, just as was Mrs. Wright's. The movement toward understanding personal freedom, accepting the range

145

of feelings in oneself for good and for ill, toward being a person of creative and even intellectual abilities and at the same time fully a woman—all such directions were evident in both women, and have a markedly religious flavor about them in that they verge on ultimate considerations.

To pastors not familiar with other types of counseling, we believe Mrs. Reede is an excellent lesson. We believe that every bit of progress Mrs. Reede made would enable her, in the proper church or pastoral relationship, to move on to a constructive religious orientation. The pastor who said that nothing of religious significance took place in her counseling would, in our judgment, be mistaken. We believe nothing could have prepared her better for the right kind of religious ministration than what occurred in her counseling.

On the other side, we believe the story of Mrs. Wright may be peculiarly instructive for other counselors. Granted she was often on the edge of letting her imaginative abstractions obscure concrete realities, this never did happen—in our judgment. Such a counselor may say, "But why did she have to go around Robinhood's Barn or Noah's Ark in order to find out about herself? Why could she not do it directly?" Of course we do not regard what she did as detour. Ethereal discussion is never a substitute for consideration of concrete internal feelings, and the counselor's skill is needed to see that the one is not used as cover-up for the other. Granted that, then a new and actually existent dimension of feelings not reducible to other terms is included in the kind of thing which Mrs. Wright did.

Chapter 6

FAILURE CASES

☐ In order to give a whole picture of what occurred in the counseling, we must include examples of the comparatively few "failure" cases among all the people in the study. We are frank to show that sometimes the dynamics of failure lay primarily in the counselee and sometimes in the counselor. Where we feel it is chiefly one or the other, we say so—not to demonstrate either undue wisdom or humility, but to "lay the cards on the table," in the hope that we have learned as much from our failures as from our successes. Furthermore, we believe that a careful analysis of the dynamics of failure is as essential to understanding the nature of the pastoral context of counseling as it is to improved pastoral relationships with people. Therefore, we present two whom we regard as representative of the failure cases in each setting.

Cora Verne (Church)

The prevailing attitude manifested by Miss Verne was apathy. She presented a total picture of a defeated person, "resigned to her fate," expressing her hopelessness in the words, "why struggle, you really can't win anyway." In spite of her overwhelmingly negative tone, she had been hopeful enough to come to the church to "try counseling as a last resort." Thus, she made it clear, early, that her move toward counseling was out of sheer desperation, that she did not expect much, and that she was rather pessimistic, because, she said, "I know me too well."

She was single, in her early thirties, and a bookkeeper in a furniture factory. At the time of our initial interview she had been employed at this job only a few months and was already disliking it intensely. She also did some part-time work on week ends, thus she was spending most of her time on the job.

Although she spoke disparagingly of the type of living situation in which she found herself, "in with a bunch of 'goofy' females," as she put it, Miss Verne reported that she stayed close to her room, went out very little socially, and had few friends. She lived in a residence for business and professional women near the university.

Constantly recurring migraine headaches practically had paralyzed her at times, she said. Medical treatment had done nothing more than to prove to her that she "couldn't take medicine," she continued, and exhaustive medical tests had shown up nothing of a definitely pathological nature organically. She noted that the severity of the headaches usually increased with the "building up of pressures on the job." Therefore she wondered if there was some connection between the headaches and her emotional patterns. Since she had never "tried this counseling bit," as she put it, and she was at the point of "trying anything," she had come hopeful that this experience would prove helpful to her.

When Colston had received assurances from her that she would continue to see her family doctor to keep a close check on the physical symptoms she had discussed, he agreed to see her under the conditions of our study, which he carefully explained to her.

She saw herself as a comic figure and used such words as "dumb," "stupid," "ridiculous," et cetera to describe most of her actions. With droll humor, she would stand off and view herself as a pathetically naïve "ugly duckling" who got herself into "messes" with reckless abandon. Although she expressed this view of herself with amusement and even glee at some moments, deeply sensitive feelings often broke through her protective façade.

Her speech, marked by a provincial "twang," was often "burlesquish," in that it tended to overplay what she was describing. She verbalized freely, but rarely expressed deep feelings.

Lost Self-Respect. In the early interviews she brought out her conflicts regarding her vocational ideals and her total ineffectiveness in most jobs she had held. She wondered whether basically she was suited to the type of work she was doing. Certainly her heart wasn't in it, she emphasized, but what else could she do? This was the only work for which she was trained. If she had a second chance or could start all over she would probably do things differently. The matter she felt most guilty about, however, was the ease with which she had fallen into the pattern of "just getting by" on the job. "I see a lot of others pulling down pretty good pay in this kind of job and not really workin' at it. At first, I was pretty disgusted with people like that—I was conscientious when I started, you see (*laughs*)—but now I'm just like all the rest of 'em, just doin' enough to get by." Although she thought she didn't care, she couldn't account for how closely her symptoms were related to her conflicts.

Now she was alarmed about her attitude toward her present job, especially since she had been employed only a short time. "I can see it's goin' the same way again," she said, "and I wish I hadn't taken this job." She said the firm's books were a "balled-up mess" she had inherited from "that man that was there ahead of me. It's always some dumb man that leaves me with a fouled-up situation like this." Of course, she hadn't been very smart herself, she quickly added, or she wouldn't have laid her own trap; in order to get the job she had represented herself as specially trained and competent to act as a kind of "trouble-shooter" for tough bookkeeping problems. "But I'm not. That's where I make my mistake everytime. Now, you see, I need to ask questions, but I won't, because then it'd all be out—how much of a fraud I am, I mean."

She saw how these and other concerns were related in such a way as to contribute to her diminishing self-respect. In the seventh interview, she began to make connections between her behavior on the job and her behavior in other situations. For example, she was living in a room which she felt was too small for her needs, but she had moved there from a larger room to reduce her housekeeping responsibilities.

MISS VERNE: There again I was dumb. I was in a double room over there by myself and I wanted a single room. And I had realized what the sitch-y-ation was—they had a lot of empty rooms and they thought (*laughs*)—and they probably didn't want to put anyone in with me. I could have stayed in a double by myself just as well as in a single—aw—I don't know (*waves her hand in disgust*).

MR. COLSTON: So you're saying, "I do such dumb things that I get disgusted with myself. Then I later regret it and kick myself for doing them."

149

MISS VERNE: Yes. Now, with this job being the way it is—having to work a half day on Saturday and the fact that I've got that other job—is a pain. And this last week I went over there Saturday afternoon and worked myself to death to finish so I wouldn't have to go back on Sunday, and of course I didn't earn any money. I probably worked only a half a day all told. I might just as well figure on spending Sunday on it, too (*laughs*). So here I am with a Saturday-Sunday job besides.

MR. COLSTON: You mean, you see yourself as foolish for getting so involved in jobs that you get in "too deep"?

MISS VERNE: Yeah—I don't know. I just get myself to where I can see what I'm doin' and then I—I just charge out there. I don't know, it seems like all this stuff all goes together.

MR. COLSTON: Almost like you purposely pile on yourself more than you can accomplish, as though you take it on—ah—rather impulsively?

MISS VERNE: It seems like about the same time of year I go to the dentist and I get into one of these deals where I can't take the medicine, or I go to the doctor for a physical and he decides to give me something I can't take. When I get on one of these "jags," that's when I start spending money—just like I was "half-sacked" or something.

I've done this before. I can go for months and months and not buy anything, then, all of a sudden, I'll start all this up at once and end up with a big fat debt on my hands. I don't know what I'm trying to prove.

MR. COLSTON: You get quite disgusted with yourself for "letting go" at certain times with the result that you just get more "bound." You wonder what it all means, I guess?

Miss Verne, thus engaged in sometimes humorous and sometimes acid reflections upon her own "stupidity," condemning herself more severely for being "taken in" by her own naïveté than for anything else. From the vantage point of elapsed time she seemed to be punishing herself with the question, "How can I be so blind to the inevitable consequences of what I am doing, or if I am, why do I seem not to care?"

MISS VERNE: Well, I go along so long and then I guess I just can't stand it. When I have a few dollars in the bank it goes to my head or something.

MR. COLSTON: As though you just have to make up for long periods of being deprived—you just have to "break out" or something like that.

MISS VERNE: Yes. And when I do it, I do it in a big way (*laughs*).

Here we see how Miss Verne reacted to her feelings of being cheated of her proper fulfillment. Her work was not supplying adequate satisfactions. She only hinted, but enough for one to see, that she was not happy about her lack of social contacts nor about her extreme discomfort in group situations. In fact, the "spending sprees" were the only satisfactions she was getting, albeit only temporary and costly ones. She felt guilty even about these periodic forms of self-indulgence, on the one hand, but felt as though she deserved them for her self-denial, on the other.

Colston sought throughout these early interviews to help Miss Verne honestly to face herself and appropriately to value herself. He tried to communicate the latter through his basic acceptance of her.

Guilty Conscience About the Job. Miss Verne did not actually come to terms with herself about her responsibility to her employer until the eighth interview.

MISS VERNE: I got a guilty conscience about this job I'm doing. I'm not doing it right. I ought to call up somebody and tell them they should relieve me.

MR. COLSTON: You just feel like you're not really finding yourself here at all. That maybe you should come clean with them.

MISS VERNE: Maybe it's me, maybe it's the job, I don't know. But I can't even keep up with the current stuff much less the stuff that goes clear back into November. And, I don't know. It seems like I got into it backwards working on the books and then I found out how the office ran, and now I forget how the books were.

I'm getting so confused myself and then all these questions keep coming up every day which make me look stupid. I don't feel like I have control of the situation. And you know when you don't have the records up to date, it's a little hard to feel

151

that you do. And right now, as time passes, more and more of it is getting so that it isn't up to date—and they can't send their records out and all that sort of thing. Who knows, maybe they aren't right.

MR. COLSTON: You feel responsible for what happens. You are expected to have answers for questions, but you are now so confused that you just feel "out of it."

MISS VERNE: Oh, yes, I've never been in such a deal as this one, where I don't feel that I accomplish anything any day. I just go from this to that to a phone call to some other dumb thing that comes along—you really don't accomplish a thing really. You go backwards. When I first came there I might have been able to understand the situation, but now I don't think I would.

My mind is more or less closed to the whole thing (laughs). But when I get like this, I can't even carry on an intelligent conversation with anyone. I get kind of antisocial and I don't have anything to say to anybody (laughs).

MR. COLSTON: You have become so worried about the job situation and are feeling so guilty about what you are not doing that you just can't face anybody, is that it?

Although Colston held up at several points what he felt were her expressions of responsibility to the job, she did not actually deal directly with them. Instead she responded in simple agreement and proceeded with self-denunciation.

MISS VERNE: Maybe the responsibility is too much. All I know is I have had responsible jobs in the past when I was all right. I don't know. Maybe it was because I worked from the bottom and knew the place inside and out. There wasn't any question that would come up that would be too much. But I get to a place where I wonder even if I ever graduated from school and majored in accounting, you know (laughs). And then there are other times when I'll be just fine and I know what I know. It's an odd feeling to question whether you know it or whether you don't. And that's the way with this job. Now, I'm beginning to wonder if I even know what the whole deal is.

MR. COLSTON: Sometimes you feel you just can't excuse yourself by saying you don't know, especially when you reflect on the training

152

you have had; and other times you wonder if you have had any such training.

MISS VERNE: That's right. And I've done the same thing other places. I don't know if it's a matter of getting something I don't like, then I start fighting it, or not. When I'm in a place like this and I'm supposed to be responsible for the job and even train others— well, either you "put up or shut up."

Miss Verne knew the "road markings" and what they meant. She saw that she could not get off the responsibility "hook" by saying she was not capable because previous experiences had proved otherwise. Thus she knew what move should be made, but stated candidly that she didn't have the courage to make it.

Avoiding Making Decisions. Characteristic of her general inertia was her inability to make even the simplest decisions. She said she was now acting only when somebody else forced her to do so. Thus, she was aware that many events involving her occurred without any responsible action on her part. She hated her own inertia, she said, but not enough to "do anything about it." In the tenth interview she said, "Take, for example, my part-time job of grading papers for City Tech."

MISS VERNE: I don't seem to know what is important or what isn't important or whether. . . . And now, grading these papers is terrible because I can't even make up my mind what grade to give them. I just can't decide what is important.

MR. COLSTON: So that you feel so pulled in so many different directions that it's hard to make decisions.

MISS VERNE: Yes, now I can't even concentrate. I went through that whole bunch of papers, and I couldn't even decide on one paper what grade to put on it. It's ridiculous. I finally ended up by giving half of them B's and the rest A's. And this not making decisions affects my job too. I'm not making decisions about anything, I'm just sitting, more or less.

My personal stuff—I'm not making any decisions on because I don't know what to make. I mean, I'm just sitting and waiting to see what's going to happen. I don't know what's going to happen. This is ridiculous. I have a feeling I should do something.

153

I don't know, you get to going round and round and get nowhere.

MR. COLSTON: Just going in circles and not being able to stop, but not getting anywhere either.

MISS VERNE: That's right. There must be a way out but I can't see it. There's no easy way out and that's probably what I'm looking for—the easy way (laughs). But I know—but I don't know what the sensible approach is to any of it.

If one wanted to make capital of the "Freudian slip" in the latter sentence, he might have a clue to Miss Verne. She had said repeatedly that she knew what she should do, but was powerless to do it. She said she was aware that the wise course would be to go to her employer and tell him the situation, but she wasn't "about to do it."

Isolation. During the fourteenth interview she described her current pattern of living as "hermitlike." She said that she rarely went out and felt very uncomfortable with other people. Laughingly, she said the only mail she received was "letters with little windows in them, that I can read without opening." She continued as follows:

MISS VERNE: I haven't written to anybody for I don't know how many weeks, so I don't get any kind of mail that you can sit down and read. My poor mother won't even write to me now, I don't suppose, because I haven't written to her. I just have nothing to say so I haven't written. And I can't seem to force myself to do anything that I'm supposed to be doing—like writing letters.

There have been plenty of times when I didn't feel like writing letters, but I've always done it because I know she worries when she doesn't hear. And I only have one sister that's a regular correspondent—and my brother. My other sisters are just periodical. I have—I haven't written to them because, as I say, I just haven't anything to say to anybody.

MR. COLSTON: You have nothing to write home about.

MISS VERNE: Well, it would just be a bunch of talk if I wrote, so . . .

MR. COLSTON: You just can't get enthusiastic about writing.

MISS VERNE: I just don't care, and I don't write. Of course, it's just something else that I'm not forcing myself to do.

MR. COLSTON: You are saying, "I just don't discipline myself to . . ."

MISS VERNE: Well, I have a feeling that I don't deserve any sympathy, and I don't want any, really. This is the end as far as all the dumb messes I've gotten into, and I don't see why anybody should sympathize with me (laughs). And I'd rather nobody would know, I guess.

MR. COLSTON: You're so ashamed that you just feel like hiding even from your own family.

She had cut herself off completely from other people including her own family. The only contacts she had with people where she lived were purely for purposes necessary to minimal living, such as taking telephone calls or paying the rent. Otherwise she was withdrawing more and more as the weeks passed. She said further, that our appointments represented her only outside activities. Furthermore, although she often missed work she was regular and prompt in keeping the appointments.

Impasse. Although she came for the eighteenth interview neatly groomed and dressed, looking and acting more feminine than Colston had ever seen her, she began talking immediately about how she was completely "bogged down." Her appearance and attitude struck him at once as being changed in a positive direction, but what she said was incongruous with how she looked and seemed.

MISS VERNE: I don't know. I'm getting so that I'm worse and worse about it. I can't do anything now. I haven't figured out for two weeks now how I was going to do my laundry (laughs). It seems like it's such a big effort to go down into the basement to put my clothes in the washing machine.

MR. COLSTON: You feel just paralyzed and this affects even your daily tasks.

MISS VERNE: Yes, and I can't—I'm scared to death to stay up too late for fear that if I go to bed, then I won't take a bath or pin up my hair or anything. If I've got the time I'll do it, but if I stay up late I'm afraid I won't even do that. I'm just clear out of the routine of what I ought to be doing. It's ridiculous. It's so much effort to do the small things.

It was effort, perhaps, but she was doing the small things. In fact she was distressed at their importance to her. She was still fighting becoming a woman, but was becoming one in spite of herself. This represented such a reorientation to her that she was experiencing loss of selfhood.

At the twentieth interview, she returned to discussing her job situation. She said now she was simply resigned to the "blow-up" which she expected momentarily.

Miss Verne: I don't know what to do. It's just waiting there— waiting for somebody to open a book and find it. Once in a while I have trouble sleeping with it. Something comes in my mind that I should have done or shouldn't have done or something—and I'm getting worse and worse. I go to bed earlier every night. It's awful.

If I go to my room I can't stand it—all I want to do is get ready and go to bed. I can't stand to read or do anything. Of course, when you go to bed at nine o'clock you can't expect to sleep (laughs). That's unusual for me because all my life I've never wanted to go to bed early. This is the first time in my life I've ever wanted to go to bed early.

I guess I can't stand my own company. I get disgusted with myself every time I do something like this. Although I don't realize when I'm getting into these messes.

Mr. Colston: As though you are just waiting for the "blow" to come, and the sooner, the more merciful. . . .

Miss Verne: Yes. And, as I say, when I get into this, I'm really not worrying about anybody but myself and so, consequently, I'm not worrying or doing anything about it. All I'm doing is maybe protecting myself for another week. So I won't have to be forced into doing something else.

And every once in a while I'll have a half way notion that maybe I could do something, and then I think of all the stuff that I haven't done and I figure that I can't do it. If I could get away with it and get another job I'd probably—just so that people wouldn't know what a dumb jerk I am, I'd probably do it.

Mr. Colston: So ashamed of how deeply you are involved and how

156

nobody can really understand it. So that if you could just shake loose and . . .

MISS VERNE: Save face. But I have a feeling that it's going to ruin me where ever I am.

MR. COLSTON: This reminds you that there is a part of yourself that you can't leave behind.

MISS VERNE: Yes, but from the standpoint that I can't seem to do anything about it—it's going to catch up with me sooner or later no matter where I am. I can't visualize exactly what could happen. I'm lost enough as it is. It's a horrible situation to be in.

At this point she brought out her resentment toward her employer for not "lowering the boom" on her. She wanted discipline from an external source so she would have something solid against which to react. "Why don't they do something about me?" she moaned. "They surely know by now what a mess their books are in. It's just this not knowin' that's killin' me." The anxiety of her own freedom in the position had become too much for her.

For the purposes of the research study, this was the termination point, however we decided to continue our appointments until Colston left the city for the summer. Shortly after he returned in the fall, he received a telephone call from her. She said that during the counseling period her headaches had ceased but she felt her improvement was due to the fact that she "was just sort of vegetating during the counseling." But now, she said, "They're coming back worse than ever." She said she had heard that several physicians at the University of Chicago clinics were doing a special study on migraine headaches and wondered if Colston could help her get in contact with them. He learned that these men had completed their study and were no longer at the hospital. Also, he was informed that there was no study of that nature in progress at that time. He reported this information to Miss Verne, suggesting, however, that she go to the hospital for a physical examination. She telephoned him shortly after this and said that the examining physician could find nothing for which to hospitalize her and recommended that she receive out-patient treatment at the clinic. However, she said she felt she was entitled to treatment at a veteran's hospital, inasmuch as she had been a nurse in the armed forces, and that she intended to telephone the large veteran's hospital in the heart of the city. A few days after this conversation, Colston called her residence to inquire about her as he had not heard from her. He learned that she had been referred to a veteran's hospital for the mentally ill near the city.

Summary on Miss Verne. The progress of counseling with Miss Verne went something like this: At the beginning she was suffering from physical symptoms which had been carefully checked out, and which she saw as directly connected to her emotional reactions to events. She was putting the blame for her frustration in her work squarely upon those who preceded her. As time went on she began to shift her focus from blaming externals to a consideration of her own responsibility for clarifying and correcting the situation. However, instead of acting on her insights, she was "acting them out" in the counseling and leaving it at that. In other words, she came to rely upon the interviews as proof to herself that she was doing something positive by dealing with her anxiety, because, as she said, here was the only place she was putting forth any degree of effort.

In theological terms, Miss Verne was confronting divine judgment on one level only—that of her understanding. She refused to take the consequences of her own decisions, whether she made them by declaration or by default, and, hence, tried to avoid taking the risk of exposing herself or of acting on her understanding of the meaning of the judgment she was experiencing.

She sought the church as a haven from the disillusioning, tangled "mess" in which she found herself. She discovered it to be so, but also realized that her anxieties did not automatically disappear. Because she did not act on her insights, she found that doors began closing for her until there was no way out which would enable her to salvage self-esteem.

Cora Verne was not finding her fulfillment as a woman. As she was approaching her mid-thirties, she feared her opportunities for radical changes might pass her by. Although she would hardly allow herself to intimate that she was interested in marriage, she mentioned the possibility several times, but quickly dismissed it as a ridiculous and incongruous idea. She just grew up with the idea she was not the marrying type, she said matter-of-factly. On the other hand, she was not interested in a career and was "bored to death out working with a bunch of men."

158

Clearly she needed depth therapy to get at the factors holding her from functioning as she was capable. Thus, another way Colston was to serve as a pastor was to make a referral to the clinics, which resulted in her eventual hospitalization. Within a short time, she was performing regular library duties within the hospital.

Catherine Frome (Center)

Mrs. Frome, in her early thirties, was the mother of two children. She had come to the counseling center because she was alarmed about her older boy, aged six, who "takes things too seriously and is too much of a perfectionist." The head of the school attended by the boy had suggested he could profit from children's therapy at the center; Mrs. Frome had followed through on this; and her son had now begun the process known as "play therapy" because much of the symbolic communication is through means other than words. At that point one of the administrators at the center asked Mrs. Frome if she would like to have some counseling concurrently, and she agreed. In the preliminary interview she put the problem entirely in terms of her son and described it as trying "to get him to take a more relaxed attitude toward his school work and other things."

What Is Counseling? During the first session with Colston Mrs. Frome discussed subjects unrelated to herself or her son personally, such as the pictures in the room and their relationship to other pictures she knew, and the like. At the second interview she was obviously agitated. The following took place:

MRS. FROME: Now before we get started today, I want to know— what does this counseling actually consist of? Am I to come and speak only of—ah—the problem with my son, and you are going to give ideas of what to try or just what is to be done, actually?

MR. COLSTON: Anything you wish to bring out can possibly get us somewhere.

MRS. FROME: For what purpose, though?

MR. COLSTON: To get at any of the concerns you feel like dealing with.

MRS. FROME: That is the only concern, actually.

MR. COLSTON: Then this is probably . . .

Mrs. Frome: (*Cutting in*) What I mean is, now, as I told you before of the problem that he has—ah—is this something in which you—are you going to give me suggestions as to what to do, or is it just a matter of sitting and talking this thing over constantly —going over the same subjects?

Mr. Colston: You mean you'd like for me to offer suggestions?

Mrs. Frome: Well, what I want to know is: What do you do? Do you just sit and listen?

Mr. Colston: I do things differently depending upon what occurs as we talk. On the whole, I guess I don't feel like trying to advise you on what to do, because I feel that this would be presumptuous, especially at this point. I guess I would prefer to see my part as working with you on whatever you bring up.

Mrs. Frome: In what respect, though?

Mr. Colston: Well, in terms of getting at a basic understanding of all that's involved.

Mrs. Frome: I feel that if I'm going to come down, and it's just going to be a repeat of this situation with no answers to the degree of what can be done at points where it's my fault in different respects—I feel that just talking about the situation with no answers is no good.

Mr. Colston: You want me to give you answers.

In this exchange Colston was quite ineffective. Mrs. Frome had put him in a particular kind of expert's role, and he could not possibly accept this in just the way she seemed to want. He was, therefore, correct in his attempt to indicate that he could not be an expert in that sense. What he failed to see and to acknowledge was that he was not eschewing every kind of expertness. As a matter of fact, if he had had no claim of any kind to expertness, he should not have been there with her. What he should have done was to define briefly to her what he felt was the positive function he could perform. This could have been done, for example, by suggesting briefly the meaning of clarification of feelings by one person as aiding the understanding of another person—her son—close to the first person. Instead of this, he was unconsciously somewhat defensive and to her must have appeared aloof. At that time the one alternative she could see to "just talking" was being told. There is an alternative, and he knew it. But his own personality stood in the way of forthright definition of the alternative. The following came immediately after what has been given above:

MRS. FROME: You can't give them all, definitely not. That I understand. But what I mean is that what I am looking for is something that will let me find out what to do, and I don't think that by just talking I will find it.

Here Mrs. Frome has suggested that she does not intend to be obstreperous, she is not expecting the moon, but that she does want to know if anything is involved beyond just talking. What Colston should have done was, without detail, to have outlined briefly the sense in which counseling, in his view, is *not* unstructured even though it sometimes appears to the person as if he is moving at random. But he had trapped himself and hence the following:

MR. COLSTON: You don't feel that you will be able to get at answers by simply discussing it.

MRS. FROME: I have tried that, and I have come to a point where I felt that somewhere within my own nature I have missed a place. I have thought it through, and I have tried different ways, and tried to help him overcome it, and somewhere I have gone wrong. That is what I am looking for.

Mrs. Frome has said that she wants to find out what her part in the situation is, that she had tried to discover this on her own but without success. Of course Colston knew that very likely behind this was the thought that what turned up would not touch the central core of her personality, whereas in actual fact it might. Nevertheless, he should have said, "You really want to find out whatever part you may be playing, however unintentionally, in this problem of your son?" But he had become far more defensive than he realized; hence the following:

MR. COLSTON: So you're really looking for a kind of formula for getting at it.

Unfortunately Mrs. Frome was not insulted by this, as she should have been, for he was really saying indirectly to her, "You want it

161

done up in cellophane." Had she responded as to an insult, this might have broken his defensiveness. But her reply was:

MRS. FROME: That's right, exactly.

For Colston the word "formula" carried a pejorative connotation of rigidity, legalism, unrealism, lack of individuality, and the like. His hostility to her had emerged in his selection of a word with such bad meanings. To her, however, the word was the equivalent of "answer." In his spontaneously defensive resort to this term, he was—in retrospect—getting back at her for a quality of rigidity which he was demonstrating while remaining, technically, within the "rules." If she had been smarter or more sensitive or more aggressive, she could have nailed him.

Mrs. Frome did have persistence, however. Toward the close of this second session she expressed resentment toward him because she felt he was interested in her mainly for research and therefore impersonal purposes.

MRS. FROME: I feel that it is kept completely unexplained—how should I say it? Oh, I don't know, but I feel that—I get the feeling that I am a layman and I have no way to collect my thoughts, and that everyone is going to be very nice and very pleasant.

MR. COLSTON: That you are kind of tolerated.

MRS. FROME: Yes, that's it exactly. That is the feeling that I have gotten.

MR. COLSTON: You're not being treated as an . . .

MRS. FROME: (Interrupting) As an adult, I feel that I am being treated as an—well, this is just a case and it takes so many weeks and that's it. That is the impression that I have received, and that is the way I feel. And that's why I'm looking for answers.

Colston can now see that this gave him an opportunity to recoup his losses. But at the time what he did was to tithe mint, anise, and cummin, and neglect the weightier matters of the law.

MR. COLSTON: Well, this prompts me to say several things about the research because I hear you saying, too, that you resent being treated as a case, et cetera. What I said originally before the interviews—I'm not sure, perhaps I didn't make this clear—what I

162

meant was that twenty interviews is the maximum limit. If you don't feel you need this many, then we will discontinue when you so desire. If you feel you need more, we will go beyond that number.

This completely avoids her real question. It strengthens her misperception that the whole thing is dangling and floating, and there is nothing definite about it. Small wonder, then, that she went on in this way:

MRS. FROME: But now, you see, when you told me—everything has been done in the manner of—this and that—and actually when it gets basically down to it, it doesn't follow that formula. It's more or less left with a—assuming that I know. That if it doesn't require twenty, there won't be twenty. If it requires only so many, that's all there will be.

MR. COLSTON: Well, that's actually it. I am really sorry if I didn't make this clear to you.

MRS. FROME: Not only yourself but the others that I talked to also (referring to her preliminary interview and the interview about her son).

Even in a counselor the human mind is a curious thing. Colston had got Mrs. Frome off onto a side road, even while giving the appearance of having spoken directly to her question. Although his defensiveness was still dominant, something in him was still after him, telling him he had evaded. This was, if you like, his own inner defensive processes trying to make a comeback but without losing face.

MR. COLSTON: Then the other thing about the research is: I feel too that if at any time it gets in the way, as I tried to indicate last time, recording or anything else, then we simply push it aside, because it's really incidental to what we are attempting to do. That is to get at what you're concerned about. The research, as I conceive it, is a means of making ourselves more effective and learning more about what we're doing, because I'm sure that we must be the first to recognize that we don't have all the answers.

If Mrs. Frome had had the wit to ask, "What else besides the recording do you push aside if it gets in the way?" we might have been

163

back in business again. Colston still had her on a detour, but it had been dressed up with road signs. Furthermore, he appealed to her sense of guilt in the latter part of his remarks, as if to say, "If we know we don't have the answers, you must recognize that as a proper mark of humility; must you not?" Caught in the pincers, Mrs. Frome had to reply, "That's right."

MR. COLSTON: And we're trying to learn. But certainly this is true, and if I haven't said it, I should like to make it clear now. There isn't any set rigid pattern to the time limit, and I regard the re-search as secondary to what is our main concern—our service to you. I don't know whether you feel that I have answered the question or not.

MRS. FROME: (Pausing) Well, but I feel that when I leave I have just repeated what I have repeated every time that I have come (laughs). And I don't feel that I'm getting any possible answer to what to try, to see if this is basically what is wrong.

Mrs. Frome was, while continuing to disclaim ordinary cantanker-ousness, nevertheless sticking to her guns, despite Colston's effort to imply to her that they are pointed the wrong way, they would hit the wrong thing if shot off, and they aren't loaded anyhow. Colston's sense of guilt was still operating—as seen later on, for at this point he conceded more than he should have.

MR. COLSTON: Well, I'm certainly willing to suggest some possi-bilities for you to try. Of course I think that you will realize that it would have to be in regard to some specific instance.

If Mrs. Frome had engraved this sentence, she could have used it later on to get him to do precisely what his better professional judg-ment would have counseled against. Even as it was, what this did, as shown later on, was to suggest to her that a continued rapping on the gates could break him down and wring "concessions" from him. None of this would have been necessary if he had redefined the situation explicitly and got off his defensive horse.

Involvement with Son. When she returned for the third session, Mrs. Frome had apparently concluded that she had better conform to what Colston seemed to want, since her questions had not brought her satisfactory answers. So she talked about her son.

Mrs. Frome: If he bought some kind of candy that I didn't want him to have, I told him not to buy it any more. He did not buy it, but his friend did. And so he thought it was perfectly all right for him to eat it. He said, "You told me not to buy it and I didn't."

Mr. Colston: So, you're saying, "I can set rules, but he uses ways of getting around them," and I guess this irritates you.

Mrs. Frome: Yes. It gets to a point where he takes things and he can—actually if you were to sit down and think it completely through there would be many ways that you could get around this. And the same way with his school. He knows how to circle, and that is the problem.

As a matter of fact, what Colston had been doing with Mrs. Frome was also to "circle" her main question. She knew it; she had tried to deal with this; but not sufficiently sure of herself, had not been able to press it home against him, as he deserved. The exchange continued:

Mr. Colston: And that worries you. You would rather he wouldn't learn how to dodge things.

Mrs. Frome: Exactly. So long as everything is going right, we have absolutely no trouble. But if an obstacle gets in the way, then he's completely unmanageable. And I feel that he has to learn that he cannot do everything that he wants to do.

Mr. Colston: In other words, "I have to set my limits with him, whether this conflicts with his wishes or not."

Mrs. Frome: That's a basic answer. It could be.

Mr. Colston: Let him know where you stand.

Mrs. Frome: His personality and my personality clash, I have felt many times. Whereas my other youngster—his personality and mine are very—ah—we get along very easily. Whereas with the older boy, he's more or less always putting a defense up, a barrier. And that is what I am trying to find out what and how to handle, especially the perfectionist part.

The fact was that she had probably tried on an alert and intelligent boy—that candy stunt shows intelligence—the same kind of justified but aggressive approach that she had tried on Colston. If he had, from the beginning, handled this without a "circle," it would have been

165

easy eventually to note how she had put even him on the spot, with the implication of what she was unintentionally doing to the boy.

Mrs. Frome did not go directly into her own feelings about her son in a self-questioning manner. Now it is easy to see why she did not. With Colston's "circle" manner, he was acting very much like the son with whom she plainly told him her personality clashed. So far as we know about the son, what he does with his mother is to satisfy all the legal requirements—e.g., don't buy that candy—but to thwart the spirit—eat it when another boy buys it. This is a clever form of resistance to being swallowed up. By anticipating demands, or fulfilling their legalistic aspects to the full, one can circumvent outside demanders. The child who not only fills the woodbox but also leaves logs across one side of the room—and mars the wall paint—can neither be asked to fill the woodbox—already done—nor scolded for injuring the wall. But if he has to resort to this kind of behavior, it is because his original sensitivity against being made demands of has not been attended to.

During the fourth interview Mrs. Frome talked about subjects unrelated to her son. That is, she was herself doing her duty in coming and talking, but keeping away from everything personal. Colston simply waited for something more significant to open up, which did not occur. This was her "circle." Since he had not admitted his own in dealing with her, he had still not seen what had happened and did not go after her "circle." Looking back, it seems so different—there were all the materials for real advance where she needed it, but Colston's own defensiveness, still up, prevented him from using them.

In the fifth interview Mrs. Frome gave expression to her strongest feeling of concern for her boy.

MRS. FROME: He's defeated. He can't think, he can't do anything. It's just like a blank wall. Oh, I get so angry at him at times because he is just so persistent, and he'll try every way. I've found recently that if I don't make anything out of what he has done—ah—he'll try a little bit more; and if I still don't make anything out of it, he stops.

This morning when he screamed the way he did I was angry, and as angry as I was at him I just said, "Well, screaming won't do you any good. You are going to go and that's all there is to that." He continued to holler some more and—ah—I said, "I don't care, you can just stand there and scream, you can holler, you can do whatever you please, but you're going to go." I don't know which would have been easier—just to haul off and pop him and say, "Get in the car!" or what.

MR. COLSTON: Very exasperating to you.

MRS. FROME: It is. What would you do if you had this problem?

MR. COLSTON: You're saying there, "Sure, he's having a chance to express his negative feelings," but there's a certain firmness in your own attitude when you say, "Well, after all, I have to have my limits too and stick to them."

Mrs. Frome continued for twelve interviews. Looking back, Colston can now see that his entire approach to her never really got off the defensive line into which he had fallen in the first session. His "circle" was in fact more rigid than her own. She represented a kind of attack upon his professional function that he was not then prepared to acknowledge and deal with forthrightly. Let her know, if she reads this, that she has taught him much. When feeling defensive in this way, what he apparently did was to retreat into reflection of feelings as a technique; while as a mere technique his own basic theory rejects this. In all the later interviews what happened was that Mrs. Frome, seeing she could not get the basic counseling situation redefined, or indeed clearly defined, utilized the relationship to get insight into certain secondary matters. That the net result of these insights was not insignificant is shown in her post-counseling test results, which demonstrated a real positive movement. If she could do this *against* Colston's defenses, it now seems probable that she could have gone much further if he had razed the ramparts himself.

Summary on Catherine Frome. Since the principal reason for Mrs. Frome's being one of our failure cases is clearly, in retrospect, not her but Colston, his contribution to this result has been set forth as honestly as possible throughout the description. Why was Colston like this in his response to Mrs. Frome? He believes he knows now, but a researcher can stand just so much self-analysis in print; so the reader can make his own psychodiagnostic guesses from here on.

As to Mrs. Frome, she was almost the perfect picture of the suburban, upper-middle-class mother who has followed Doctor Spock down to the smallest detail but unaware that half his paragraphs tell a parent when to take it easy. Of course Mrs. Frome was defensive, but her concern for her son was nevertheless genuine. The latter could have been acknowledged in such a way as to diminish the former.

Even despite Colston's ineptitude, the test results showed Mrs. Frome as making personality gains. Undoubtedly this shows that she was, inwardly, very much more prepared to benefit from counseling than she directly, at any point, revealed. Hence the failure seems due not to her except in the most minor degree, but to the counselor. Other cases in our study were different, as indicated in some of the life sketches.

Cora Verne and Catherine Frome. Although Cora Verne rated herself as a failure, and the results of the self-concept test supported her evaluations, her performance on the Thematic Apperception Test showed marked personality gains from the beginning to the end of counseling. Paradoxically, these gains came primarily in the area of ability to move toward her goals, the very factor which seemed least evident in the counseling!

Actually Mrs. Frome made gains in all areas measured by the TAT, despite Colston's poor counseling, and scored all around better than Miss Verne. Yet, Miss Verne's numerical scores on the TAT were higher to begin with and any improvement was significant, especially in view of her low self-rating.

The marked similarity in beginning scores on all tests between Mrs. Frome and Miss Verne tends to show how well-matched they were. However, the dynamics of failure were different in each case.

Chapter 7

TEST RESULTS

◻ The original goal of the study was to have ten matched pairs, that is, to examine the counseling with ten persons at Bryn Mawr Community Church and with ten persons at the University of Chicago Counseling Center—with certain formal characteristics corresponding, such as age and sex.[1] We succeeded in this except that one person, Laurie Day, was not available for post-counseling tests. In addition to the twenty persons in the matched pairs, five other persons were included in the research, three at the church and two at the center. Precounseling test scores are available for all twenty-five persons. Post-counseling scores are available for twenty-two persons. Follow-up test scores—six months or later after counseling— are available on twelve persons.

How many cases does it take to prove something? The one possible general answer is that it depends on what we are trying to prove. One case of smallpox or typhoid fever would be enough completely to alter the public-health work of a district until all special measures had been taken. The same public-health officers could hear of a hundred cases of the common cold, or even of pneumonia, without changing their work, unless some common factor within their area of responsibility could be identified.

We regard the principal merit of our study as the actual case reports of counseling by the same counselor in two different settings. Nevertheless, we wanted to go as far as possible, consistent with time and resources, in studying a sufficient number of cases to make the results of tests significant from a scientific point of view. Our psychologist advisers felt that ten matched pairs *might* be enough to be statistically significant—they did not guarantee it—in terms of the hypothesis of our study. The possible significance of the test results, they further indicated, would depend partly upon the tests chosen, that is, especially upon whether one test tended to check up on another at some point relative to the central concern of our study. Tests were selected partly with this mutual check-up in mind.

When the findings of the tests are examined overall, they are mostly not, by the standards of the psychologist, statistically significant. That is, they will not prove to the person skeptical of pastoral counseling that, contrary to his views, a pastor with skill in counseling equal to that of another type of counselor tends to get more constructive change in his people for the same amount of counseling time expended. On the other hand, the results suggest that the trend, if there is a trend, is in the direction of the pastor and not the other way, even though the degree of difference is not significant statistically. Thus the general finding is, according to the tests, suggestive, but far from conclusive in relation to the hypothesis. The conservative but important moral for the pastor to draw is that his being a pastor is certainly no disadvantage to him in counseling with those people who are prepared to consult him. If our findings suggest that he should set aside any notion of having a great margin of advantage over other counselors, he may not be wrong in believing he has a slight edge. In the counseling business, however, if it is results he wants, he has no reason to want to be something other than a pastor in order to help people.

The People in the Study

A very brief recapitulation of the people who cooperated in the research is inserted here as a convenient guide to the use of the tables, on which all actual scores of the tests are shown. The fictitious names of the people appear here in the same order as on the tables for a handy reference in identifying them and their test results.

THE PEOPLE IN RESEARCH

Church

Esther Merz	37	widow	Anne Vick	38	married
Helen Wright	42	married	Margaret Reede	45	married
Cora Verne	32	single	Catherine Frome	31	married
Betty Earle	30	married	Sharon Troy	27	single
Alfred Johnson	33	married	Bruce Charles	41	married
Susan Graham	18	single	Laurie Day	19	single

Shirley Vance .... 42 married
Amy Tone .... 35 married
Evelyn Brent ..... 26 divorced
Mary Keene ...... 30 married
Martha Williams . 52 divorced
Thelma Phillips .. 62 divorced
Erma Austin ..... 34 married

Ruth Farr .... 36 married
Sarah Bloom ..... 34 married
Jane Young ...... 24 single
Lucy Todd .... 34 married

Bart Lowe .... 41 single
Nancy Kane ...... 33 married

Precounseling test scores are available on all twenty-five persons.

Post-counseling test scores are available on all persons except Laurie Day, Erma Austin, and Nancy Kane.

Follow-up test scores are available on: Esther Merz, Anne Vick, Helen Wright, Catherine Frome, Alfred Johnson, Susan Graham, Sarah Bloom, Evelyn Brent, Jane Young, Martha Williams, Thelma Phillips, and Bart Lowe—12 persons out of 25.

Selection of the Tests

Three tests were used with all persons who participated in the study. Our aim was to have the same three tests taken by each person three times—before the counseling began, immediately on its termination, and six months after termination. All eighteen persons in the matched pairs, and the four additional people reported on, received the tests before counseling and immediately afterward. Circumstantial difficulties were encountered in the follow-up testing, where it proved possible to test only about half the total number.

In addition to the three tests administered to all the persons before and after counseling and to half of them a few months after counseling, two types of subjective ratings were also made. With the aid of rating scales to quantify the subjective judgments, each person who received counseling was asked at the time of his termination to rate himself by evaluating the degree of progress he felt he had made, how effective he felt the counseling had been, and so on. Also at the point of termination of each case Colston used a rating scale to pin down his subjective judgment of the progress, if any, made by each person during counseling. These two types of subjective judgment of progress are later compared with each other and with the findings from the tests.

A preliminary description of each of the three tests at this point will make it easier to indicate why each was chosen.

171

Because of the uncanny ability of the so-called projective tests to get underneath the surface of personality when interpreted by psychologists of special training, we were eager to have one test of this kind. The oldest and most widely used test of this kind is the Rorschach or ink-blot test. Of the same type, although different in details, is the Thematic Apperception Test, so called because it tries to get at "themes" or patterns beneath the surface of consciously controlled perception.[2] We concluded that the latter test, or TAT as it is usually known, was superior for our purposes, and we had skilled interpreters of this test in the persons of Harold Boris and Rosalind Dymond Cartwright.

We wanted also to have a test that would get as directly as possible at a person's feeling about himself, what Carl R. Rogers and his associates call his "self-concept."[3] Just such a test was then being tried out by its creators, John M. Butler, now director of the counseling center, and Gerard V. Haigh.[4] Not a test that had been "standardized,"—that is, tried out over a period of time on relatively large numbers of people—it was in an experimental stage, so much so that it had no precise name. Its aim was to give an index of personal adjustment by getting at a person's conscious feelings about himself. It used the so-called "Q-technique" devised by William Stephenson, but the content of the test was constructed by Butler and Haigh.[5]

Our third test was one of social attitudes, consisting of portions of several interrelated tests that had been devised by Adorno, Levinson, Lichtenberg, and others in their monumental study, The Authoritarian Personality.[6] We used three sub-tests, or "sub-scales" as the technical jargon puts it. The first is called the "ethnocentrism scale" and assesses the extent to which a person is rigid in evaluating the standards of all other groups from the point of view of those of his own group. It has proved effective in detecting attitudes such as anti-Semitism, antinegro prejudice, and similar attitudes even when they may not be fully conscious to the persons holding them.

The second sub-scale of the social attitudes test was that called "religious conventionalism." It assesses the degree to which a person adheres to religious ideas that are conventional within our culture, whether they have much personal meaning to him or not. It is not at all, therefore, an appraisal of one's faith, of the depth of his religious insight, or of the theological adequacy of his beliefs.

The third part of the social attitudes test that we used is called "traditional family ideology." Here the attempt is to appraise the degree to which a person holds to ideas about the kind of relationships that ought to obtain in family life in terms of the standard that has been traditional in our culture—but which is now, plainly, changing rapidly.

Even these brief general descriptions of the three tests suggest some of our reasons for their selection. The TAT gets at factors beneath the surface, helps to correct, if need be, the findings of the other tests that lend themselves more easily to being "rigged" by a sophisticated person. It also has suggestive value in warning about possible psychotic trends in a person. We felt this quality would be an additional check against our becoming involved in counseling with persons who need, not counseling, but some form of psychiatrically directed therapy. The TAT cannot be effectively interpreted even by a generally qualified psychologist unless he has had special training in it, and we were fortunate in having Harold Boris, one so equipped. Some TAT interpretations were done by Rosalind Dymond Cartwright, recognized as an authority in this type of test interpretation. She also analyzed some of the test results to determine their significance and provided expert counsel in helping Colston to analyze the others. The conclusions we have drawn, however, on the basis of the test interpretations are entirely our own.

The adjustment-through-self-concept test of Butler and Haigh was used partly to contribute data to the experimental construction and checking of this test at the counseling center, partly because it aimed at a direct appraisal of a person's feeling-tone about himself, partly because of its relative ease of administration, and partly because its use of the Q-technique simplifies the statistical handling of data derived from it.

We were first intrigued by the social attitudes test because it included the "religious conventionalism" sub-scale. Would the people we saw at the church be very much more rigidly conventional in their views of and adherence to a religious stereotype than persons at the center? Whatever the answer, the question seemed important and this test seemed able at least to give clues to its answer. Having decided on that, we included the "ethnocentrism" and "traditional family ideology" sub-scales also partly because of what they appraise directly and partly because their findings tend to be correlated highly with the results of the "religious conventionalism" scale.

Some practical considerations were involved in our criteria of selection. The funds available for testing purposes were limited. Even more important, each person in the study had to give a considerable block of time both before and after counseling—and in some cases six months after counseling as well—to taking our three tests. We felt that this time just about reached the upper limit of what we could legitimately expect of our people without having the time spent in testing affect adversely the counseling. The testing time given by each person in the study was about six hours and, for the twelve who also took the follow-up tests, about nine hours.

Adjustment-Through-Self-Concept Test

This test used the Q-technique devised by Stephenson. This is a technique and not itself a test. A certain number of cards is given to each person, and he is asked to read the statement on each card and put it in a particular pile depending on his reaction to the content of the statement. In the usual application of Q-technique there are 100 cards divided into nine piles of different sizes. The difference in the size of the piles has been designed to make statistical computations easier.

The merit of the Q-technique is that it provides a relatively simple means of getting at the subjective opinions or feelings of people. For instance, it can give a rough measure of the degree to which a person responds positively or negatively to such statements as "I am a submissive person" or "I am an aggressive person."

In the test devised by Butler and Haigh, which we used, there were seventy-four items instead of 100. In examining the tables giving results on this test, seventy-four would have been a "perfect score." The seventy-four items in this test were designed to elicit the person's concept of or opinions about himself. Sample items were "I put on a false front," "I am responsible for my troubles," "I have the feeling that I am just not facing things," and "I am a rational person." The items are not reproduced in detail here, but they are available elsewhere.[7]

Findings of the Adjustment-Through-Self-Concept Test. The findings of this test are presented in Table 1. Let the reader first scan

174

the column under church marked "Diff." for "Difference." This shows the individual changes in scores on this test from the period immediately before, to that immediately after, counseling. With one exception, all the mathematical signs are positive rather than negative— and there is one zero, indicating no change. From the point of view of statistical significance, the collective amount of change registered from precounseling to post-counseling by the people at the church is not significant—i.e., it does not constitute conclusive proof of anything. On the other hand, if the one case with the big "–25" were excluded from the average amount of change registered by this test, the result would be significant statistically.

If the reader's eye runs down the plus and minus signs of the counseling center clients, he sees a different situation. He sees six plus and five minus signs. The amount of change from precounseling to post-counseling in these persons, as registered by this test, is almost zero viewed collectively. Two of the individuals demonstrated very significant positive changes according to this test, while the others registered slight or negative changes.

TABLE 1

Findings of the Butler-Haigh Adjustment-Through-Self-Concept Test on Individual Persons

FORMALLY MATCHED PAIRS

Bryn Mawr Community Church				Counseling Center				
Name	Pre	Post	Diff.	FU	Name	Pre	Post	Diff.	FU
E. Merz	30	43	+13	38	A. Vick	37	43	+ 6	39
H. Wright	48	58	+10	51	M. Reede	31	43	+12	—
C. Verne	39	14	−25	—	C. Frome	32	38	+ 6	45
B. Earle	36	55	+19	—	S. Troy	25	40	+15	—
A. Johnson	26	32	+ 6	43	B. Charles	38	30	− 8	—
S. Graham	37	51	+14	52	L. Day	(22)	—	—	—
S. Vance	37	42	+ 5	—	R. Farr	.37	36	− 1	—
A. Tone	30	34	+ 4	—	S. Bloom	42	31	−11	39
E. Brent	28	28	0	29	J. Young	52	48	− 4	43
M. Keene	39	48	+ 9	—	L. Todd	37	36	− 1	—
Mean									
Average	35.0	40.5	+ 5.5	42.6		36.8	38.3	+ 1.6	40.2

UNMATCHED

Bryn Mawr Community Church					Counseling Center			
Name	Pre	Post	Diff.	FU	Name	Pre	Post	Diff.	FU
M. Wil- liams	43	48	+ 5	42	B. Lowe	45	52	+ 7	—
T. Phillips	36	45	+ 9	40	N. Kane	(46)	—	—	—
E. Austin	(27)	—	—	—					
Mean Average	39.5	46.5	+ 7.0	41.0		45.0	52.0	+ 7.0	—

TOTAL								
MEAN AVERAGE	35.8	41.5	+ 5.8	42.1		37.6	39.7	+ 2.1	40.2

Table 2 presents the *collective* results of the changes as measured by this test. The first set of columns shows the sums of the twenty persons in the ten matched pairs, while the second set shows the total for the entire twenty-five persons.

Immediately on termination of counseling by each person Colston made a subjective rating of degree of success or failure in the counseling, the details of which are explained later in this chapter. However, while the reader's mind is immersed in the findings of the Butler-Haigh Test, it is instructive to consider a gross correlation between these findings and the success-failure ratings of the counselor. At this point the latter are considered also in gross terms, as leaning either on the success or the failure side but without reference to the gradations. Table 3 demonstrates this comparison of gross success and failure as measured by the Butler-Haigh Test and assessed by the counselor's subjective ratings. The correlation of the two with the persons seen at the church is statistically significant, while that at the center was not. What this probably means is that the counselor evaluated his successes and failures better at the church than at the center. In Table 4 the actual scores on the Butler-Haigh Test are given in comparison with the counselor's ratings of success and failure. This table simply individualizes what is given collectively in Table 3 and does not add to the general conclusion.

TABLE 2

Adjustment Scores of the Matched Groups
on Butler-Haigh Q-Technique Test

(For 22 total persons, and 9 matched pairs, who completed pre- and post-tests.)

Group	Adjustment Bryn Mawr Comm. Church		Adjustment Counseling Center	
	Mean	Range	Mean	Range
Precouns. (N=9)	34.77	26-48	36.78	25-52 (N=9)
Post-Couns. (N=9)	39.33	14-58	38.33	30-48 (N=9)
Follow-Up (N=4)	42.60	29-52	40.15	39-45 (N=4)

Adjustment Scores of the Total Group
on Butler-Haigh Q-Technique Test

Group	Adjustment Bryn Mawr Comm. Church		Adjustment Counseling Center	
	Mean	Range	Mean	Range
Precouns. (N=12)	35.75	26-48	37.60	25-52 (N=10)
Post-Couns. (N=12)	41.50	14-58	39.70	30-52 (N=10)
Follow-Up (N=7)	42.14	29-52	40.15	39-45 (N=4)

Note: "N" in the above table refers to the number of persons whose scores were
included in the scoring.

TABLE 3

Comparison of Butler-Haigh Adjustment Test
Scores with Counselor's Ratings of Success and Failure

| Matched Pairs | Counselor Ratings | | Up or Down on Test Scores | | | |
	Success	Failure	Pos.	Neg.	Same	No Data
At Church ... 7	3		8	1	1	0
At Center 6	4		4	5	0	1
Total Group						
At Church ...10	3		10	1	1	1
At Center 7	5		5	5	0	2

TABLE 4

Comparison of Butler-Haigh Adjustment Test Scores with
Counselor's Ratings of Success or Failure of Individual Persons

Persons Rated as Success by Counselor

Church				Center		

MATCHED PAIRS

	Pre	Post	Diff.		Pre	Post	Diff.
E. Merz	30	43	+13	A. Vick	37	43	+ 6
H. Wright	48	58	+10	M. Reede	31	43	+12
B. Earle	36	55	+19	S. Troy	25	40	+15
A. Johnson	26	32	+ 6	B. Charles	38	30	− 8
S. Graham	37	51	+14	(Failure)			
S. Vance	37	42	+ 5	R. Farr	37	36	− 1
(Failure)				J. Young	52	48	− 4
M. Keene	39	48	+ 9	(Failure)			

UNMATCHED PERSONS

M. Williams	43	48	+ 5				
T. Phillips	36	45	+ 9	B. Lowe	45	52	+ 7

Persons Rated as Failure by Counselor

MATCHED PAIRS

C. Verne	39	14	−25	C. Frome	32	38	+ 6
(Success)				L. Day	(22)	—	—

178

A. Tone	30	34	+ 4	S. Bloom	42	31	−11
E. Brent	28	28	0	(Success)			
(Success)				L. Todd	37	36	− 1

UNMATCHED

| E. Austin | (27) | — | — | N. Kane | (46) | — | — |

The findings on the Butler-Haigh Test at the church are, as a whole, almost but not quite—due to Miss Verne—statistically significant. What this means is that the changes in adjustment, as registered by this test, from the precounseling to the post-counseling period are almost conclusively, but not quite proved to be due to the counseling in the persons who received counseling at the church, when they are considered collectively. No such proximity is approached in the persons counseled at the center. Since we believe that the counselor did the same kind and quality of counseling with the persons at both places, the tentative but not conclusively proved suggestion is that the persons at the church collectively were more ready to profit from counseling than were those at the center.

For whatever it may mean, six of the nine people who completed post-counseling tests at the church changed positively to a slightly higher degree than the people with whom they were matched at the center, while one person, Evelyn Brent, showing no change, was still better off than her matched partner at the center, Jane Young, who slipped from her initial score. Margaret Reede (center) showed a slightly more positive change than Helen Wright (church), while Catherine Frome (center) scored much better than Cora Verne (church) whose grossly negative score pulled down the total of the church group.

Social Attitudes Test

As indicated early in this chapter, we used three sub-tests—"sub-scales"—of the overall and interrelated test of attitudes on social issues, involving respectively "religious conventionalism, ethnocentrism, and traditional family ideology." The three sub-tests jointly contained thirty-nine items, to which the person had to respond with a choice on a six-point scale described below. Here are some illustrations of the actual items in the test.

179

Religious Conventionalism. "Every person should have complete faith in a Supreme Being whose rules he obeys without question."

Ethnocentrism. "One trouble with Jewish business men is that they stick together and prevent other people from having a fair chance in competition."

"Negroes have their rights, but it is best to keep them in their districts and schools, and to prevent too much contact with Whites."

"The first principle of our foreign policy should be to join forces with any country just as long as it is strongly anti-communist."

Traditional Family Ideology. "Women who want to remove the word 'obey' from the marriage service don't understand what it means to be a wife."

"A child should never be allowed to talk back to his parents, or else he will lose respect for them."

"If children are told much about sex, they are likely to go too far in experimenting with it."

"The most important qualities of a real man are determination and driving ambition."

The order of the items in the total social attitudes test was to mix them up, that is, the person taking the test did not realize that three separate sub-tests were involved.

The principal purpose in the original design of this test, and of each of its parts, was to distinguish a certain rigid, conventional, and socially unprogressive type of person—named the "authoritarian personality"—from other people, a task in which it is generally regarded by psychologists as being successful. To what extent the test, and its parts, distinguishes any other shades of social attitude is much more open to question.

Findings of Social Attitudes Test. The findings of each of the sub-tests or parts of this test are given in Table 5 for each person individually in our study. As in golf, low scores are good, and high scores, bad. The first series of columns is about ethnocentrism, the second about religious conventionalism, and the third about traditional family ideology—as we have previously defined each of these. The changes in the church group viewed collectively and the counseling center group viewed collectively are shown in Table 6.

No instructions are given the reader about what to look for in these tables because none of the results is statistically significant. Very

180

slight, but statistically insignificant, trends toward greater ethnocentrism after the counseling were suggested in the church group, and a slight trend in the other direction was evidenced in the counseling center group. Collectively, the church group moved very slightly away from religious conventionalism, while the counseling center group moved slightly toward it. Both groups moved very slightly away from traditional family ideology, the center group more than the church. But no one of these trends was even close to being statistically significant. Several tries were made at grouping the persons in different ways—success as against failure cases, high versus low scores on other tests—but no type of regrouping produced statistically significant differences.

In all probability, the main conclusion that may be drawn from these findings is that this test and its sub-tests were not well suited to making significant differentiations among the kinds of people with whom this study was carried out. This test and its parts were designed not as a subtle test of social attitudes across the whole range of the American population, but specifically to discover a certain type—unfortunately large in number—of rigid, conventional, socially unprogressive, "authoritarian" person. Most of the people in our study, even though they may have some attitudes that both Christian and democratic social ethics would like to correct, were not authoritarian personalities—even though the scores of a few come uncomfortably close to it. Since the test is not especially designed as a fine-line indicator among gradations of anti-authoritarian personality, it is therefore small wonder that it demonstrated no statistically significant general changes in social attitudes.

There is of course no automatic guarantee that a person who has received genuine help in counseling on the kind of personal and interpersonal problems that have most troubled him will go right on to remake his social attitudes consistent with his newly acquired personal freedom and vision. Perhaps the test is important at least in showing that counseling did not take our people backward on social attitudes! Our hunch would be, however, that a sense of social responsibility of a proper kind would tend to be increased, or at least the possibility of it released, by effective counseling. But we would also be inclined to think that it might take some time for it to crystallize and that circumstance and happenstance would affect it too.

181

A test designed to measure gradations of a more subtle kind would be needed to get at this properly.

TABLE 5

Attitudes of Individual Persons Toward Social Issues

	Ethnocentrism			Religious Conventionalism			Traditional Family Ideology		
	Pre	Post	FU	Pre	Post	FU	Pre	Post	FU
E. Merz	2.27	2.47	2.00	6.33	5.83	5.92	4.67	3.75	3.92
A. Vick	2.53	2.13	2.20	3.67	2.50	2.17	2.75	1.58	2.00
H. Wright	1.93	1.07	1.20	5.83	4.83	5.33	3.00	2.17	1.75
M. Reede	2.80	3.00	——	2.75	2.67	——	2.33	2.42	——
C. Verne	3.00	3.86	——	5.17	5.55	——	3.75	5.00	——
C. Frome	3.60	3.33	3.00	6.25	6.50	5.50	3.33	3.67	3.67
B. Earle	4.80	5.07	——	6.83	6.50	——	2.75	3.17	——
S. Troy	1.20	1.07	——	1.58	1.75	——	2.08	2.00	——
A. Johnson	5.47	5.33	4.93	6.42	6.58	6.67	5.33	5.58	5.50
B. Charles	2.13	2.13	——	4.92	4.58	——	3.08	2.92	——
S. Graham	3.00	2.86	2.27	4.50	3.42	3.17	1.67	2.00	1.83
L. Day	2.60	——	——	5.67	——	——	2.42	——	——
S. Vance	3.33	4.00	——	5.33	5.50	——	3.67	4.00	——
R. Farr	2.94	2.73	——	3.50	4.50	——	2.42	2.17	——
A. Tone	3.67	4.46	——	5.25	3.92	——	2.17	2.33	——
S. Bloom	3.33	1.47	2.20	2.75	4.08	3.00	3.50	2.08	2.50
E. Brent	4.40	4.33	4.40	5.08	5.08	5.25	4.33	3.83	4.67
J. Young	1.86	1.67	1.60	5.30	5.50	5.17	3.08	3.08	3.08
M. Keene	3.80	4.13	——	6.33	6.42	——	4.25	3.00	——
L. Todd	2.20	1.26	——	5.25	6.25	——	2.50	3.42	——
M. Williams	3.00	3.20	2.86	4.50	4.00	4.50	3.33	3.17	3.25
T. Phillips	4.27	5.90	4.80	4.92	6.00	5.58	4.08	4.83	4.17
B. Lowe	1.07	1.07	——	2.42	2.25	——	1.50	1.42	——
E. Austin	4.93	——	——	3.83	——	——	3.92	——	——
N. Kane	3.13	——	——	6.00	——	——	2.50	——	——

TABLE 6

Collective Differences Between the Two Groups
on Attitudes Toward Social Issues Tests
(22 persons who took both pre- and post-tests.)

Sub-scale	Matched Groups Mean Difference	
	Church Group (N=9)	Counseling Center Group (N=9)
Ethnocentrism	+0.23	—0.42
Religious Conventionalism	—0.26	+0.27
Traditional Family Ideology	—0.11	—2.20

Sub-scale	Total Groups Mean Difference Between Pre- and Post-Counseling Scores	
	Church Group (N=12)	Counseling Center Group (N=10)
Ethnocentrism	+0.31	—0.38
Religious Conventionalism	—0.24	+0.22
Traditional Family Ideology	—0.01	—0.18

The Thematic Apperception Test

The TAT—one scientific abbreviation we shall adopt—consists
of twenty pictures that are shown to the person one at a time. With

a careful and standardized—but not coldly formal—statement, the test administrator presents one picture to the person, asking him to look at it and then tell in his own words the first story or narrative that occurs to him after looking at the picture. The pictures range from those of real people in various kinds of situations to those of sheer fantasy, which could give rise to all kinds of imaginative responses. None, however, are mere forms, shapes, and colors as in the Rorschach test of which the aims are similar. Yet these pictures are without a kind of photographic detail that would inevitably send a person's story along one direction rather than another.

To show the reader what is involved, we may use a hypothetical illustration of our own. Suppose one card pictures a child sitting in a window. One person may then tell a story involving the child's waiting with eagerness for his father to return home. Another's story may be about a disillusionment that makes the child think of jumping out the window. Still another's narrative may show the child wistfully watching other children playing in the distance, in which desired activity he is prohibited by his parents from participating. That is, the pictures are such that the direction of the story is not preconditioned. Thus the person can be faithful to the picture and yet "project" his story from within himself. This is why this is a so-called "projective test."

Instead of the full twenty-card test, we used an abbreviated form, which has been well checked, of eleven cards, mainly to save the time of the psychometrist and of our parishioners and clients. So far as the checking has shown, there is no significant difference between the findings from these eleven cards and from the twenty of the entire test.

When the test was being given the entire proceedings were electronically recorded. That is, every word of every story told by the person was available for study by the psychometrist, and he could also check on the directions that had been given to each person at every point.

Since Colston as the counselor did not wish to prejudice the study in any way by entering into a relationship with the people, in which either positive or negative images of him were created before the counseling began, he secured the services of two trained psychometrists, Richard Robertson and Mary Lou Bridges, both employed at the counseling center, for the test administration.

Genuine skill is required also in the interpretation of the tests, which was ably done by Harold Boris. A few of the tests were subjected to complete and comprehensive analysis by Rosalind Dymond Cartwright. These were thoroughly and skillfully done and were immensely interesting.

At the risk of oversimplifying, we may say that the TAT appraises: (1) the person's capacity to mobilize himself for a course of action that is appropriate; (2) his capacity for tolerating his own real feelings good or bad; (3) the degree of intensity of his feelings; and (4) the relative degree within him of rational as against prerational or magical thinking.

Since the pastoral reader is more interested in what the test can demonstrate than in how it does so, we present here the raw TAT report on Catherine Frome, both before and after her counseling, as an illustration of the penetration of this test in the hands of a skilled interpreter.

A Comprehensive Analysis of the Pre- and Post-Counseling Thematic Apperception Tests of Catherine Frome

Pre-Counseling TAT:

Mental Approach

This is a subject of average intelligence who is straining to operate at a higher intellectual level than she is capable of. She is a matter-of-fact person who likes to get at the heart of the matter and deal with it quickly and directly. In this she is pretty efficient except where the material touches her emotionally, and then she is completely blocked and can only deny that the stimulus has any meaning.

Imaginative Processes

Her imagination is rather limited to popular concepts. She views this side of herself as rather a waste of time.

Inner Adjustment

She has strong needs to determine her own life and make her own choices. This is her main orientation toward action. Her impulses and thoughts are used to determine what she wants and how to get it and then she drives straight toward her goal. This is fine, and she seems capable of meeting with frustration from others or from the outside world, but she can't handle her own affect life. This throws her. In other words, her in-

185

ner adjustment is poor, her outer pretty good. She is hesitant even to attempt to understand herself. It seems dangerous as if she is opening a Pandora's box. She has no idea of what's inside and fears it.

Her general mood tone is fairly happy which she manages by maintaining strict control and denial of her own inner life.

Emotional Reactivity

Her emotional reactivity is low. She tends to deny the presence of unpleasant affect and to keep it under strict control.

Interpersonal Relations

The subject is going-it-alone. She does not relate to others at this point because they are seen as getting in her way. She admits that at times she bites off more than she can chew and needs help but she feels happiest when alone and prefers to have others only as an appreciative audience in the background. She does not enjoy close contacts or integrating with others where this means sacrificing her wants to theirs or compromising. She realizes this is sometimes necessary, but other people are merely necessary evils, not human beings with rights and emotional lives to be understood and appreciated.

Work and career are her main preoccupations and she wants most of all a feeling of success.

Summary

This subject is one with a strong drive toward self-determination. She dislikes interference and pressure and needs to feel competent. She feels other people are hindrances. She has a strong block against introspection and refuses to deal with her emotional problems.

Post-Counseling TAT:

Mental Approach

The major change here is in the reduction of the excessive tension for intellectual mastery. Where she previously used complicated words incorrectly, she is now content to use simpler ones correctly. She still has her direct manner of approach and no longer has the blocking on the affect-laden material. She now can deal with this adequately. (See page 187, Stories 3 and 10.)

Imaginative Processes

She is now a little more tolerant of her inner life and her creativity and imagination, although this will never be a strong point with her.

Inner Adjustment

The pattern here is much the same as previously except that there is

186

more tolerance in inner life for thought and much more tolerance for emotion. No longer is she afraid of herself. She even finds she enjoys knowing herself better. Negative emotions are not so frightening. They can be experienced and handled.

Interpersonal Relations

The subject changed in this area considerably. She now is more willing to give other people a place in her life (see Story 16) and to give and take comfort from others (card 10). Whereas previously parents were seen as people to be circumvented and left behind so that she could do what she wanted, they are now seen as having some good ideas but having to have her interests explained to them, and then they are reasonable (1, 2, 6). Her husband was and still is impractical and an emotional someone to be handled, but is now seen as someone to share things with and with whom success can be won. This is still an important goal to her—success and admiration from others, but it seems to be in better balance with the breaking down of her defenses against having an emotional life and against accepting others into her emotional life. Her record now reads as an essentially normal one rather than that of a highly defensive, cold person whose main concern was self-satisfaction.

Illustrative Stories

Pre

Card 3. It appears to be someone who is just lying there, completely confused and tired. I didn't get too much from the picture. Just despondent. I really don't know how to make up a story out of it. I get nothing.

Note: Essential rejection of the situation.

Card 10. I don't get much out of this—it could be a romance about to take place and it could be a couple in deep sorrow. I don't get much of a story out of it other than it could be one or the other. I see no story.

Post

I would say that he is only depressed. Possibly he's completely unhappy and bewildered. He's thrown himself down in despair. I would say he'll sulk a while, and he'll snap out of it.

Note: Negative emotion accepted and dealt with. Need not be overwhelming.

I would say this couple are trying to comfort one another. There has been a great unfortunate thing that has happened in the family and through love and understanding on one another's part they will get over the hump and be happy again.

Note: Rejection of both tenderness and support.

Card 16. I'm taking a trip through the mountains and I'm enjoying it immensely. There is this tremendous landslide in which I am, in fact, completely cut off from everyone. There's no way to get out so I park my car and set out to climb over the nearest mountain. All the roads are blocked. It seemed sensible until I started to climb. I have to return and sit and wait until they clear the road and let me through.

Note: Taking the trip alone (running away?) is blocked and she can't surmount her difficulties until she is helped.

Card 19. A little house out of a story book. It has the intrigue of asking you to come in, but you will hesitate because of its weirdness—things going on to frighten a person. After much thought you will proceed to find out what is in this weird little house.

Note: Self-exploration, dangerous, weird, frightening, unknown.

Note: Acceptance of tenderness and support.

This morning we are going on a lovely trip—to ride up to Cedar Lake. Then we're going to have a picnic, et cetera. We go home after a lovely day at Cedar Lake.

Note: The whole family goes and enjoys itself as a group.

I think I am going to visit this house. It looks quite intriguing, doesn't it, and kind of inviting. Looks like I'm going to have a nice time there. That's about all —I'll enjoy myself.

Note: Self-exploration, fun.

Findings of the Thematic Apperception Test. The total score of each person on the TAT—as registered before counseling began, after it was over, and some months later—is given on Table 7. The dash means we do not have a score for the person on that test at that time. First are given the scores on each of the four sub-tests, which we include here for the sake of the psychologists. The technical designations of these parts are: Motility Potential, Affective Complexity, Primitive-Neutral, and Primary-Secondary. We tried, but found that these technical designations could not be explained without using more space than we could afford. For our purposes, what is significant is the total score.

If the reader lets his eye wander over the changes in total scores of the church group, he will see that the movement was upward in nearly all the cases. In the center group, on the other hand, the movement was almost evenly divided between upward and downward. Statistical treatment suggested that the net collective changes in the church group were significant—i.e., were produced by counseling and not by chance or circumstance. On the other hand, there was no statistically significant change in the center group viewed collectively.

The significance of these differences is uncertain, and they are not overwhelming. Whatever importance they have, however, is augmented by the general way in which these TAT findings coincide with those from the Butler-Haigh.

TABLE 7

Thematic Apperception Test Scores on Individual Persons

Name	Testing Point	M-P	A-C	P-N	P-S	TOTAL SCORE
E. Merz	Pre	17	1	4	10-2	3.0
(Church)	Post	21	0	X	8-3	5.5
	FU	19	0	X	10-4	6.5
A. Vick	Pre	21	4	2, 2, 2, 2	10-5	17.5
(Center)	Post	22	1	2	10-5	9.0
	FU	19	1	2	9-4	7.5
H. Wright	Pre	23	0	X	10-5	6.5
(Church)	Post	25	1	2	9-4	10.5
	FU	26	1	4	10-5	11.0
M. Reede	Pre	23	0	X	10-2	3.5
(Center)	Post	14	2	2, 1	10-1	3.0
	FU	—	–	–	—	—
C. Verne	Pre	18	0	X	8-5	6.0
(Church)	Post	26	0	X	9-5	9.0
	FU	—	–	–	—	—
C. Frome	Pre	20	0	X	7-2	5.0
(Center)	Post	22	1	2	10-4	8.0
	FU	16	0	X	10-5	3.0
B. Earle	Pre	23	0	X	8-4	7.5
(Church)	Post	22	1	2	10-4	8.0
	FU	—	–	–	—	—

S. Troy	Pre	21	0	X	9-5	6.5
(Center)	Post	28	2	2, 2	7-4	17.0
	FU	—	–	–	—	—
A. Johnson	Pre	21	0	X	9-4	5.5
(Church)	Post	23	0	X	9-4	7.5
	FU	25	0	X	10-5	7.5
B. Charles	Pre	25	1	4	8-5	12.5
(Center)	Post	23	0	X	9-4	6.5
	FU	—	–	–	—	—
S. Graham	Pre	29	0	X	7-5	12.5
(Church)	Post	23	0	X	10-5	8.5
	FU	29	1	2	9-4	12.5
L. Day	Pre	24	0	X	9-4	7.0
(Center)	Post	—	–	–	—	—
	FU	—	–	–	—	—
S. Vance	Pre	18	0	X	9-3	3.0
(Church)	Post	20	0	X	8-3	5.0
	FU	—	–	–	—	—
R. Farr	Pre	21	0	X	10-3	3.5
(Center)	Post	26	1	4	8-5	13.0
	FU	—	–	–	—	—
A. Tone	Pre	17	0	X	9-2	1.5
(Church)	Post	17	0	X	6-0	2.5
	FU	—	–	–	—	—
S. Bloom	Pre	14	0	X	9-3	1.0
(Center)	Post	23	0	X	10-5	6.5
	FU	24	0	X	9-4	7.0
E. Brent	Pre	19	0	X	8-2	3.5
(Church)	Post	20	0	X	8-2	4.0
	FU	18	0	X	9-3	3.0
J. Young	Pre	29	4	4, 2, 3, 3	9-5	24.5
(Center)	Post	26	2	4, 2	9-5	15.0
	FU	25	0	X	7-5	10.5
M. Keene	Pre	19	0	X	8-3	4.5
(Church)	Post	21	1	2	6-3	10.5
	FU	—	–	–	—	—
L. Todd	Pre	23	0	X	10-2	1.5
(Center)	Post	18	0	X	10-0	−1.0
	FU	—	–	–	—	—
M. Williams	Pre	26	3	3, 3, 2	8-5	24.0
(Church)	Post	25	1	2	7-5	13.5
	FU	19	0	X	10-4	3.5
T. Phillips	Pre	19	0	X	9-5	5.5
(Church)	Post	23	0	X	8-3	6.5
	FU	16	0	X	8-3	3.0

E. Austin	Pre	23	0	X	8-5	8.5
(Church)	Post	—	–	–	—	—
	FU	—	–	–	—	—
B. Lowe	Pre	22	0	X	7-5	9.0
(Center)	Post	20	0	X	8-5	7.0
	FU	—	–	–	—	—
N. Kane	Pre	28	4	2, 2, 2, 3	5-5	27.0
(Center)	Post	—	–	–	—	—
	FU	—	–	–	—	—

The correspondence of the *collective* findings is very high. Both tests show the people at the church to have made more significant positive changes as a result of the counseling than did the people at the center. The results are clearer with the TAT, where they are statistically significant; but with the Butler-Haigh test they are on the verge of statistical significance; so the trend is the same. Table 8 shows the changes in the groups collectively.

The Counselor's Ratings

At the termination of counseling by each person Colston made a rating of the relative success or failure with each person by marking on an eleven-point scale of change positive or negative and on a nine-point outcome scale ranging from complete failure to marked success. These scales are represented schematically at the top of Table 9.

Colston's ratings were subjective in nature. In making them, however, he had particularly in mind such things as change in ability to communicate, a change in feeling of rapport with him by the person, degree of demonstrated ability by the person to move into deeper levels of his feeling and whatever he had reported to Colston, pro or con, about his relative change in ability to cope with the world through action.

Colston's actual ratings of each person's change, made at the termination of counseling, are indicated in the latter part of Table 9. Simple arithmetic shows that the average change of the persons viewed collectively, according to his ratings, was plus 1.66 at the Bryn Mawr Community Church and plus 1.50 at the counseling center. On the nine-point scale of outcome his collective ratings showed the church people as averaging 6.08 at termination while the center people averaged 5.90.

191

TABLE 8

Thematic Apperception Test Scores of the
Matched Pairs Considered Collectively

(22 persons, including 9 matched pairs, who completed pre- and post-tests.)

Group	Church		Counseling Center	
	Mean	Range	Mean	Range
Precouns. (N=9)	4.55	1.5- 7.5	7.83	1.0-25.0
Post-Couns. (N=9)	6.94	2.5-10.5	8.55	—1.0-17.0
Follow-Up (N=4)	7.00	3.0-11.0	7.00	3.0-10.5

TAT Scores of Total Group

Group	Church		Counseling Center	
	Mean	Range	Mean	Range
Precouns. (N=12)	6.42	1.5-18.0	7.75	1.0-25.0 (N=10)
Post-Couns. (N=12)	7.58	.2.5-13.5	8.60	—1.0-17.0 (N=10)
Follow-Up (N=7)	6.71	3.0-12.5	7.00	3.0-10.5 (N=4)

TABLE 9

Ratings by Counselor of Change and Outcome

Scale of Change (assessed amount of change person has made)

—5   —4   —3   —2   —1   1   2   3   4   5

Changed   No   Positive
for the worse   change   Change

192

Scale of Outcome (*assessment of counseling as failure or success*)

1	2	3	4	5	6	7	8	9

Complete   Marked

Failure   Success

Ratings by the Counselor

	Change	Outcome		Change	Outcome
E. Merz	3	8	A. Vick	3	7
H. Wright	5	9	M. Reede	3	7
C. Verne	−3	3	C. Frome	−1	4
B. Earle	3	7	S. Troy	5	9
A. Johnson	4	7	B. Charles	1	5
S. Graham	1	6	L. Day	−	−
S. Vance	1	6	R. Farr	3	8
A. Tone	−1	4	S. Bloom	−1	3
E. Brent	0	4	J. Young	1	6
M. Keene	4	7	L. Todd	−1	4
M. Williams	2	6	B. Lowe	2	6
T. Phillips	1	6	N. Kane	−	−
E. Austin	−	−			

Mean Counselor's Rating at Church: Change, 1.66; Outcome, 6.08.
Mean Counselor's Rating at Center: Change, 1.50; Outcome, 5.90.

Parishioner-Client Self-Ratings

Upon the termination of counseling by each person, he was asked to rate himself, that is, to indicate the degree of change for good or for ill and the relative success of the outcome, using the same two scales as were used by the counselor, and which appear at the top of Table 10. The directions given him were as follows: In regard to the eleven-point scale of change, he was asked to rate the amount of change he felt in either direction from the precounseling to the post-counseling occasions. On the outcome scale he was asked to give his estimate of what had happened in three ways: First, his appraisal of the degree of positiveness of the counselor's attitude toward him; second, the degree of his positive feeling toward the counselor; and

193

third, his estimate of the outcome of the counseling for him. The result of these self-ratings is shown in the latter part of Table 10.

TABLE 10

Parishioners' and Clients' Self-Ratings of Change and Outcome

All persons in the study were asked to rate themselves on a nine-point scale immediately at the end of their counseling. A reproduction of the scale is below, followed by the actual ratings made by the people.

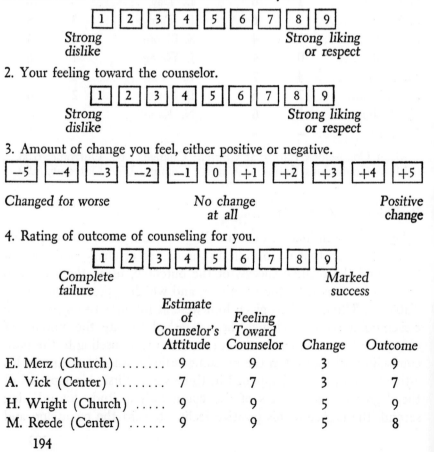

SELF-RATING SCALE

Directions: This rating scale is designed to give us some information on your reactions to your counseling. Please mark an X in the box which you feel applies to you.

1. Estimate of the counselor's attitude toward you.

| 1 | 2 | 3 | 4 | 5 | 6 | 7 | 8 | 9 |

Strong   Strong liking
dislike   or respect

2. Your feeling toward the counselor.

| 1 | 2 | 3 | 4 | 5 | 6 | 7 | 8 | 9 |

Strong   Strong liking
dislike   or respect

3. Amount of change you feel, either positive or negative.

| −5 | −4 | −3 | −2 | −1 | 0 | +1 | +2 | +3 | +4 | +5 |

Changed for worse   No change   Positive
        at all   change

4. Rating of outcome of counseling for you.

| 1 | 2 | 3 | 4 | 5 | 6 | 7 | 8 | 9 |

Complete   Marked
failure   success

	Estimate of Counselor's Attitude	Feeling Toward Counselor	Change	Outcome
E. Merz (Church)	9	9	3	9
A. Vick (Center)	7	7	3	7
H. Wright (Church)	9	9	5	9
M. Reede (Center)	9	9	5	8

194

C. Verne (Church)	4	8	−4	3
C. Frome (Center)	6	7	1	5
B. Earle (Church)	9	9	5	9
S. Troy	9	9	4	9
A. Johnson (Church)	9	9	4	8
B. Charles (Center)	5	6	1	6
S. Graham (Church)	5	6	4	5
L. Day (Center)	−	−	−	−
S. Vance (Church)	8	9	5	8
R. Fair (Center)	5	5	2	6
A. Tone (Church)	9	9	5	9
S. Bloom (Center)	9	9	3	5
E. Brent (Church)	7	6	3	5
J. Young (Center)	8	9	3	7
M. Keene (Church)	9	9	3	6
L. Todd (Center)	6	9	0	9
M. Williams (Church) ..	6	9	2	7
T. Phillips (Church)	7	9	2	7
E. Austin (Church)	−	−	−	−
B. Lowe (Center)	7	7	3	6
M. Kane (Center)	−	−	−	−

The mean or average change collectively for the people at the church was plus 3.08 on the eleven-point scale, as the people saw it themselves; while that for the people at the center was plus 2.50. On the nine-point outcome scale, the church people collectively rated themselves, at termination, at an average of 7.08; while the people at the center had a comparable figure of 6.80.

Table 11 shows the rating by the persons collectively, at the termination of counseling, of the four aspects of the counseling previously indicated. The changes were indicated on the eleven-point scale from minus five to plus five. The three other characteristics were rated separately on the nine-point, from one to nine, outcome scale. At all points the ratings are slightly higher for the church than for the center people.

TABLE 11

Collective Averages on Self-Ratings of Change and Outcome

(on 22 persons who completed such self-ratings.)

Estimation of Counselor's Attitude Toward Person:	
Matched—	
Bryn Mawr Church	7.80
Counseling Center	7.10
All—	
Bryn Mawr Church	7.58
Counseling Center	7.10
Person's Attitude Toward Counselor:	
Matched—	
Bryn Mawr Church	8.30
Counseling Center	7.67
All—	
Bryn Mawr Church	8.41
Counseling Center	7.60
Changes over Counseling Period:	
Matched—	
Bryn Mawr Church	+3.30
Counseling Center	+2.44
All—	
Bryn Mawr Church	+3.08
Counseling Center	+2.50
Outcome of Counseling:	
Matched—	
Bryn Mawr Church	7.10
Counseling Center	6.89
All—	
Bryn Mawr Church	7.08
Counseling Center	6.80

196

Comparison of Counselor- and Self-Ratings

In general there was a high correlation between the ratings by the counselor and the ratings by the persons themselves. Colston's ratings were usually a bit lower than theirs, and hopefully this is due to professional experience and acumen and not simply to the caution resulting from knowledge that the findings are to be published.

On the eleven-point scale of change, from minus five to plus five, his ratings for the church people collectively averaged plus 1.66 while the self-ratings averaged plus 3.08. For the center people, his average was plus 1.50, whereas their own ratings averaged plus 2.50. On the outcome scale his average ratings for the church people was 6.08, while they rated themselves collectively at 7.08 on the nine-point scale. His rating for the center people, average, was 5.90; while their self-rating on outcome was 6.80. The general agreement in individual cases, as can be seen by comparison of the tables, between Colston's ratings and the self-ratings was remarkably high, with exceptions that can be clarified by reference to the case histories.

Conclusion

On the basis of general congruence of findings from the TAT and the Butler-Haigh Adjustment Test, which are roughly in agreement with the counselor's ratings both of change and of outcome, it can be said that the validity of our hypothesis is given some suggestive support and is just on the edge of being statistically significant in the sense that the comparatively greater collective progress of the people at the church could not have been produced by chance. It is only on the edge, however; it is not proved.

We find ourselves, frankly, surprised that the test data went as far as they did in substantiating our hypothesis and relieved that they did not go further. In the latter instance our pedagogical instinct warns us of the dangers of clergy readers concluding from substantiation of our hypothesis that they can help nearly everybody better than anyone else. Our hypothesis was much more guarded than that. We hypothesized that people who seek help from a pastor in a pastoral setting may make more, or more rapid, progress than if they seek another type of counselor. Apart from the data given in the individual cases, we have not studied the factors that bring someone to the pastor rather than to another helper. Further, we should cer-

197

tainly not assume that the Counseling Center of the University of Chicago is to be understood as typical of all counseling other than that by pastors. We are prepared to attest its quality. But the issue here is context. A medical context might be very different in the eyes of the people seeking help, and so might other contexts, such as a social case work agency. Our job was not to study all these, but to study pastoral counseling in relation to one other context. Of the representativeness, contextually speaking, of the one we studied, we can only guess.

We do believe we have demonstrated that the best tests so far devised by astute psychologists may be applied in a pastoral situation, if proper care is taken, without injury to the pastoral relationship. And although our hypothesis is now shown to require correction and greater precision for future study, we believe our general line is important to pursue further. Studies attempting to show that the pastor, in counseling, has all or nothing are doomed by our findings. It remains to further research to find out more precisely what is his proper context, what kinds of people can be helped within this context, and how he can maximize his own helping while also making maximum capital out of the immense boon that exists in the presence of other trained helpers who can often do things he cannot.

Chapter 8

CONTEXT AND THE PASTOR

◻ It is our hope that the pastoral reader will receive practical help from three aspects of this book: First and most important, from the cases and sketches; second, from the reports on tests; and third, from our interpretative generalizations. We have presented interpretations throughout the volume. In the present chapter we focus on such interpretations.

Every case or sketch, in our judgment, offers some unique contribution to the pastor's understanding. We shall first lift up the unique contributions made by each of the six cases set forth in detail in the text. More briefly, we shall then summarize the additional insights that are available from the study of the remaining nineteen cases involved in the research. These are so presented that the reader need not be familiar with the details of these cases in order to understand the contributions noted here in summary form. He may, however, if he wishes, check our discussion by referring to the sketches in Appendix B.

We shall then consider briefly the general significance of the testing procedures, results, and methods. After brief discussions of counseling with persons at various ages and stages of life and counseling with persons who have been divorced, we shall conclude by summarizing what our study seems to have shown about the four dimensions of context set forth in Chapter 2.

The Pastor and the Cases

Our discussion of what each of the cases and sketches suggests to the pastor concerning his counseling begins with the six cases that were treated in detail, and then moves to those that were reported as briefer life sketches.

199

Esther Merz (*Representative Case from Church*). Perhaps the most important contribution made by Mrs. Merz's story is its demonstration that a sincere yearning for religious truth, confused and full of doubt as it may be, may nevertheless serve as the avenue or channel leading to a reconsideration of the self in all dimensions of its relationship—to itself, to other people, and to God. During difficult and frustrating years immediately before her counseling, it was the search for religious meaning that kept Mrs. Merz going in all realms of her life. When she entered upon pastoral counseling, she increased her religious understanding, but went right on also to a greater capacity to reconsider critically her relationships to herself and to other people. A religious yearning, problem, or doubt may indeed have significance in and of itself, and it may serve, at the same time and without compromise of its independent status, as a channel to reconsideration of all dimensions of life.

Mrs. Merz also provides some light on how to deal with serious and deeply personal religious questions. She began her counseling by posing the most basic of such questions. Yet since she knew in her head the right answer, but this answer had not become inwardly meaningful to her, the one chance of helping her to assimilate it was to go with her while she pursued the personal conflicts and involvements that prevented her from feeling all over what her mind already knew. Right answers, intellectually speaking, are indispensable. But presenting them to a person is by no means always the most effective way to help him assimilate them.

Mrs. Merz helps us to explode the modern form of the childless-woman stereotype. Our society tends to believe that every woman in her late thirties or early forties who is unmarried or who, if married, is childless, is *ipso facto* neurotic.[1] It is not necessary to deny the centrality to most women of a spouse relationship and children in order to deny the universality of this neurotic stereotype. During the course of her counseling Mrs. Merz changed her mind and her feelings about this. Not being married—her second husband had died, and she had been divorced from the first—and having no children were real lacks from her particular perspective. Yet she changed from feeling her life meaningless unless she had them to a realism which still acknowledged its desire but moved ahead to find meaning and satisfaction in her life as it was.

200

In Mrs. Merz too we see the connection that often exists in hypersensitive people between self-blame and suppressed selfhood. Conscience rode Mrs. Merz perennially. She judged herself—and found herself wanting not by standards that were appropriate to the kind of person she really was, but according to the criteria constantly set forth by her aggressive and compulsive older sister. From this bondage counseling began to free her. At the same time her sensitivity, instead of disappearing, became more relevant to the real needs of other people, and she became better able to distinguish the trivial from the serious.

Finally, but certainly without exhausting what may be learned from Mrs. Merz's story, we are indebted to her for insight into counseling as deepening and counseling as broadening. Mrs. Merz, perhaps halfway through her counseling, had achieved a deeper level of considering her situation than had been possible at the beginning. From then on, however, that level remained relatively unchanged. Yet there was a working out of many implications from the new level, both in feeling and in life action, what we have called consolidation. At the proper time, both depth and breadth are relevant. To appreciate only one at the expense of the other in counseling is to run risks of serious distortion.

Anne Vick (Representative Case from Counseling Center). According to our interpretation, Mrs. Vick was confronted with a difficult life situation of such a kind that the very qualities in her which, by such standards as the TAT, give her a wide range of feeling and sensitivity—positive—instead made her vulnerable and paralyzed in her actual situation—negative. We saw the counseling, in retrospect, as having helped her to build a "callus" or defense where she had to have it in order to meet the immediate situation. She had to narrow herself in order to deal with crisis. We found ourselves shocked to find that we had aided her to limit her freedom. We are not certain our counseling could not have been improved had we recognized, at the time, what was really taking place.

Yet counseling may not always be a matter of going on from more to more. Some people may, like Mrs. Vick, be caught in situations where their virtues betray them and where, for the time being at least, they must pull in their horns in order to survive. The process is not wholly unlike that in bereavement. It differs in that grieving is

201

normally followed, in time, by a gradual re-extension of the capacities for relatedness that the grief has temporarily confined to a narrow and hopeless channel. The danger in people like Mrs. Vick is that the new defense acquired may remain permanently.

Mrs. Vick showed us, we believe, that sometimes narrowing is necessary or is at least the best that can be had under the circumstances. Yet we still wonder whether a more adequate effort on our part to redefine the nature of the counseling process and relationship might not have been better. With this, it is possible that the true but temporary nature of the narrowing could have become clear to Mrs. Vick, thus guarding against its becoming a permanent limitation on her potentialities.

The final contribution we shall mention from Mrs. Vick is her demonstration to us of what external handicaps—her size and weight —may do to the internal frame of reference of the handicapped person. Not all handicaps tend to produce the same inner point of view, and by no means all people with the same handicap respond in the same way. Society is full of pity for the blind, for crippled children, and for many others; it is contemptuous of the very small man and the very large woman, amused by the gawky and lanky teen-ager; and is afraid to acknowledge that the mentally deficient exist. Both Mrs. Vick and her husband had, externally speaking, the same kind of handicap. We attempted to show the probability that some aspects of their respective reactions to this were similar, but that crucial ones were quite different. Certainly we can never assume that our untutored and uncriticized responses to someone with a handicap will correspond with his own feelings about it.

Helen Wright (Success Case from Church). Probably heading the list of contributions from Mrs. Wright's story is her demonstration that she could, frequently, work through her problems of relationship to herself and other people only *after* she had begun to work through the same problems at the religious level. Her marked progress in getting along with her niece followed genuine insight into receiving and accepting the forgiveness of God. People of the "down-to-earth-facts" type, especially if they are also religious skeptics, are inclined to write off the Mrs. Wrights. For our part, we believe some people may operate and think in this way, and that there is no good a priori reason for regarding them as neurotic evaders because of the order in which various dimensions of their focal problem are considered. Mrs. Wright, after all, did finally deal with the hard facts.

Closley related to the first point is what can be learned from Mrs. Wright's rather unusually abstract level of discourse during her counseling. This could mean keeping at arm's length the concrete situations that hurt if voiced realistically. Such a danger should be watched in people whose natural discourse is of this type. Yet Mrs. Wright came out of her clouds, and quickly. So long as the danger is watched, there is no demonstrated reason why the mode of discourse in counseling must be dull prose rather than romantic poetry, unless the counselor is wholly unpoetic.

We owe a debt to Mrs. Wright also for showing us how the pastor, who represents "ideals" to most people in some sense or other, may be in a position, if he is wise and knows what is happening, to help expose those "ideals" when they need it. Mrs. Wright, as we interpret her, had projected her ideal values into her niece, and therefore felt justified in being disturbed when the niece fell below these standards. But whatever validity there might have been in this or that aspect of the content of the ideals, the whole procedure was negative because the "ideals" were being used as a means of gaining control. Relevant ideals emerge, as they did later in Mrs. Wright, out of a different atmosphere.

Our next point goes rather beyond the clear evidence, and yet we feel it is true that Mrs. Wright has suggested to us some very important things about the conditions under which suffering may be remedial. For approximately eighteen years, she and her husband had been parents of a mentally deficient boy. The most acute crisis of their lives came when they had to decide whether to send him to a school for such children away from home or to try to keep him at home. Long before Mrs. Wright's counseling began, she had come to terms with all the acute aspects of this situation, and yet a deep unvoiced question continued to rankle under the surface. Was she guilty, before or after? There was no doubt that, over the years, she and her husband had both suffered. There seems little doubt that her self-reflection over the suffering and the haunting sense of guilt affected her religious search finally leading to the counseling. Yet the unaided interpretation of her suffering was not in itself remedial. For it to become remedial there had also to be articulation in just the kind of relationship she found in counseling. Oversimplified under-standings of the connection between suffering and triumph are dis-tinctly warned against by Mrs. Wright. Yet we may also be justified in suggesting that pastoral counseling may do much to turn suffering that is unavoidable into something other than defeat. Christian faith does *not* assert the connection between suffering and triumph to be automatic. It says rather that the ultimate meaning of suffering may be transformed by the perspective of faith. Mrs. Wright shows us one way in which that perspective may be found and assimilated.

Margaret Reede (*Success Case from Counseling Center*). The story of Mrs. Reede makes one immensely important and wide-ranging contribution to our pastoral understanding. There can be no "book-keeper's" approach to dealing with the range of feelings within our-selves and other people. "I like him 42 per cent for this, and dislike him 23 per cent for that; therefore my net score for liking him is plus nineteen." Plus nineteen could hardly produce a date or a dinner much less maintain a marriage. It is immensely difficult for any-one to recognize, as Mrs. Reede came to do, that *both* her feelings of resentment and her feelings of closeness and appreciation toward her husband were greater than she had previously realized. If, during counseling, she had recognized one was more than she thought and the other less, a bookkeeper could still have helped her. What she found, however, was that both were greater, hence the contrast be-tween them was more, rather than less, intense. To deal with this, even double-entry bookkeeping not letting its left-hand column know what was in the right-hand column, would not do. Decision had to be made acknowledging the ambiguity to continue in view of the range of actual feelings.

To the bookkeeper who is part of the mind of each of us it seems unfair that the Mrs. Reedes of this world even have to confront such a dilemma. "If he's systematically unfaithful, why doesn't she leave him?" "Has she made herself attractive enough to hold his attention?" "A woman married her man for better or for worse; so why doesn't she just do her best?" These are all bookkeepers speak-ing. Each uses a different numbering system but each wants to get it settled, done, rounded off. Life and our interior feelings are not helped by such coercion. When there is a range of feelings, the best long-term interests are served if these are actually acknowledged to the degree that the person can tolerate the real ambiguity. If his tolerance is low he may be shattered if the reality is forced upon him. When sensitivity is great, as in Mrs. Reede, and the range of feelings is wide, the acknowledgment and toleration of the range of feelings may be encouraged.

Besides this overridingly important contribution from Mrs. Reede's story, there are others. One emerges from reflection on the morality or immorality of Mrs. Reede's returning to her husband or maintaining her separation from him. We believe the account demonstrates that the basis of morality in her decision—either way—lies in something deeper than the action itself, and without that, a decision either way could be a movement toward immorality.

There is also, from Mrs. Reede, an interesting suggestion about what may help to release potential productivity. Preoccupied and in conflict about her relationship to her husband, Mrs. Reede discovered during her counseling that, although this did contain some inevitable hindrances to her productivity, it was not in itself the crucial factor. That lay, instead, in her secret conviction that everything must be settled before she produced. The artist or scholar may still have to live in an emotional attic if he is to get his work done.

Finally, we believe that Mrs. Reede's refusal ever to permit anything to be discussed that she regarded as religious in character—and yet her dealing with issues that bordered steadily upon ultimate concerns—provides a significant warning for and challenge to us. Because we are Christian, do we insist that everyone consider his problems within our frame of reference before we will have dealings with him at all? In a world where there are many Mrs. Reedes, unaware that Christian faith deals with just those issues that confront them on the deeper ranges of their problems, that is to cut off all possible contact.

Cora Verne (Failure Case from the Church). Probably the most important contribution of Miss Verne's story to our understanding of pastoral responsibility in counseling is to illustrate the degree to which the parishioner's "acting out" his insights in counseling may become a substitute for decisive action where it really counts—in the actual situation creating the anxiety. Colston had to learn this from a failure case. We should point out, however, that all was not lost in our contact with Miss Verne. She made some significantly positive

205

gains in crucial areas within her personal development as assessed especially by the Thematic Apperception Test.

Nevertheless she was taking the road of personality impoverishment as the way out of her immediate problem. She escaped one kind of anxiety by exchanging it for another which arose out of her extreme loneliness. The counselor served as a "confidant," but not much more than that because the counseling did not move to deeper and more complex levels.

The "tip-off" as to the ultimate ineffectiveness of the counseling was in her progressive withdrawal from social situations, even in her work where her participation was essential to doing the job. Although in the counseling she was demonstrating considerable insight in actual situations she was retreating further. In other words, her insights in counseling actually raised more anxiety from which she continued to withdraw. Although she knew she was maintaining a "head-in-the-sand" attitude, she hoped decisions would be made for her by default and for which she was really not responsible.

Clearly, therefore, Miss Verne exhibited behavior through several interviews which warranted referring her to a person of special competence. As it was, she would not hear of this, and our primary function was to help to prepare her to accept such treatment as we felt was necessary.

Catherine Frome (Failure Case from the Counseling Center). Our analysis of the counseling with Mrs. Frome was severely critical of our own work as counselor. In speaking of the son who was causing her difficulty, Mrs. Frome spoke of his using a "circle" in evading her. We concluded that we had in effect been using our own form of "circle" in dealing with Mrs. Frome, that our defenses never relaxed enough for us to be genuinely straightforward and honest with her and that the failure was due far more to us than to her. A particular pastor's "circle" may be quite different from that of the counselor in this case. The "circle" of one pastor may emerge with passive people who at the same time are aggressive, even though he may deal effectively with open aggressiveness. The "circle" of another may come with detached people who have long pauses and seem not to keep the ball rolling. Whatever the particular temptation, no pastor is without his tendency to "circle." Indeed, Mrs. Frome has even contributed a useful metaphor to our thinking about the individuality of our professional temptation.

Our own defenses were so important in the failure of the counseling with Mrs. Frome that anything else she may have taught us is secondary. And yet, by implication, her story suggests that a firmer grasp upon the ability to redefine the situation, as needed, honestly if briefly, might have made success out of failure here as elsewhere.

Some Clues from the Other Parishioners or Clients. Reflection on our work with the nineteen additional persons involved in the research, who are reported in Appendix B but not in the main text, has given us some clues, warnings, and resources for future pastoral counseling. We shall consider these in order. By "clues" in this section we mean important but not obvious signals that reveal something underneath different from what appears on the surface. This account is in no way exhaustive about all such clues, but lifts up those that became plain in our counseling with these persons.

One clue concerns hidden characterological affinities between marital partners. This was brought home to us by Mary Keene. During every counseling session except the last, Mrs. Keene bemoaned her husband's faults and especially his irresponsibility and infantilism. As a result of her striking him on the nose and then discovering she had more positive feeling for him than she had acknowledged, she decided to begin accepting him as he was. The evidence suggested to us that Mrs. Keene herself had more traits of infantilism in her character than were apparent on the surface and that recognition by us of this secret affinity was indispensable to realistic aiding of her or of her marriage. It is our hunch that such secret affinities are present in a large number of the married couples who seek help.

Another clue alerts us to the possibility that some people find unusual difficulty in entering upon a counseling relationship because they are reacting against a cultural stereotype. We saw this in Lucy Todd. A Negro of high intelligence and sensitivity, Mrs. Todd was nevertheless never able to open up in counseling in even a minimal degree. Her detachment, we concluded, was precisely the opposite of the cultural stereotype of the "emotional" Negro. With her our counseling failed to get off the ground. Subsequent reflection suggests that our one chance with her would have been to help her see that "opening up" was not just "emoting." The barriers to gaining help

207

from counseling must always be seen individually, but they may receive added impetus from specific cultural pressures. A similar point emerged from our reflection on Erma Austin whose own individual reluctance to acknowledge the need for help because this implied "weakness" was augmented by the autonomous respectability pattern of middle-class culture.

A third clue is that diligent and persistent work by a person in his counseling does not necessarily mean that he is shifting an inch from internal rigidity. For this we are indebted to Martha Williams, who sought help in dealing with her teen-age children. She was honest, sincere, and diligent in her counseling, and did get help by trying out various approaches to her children and then discussing these and their results in the counseling. But she never, in her imagination, put herself within the perspective of a teen-ager to find out how things really look to him. We believe such clear absence of imaginativeness exists for dynamic reasons, that such people fear that to "understand" is to "lose out."

A fourth clue that struck us involves suggestions on how to distinguish between wit that helps and wit that hinders counseling. Amy Tone was full of wit and saw the ludicrous side of all her troubles. We saw that Mrs. Tone sometimes used this regressively, that is, her recognition that she got herself into "messes" became a substitute for overhauling the propensities that produced the messes. On the other, we felt that the ability to stand aside and see herself humorously and the ability to make progress in self-examination through counseling were closely related in Mrs. Tone. If a pastor is heavy-handed and lacking in a sense of humor, his parishioner will rightly regard him as incapable of that very shift in perspective that counseling requires. If he is, on the other hand, naïve enough to believe that anyone with a sense of humor has no real problems, he will fail to see that an appeal for help may often be concealed beneath even sophisticated wit.

A fifth clue suggested to us that the relative clarity or distortion of a person's vision of his problem may need to be appraised not solely in terms of what he says but also in terms of his stage in the developmental sequence of life. Army Officer Bruce Charles spent much of his counseling time discussing whether he should remain in military service or seek a civilian occupation. Much of the content of his discussion would have suggested clear vision provided he had been at some such age as the mid-twenties. Since he was in fact in his early forties, it seemed to us that his vision was more distorted than he realized. True, he might yet be able to change his career if he and his family would fully count the cost, but his discussion was as if there were no real cost involved in such a change. The content of any presentation in counseling, considered solely of itself, may nevertheless miss the meaning unless the more general life situation is also considered, especially one's place in the stages of life.

Although many additional clues came to us, the last to be noted here concerns the understanding of the individual person who has become a social outcast. We differentiate sharply here between persons whose outcast condition results from some arbitrary social judgment or prejudice, for example, anti-Semitic or antinegro biases in the culture. We mean a person like Bart Lowe, white and not Jewish, who frittered on the fringes of organizations working for peace, who held no regular job in order that he might pursue his intellectual interests, and then wasted his time on obsessional detail. Such persons tend to be objects of both pity and contempt. What we saw is that dynamic forces are operating in such people, that they do "lose" in terms of social acceptance but that they also "gain" in not having to produce and hence admit themselves to social judgment.

Some Warnings from Other Parishioners and Clients. Sharon Troy warned us that the person who manifests some sophistication about psychological matters does not necessarily use these to conceal feelings. Jargon and sophistication may of course serve as defenses. In these days, however, when most intelligent people know something about psychology it should not be assumed that a bit of such knowledge is bound to be false in nature and defensive in function.

Evelyn Brent warned us that people who seek counseling only on the suggestion of others are unlikely to be capable of help until they reach a point of desiring it for their own sake. Mrs. Brent, who was willing to talk only about her son and not about herself, said, "It's not me that I'm concerned about." This sentence has a double meaning. It intends to suggest selflessness, but what it really connotes is untouchability.

Mrs. Brent also warned us against concluding that mousiness is a mark of recognized weakness. Mousiness like hers is not the meek-

209

ness that shall inherit the earth. It wishes precisely to inherit the earth as a matter of right, but believes the best way to have the earth thrust upon it is constantly to disavow the desire to inherit. Thus some mousiness represents an attempt to control. It may be high in hidden aggression.

From Laurie Day's experience we were warned against concluding that teen-age problems will simply work themselves out in time. Part of Miss Day's problems came from the requirements of these intermediate years between childhood and adulthood, but some of them came from factors that were individual to her. Teen-agers may be disturbed over things that cannot be accounted for simply because of their being teen-agers.

Warnings about the extreme complexity of what having children may mean to childless people were given us by three of our people, Alfred Johnson and Mary Keene as well as Esther Merz whose story has been given in detail. As we have already seen, during the course of her counseling Mrs. Merz became able to accept herself as a person and a woman whether she ever had children or not. Alfred Johnson had been afraid to have children and considered himself an unfit prospective father, while yet feeling guilty over depriving his wife. When his counseling enabled him to deal better with his timidity and cowardice his attitude concerning fatherhood changed, and a baby was happily received. Mary Keene's husband did not want children. After several years of marriage in which she had apparently been content without them, Mrs. Keene decided that her deprivation of children was solely due to her husband's attitude. We not only doubt this conclusion in her case but believe also that she is perhaps as unprepared for motherhood as is her husband for fatherhood. What prospective children may mean to persons or couples should not be inferred merely from casual or conventional statements. It is likely to be very complex.

A similar warning concerning the complexity of meanings in interfaith marriages—or prospective marriages—was given us by Ruth Farr and Jane Young. We encountered Mrs. Farr only after she, a Roman Catholic, was already married to a Protestant. Even though both she and her husband had been lax about exploring the meaning of their situation at the time of the marriage, Mrs. Farr showed us that an intelligent confrontation of the problem may be very important even

210

if it comes late. Jane Young, also a Roman Catholic, showed us that an inability to confront the situation posed by such differences—she had a Jewish friend—may be due far less to the interfaith situation than to intrapsychic factors. Miss Young could not understand why her friend became so worked up over the fact of religious differences. Whatever attitudes a pastor may take in general or in particular instances toward interfaith marriages—actual or prospective—he can be sure that the interweaving of the interior personal problems and the actual situational problems will form many complex patterns.

Many of our parishioners and clients warned us to have the peculiar kind of patience that counseling requires, among them Amy Tone to whose wit we have already referred. Mrs. Tone was able, rather early in her counseling, to put her finger on the crucial area of her problem, but this in itself proved insufficient to help her. She had, laboriously, to work through various aspects and dimensions and implications. Whatever else counseling may be, it is seldom the cry of "Eureka," after which every one—including the pastor—lives happily ever after. Patient pursuit of implications, which the psychiatrists call "working through," is as important as the basic clue.

Some Resources Suggested by the Other Parishioners and Clients. Reflection on our counseling showed us that there were some resources working "on our side," the full significance of which we had not recognized at the time. There was, for example, Betty Earle's activities in the church. Mrs. Earle had some difficult problems in her life situation. But before, during, and after the counseling, including a period of very tough going, Mrs. Earle was responsibly active in her church. When it is possible for a person to do this, despite inner turmoil and personal problems, it is in itself a prognostic indicator of the most positive kind. It would be worse than useless, however, if it were forced. Any suggestion that "Your problems will be solved if you are active in our church" is entirely misleading. It is the interior strength that makes such participation possible, not the activity that produces the strength.

Sharon Troy taught us something of the hidden resources in the person intelligent enough to seek "preventive counseling." Unlike most of the persons in our study, Miss Troy had made no obviously troublesome decisions in her past life, nor was she now at some peak of desperation. She loved her fiancé, planned to marry, but she wanted

211

to ensure that her admiration for him was not mere dependency. The pastoral temptation would be to suggest that if she were as clear-headed as that there was no problem and she needed no counseling. But she did in fact need counseling. Her passivity of personality might very well have wrecked her forthcoming marriage. She sought help at an early age, and thus shows us that the virtues of "preventive counseling" are very great. Most people seek help only when desperate. Have we the wit to recognize that people can be helped more when they approach us before desperation? Or may we be tempted to tell them their problem is already solved?

Another lesson about resources came to us from Shirley Vance, who approached life and her husband like a bulldog, holding a particular question in her teeth and never letting go. Even though our counseling did not succeed in moving Mrs. Vance beyond the realm of her single-minded preoccupation, she nevertheless made progress judged by all standards including the actual life situation. We believe this was because it became possible to help her to use her bull-doggedness in examining the real nature of her home situation, rather than dealing with the concentrated tenacity itself. For more thorough change, of course the latter would be needed. But here it proved possible to utilize the focal characteristic for constructive rather than destructive purposes, even when it could not be centrally altered.

Martha Williams taught us that the "try out and then discuss" procedure in counseling may be a resource altering the real life situation even when the person seems not capable of any imaginative movement beyond his own rigidities. Bothered about her teen-age children, Mrs. Williams tried out various new tacks with them, then returned to discuss the results of these in her counseling sessions. Even though she did not emotionally switch her perspective, her changing methods apparently made her children feel she was not as rigid as they had supposed, and actual relationships improved. It is possible to press too hard for responses of genuine feeling, when a person may not be capable of that. "Try out and then discuss" will not move as deeply as direct discussion of feelings, but if it is as far as a person can go, then the resources within it should not be denigrated.

Several of our people taught us how great and deep a resource it is simply to confess that one needs help. Ruth Farr showed this in an especially vivid way. Her entire counseling experience was one of swallowing pride. First she sought psychological help for her small daughter, and then for herself. In her own counseling she became aware, painfully, of the hostile chips on her own shoulder that she had previously not seen. She demonstrates to us that the setting aside of pride is made possible by strength, not weakness. It is a mistake ever to underestimate the extent to which a person has swallowed pride— and hence demonstrated strength—in seeking help at all.

Our two teen-agers, Susan Graham and Laurie Day, and Thelma Phillips, our grandmother, show us that counseling may be relevant at almost any age after childhood, and that the principal resource at any age lies in the serious readiness to reconsider one's overall situation. The capacities to pursue the implications may differ from age to age, as well as from person to person. Mrs. Phillips, for example, swallowed her pride and confronted the basic fact that her apparent altruism was attempted domination; yet the fact that she did not work through many of the implications of this was perhaps due in part to her age. Teen-age Susan Graham, we felt, got some real help from her counseling in what was, generally speaking, a normal problem of adolescent development. Yet she, not yet having lived with any of the tragedies and irreversibilities of life, could not go on imaginatively to consider problems yet to come. The implicative potentialities of counseling seem generally greater for persons in the intermediate years —from the twenties through the fifties—but counseling may help both teen-agers and older people also.

Betty Earle taught us that the pastor's intelligent and sympathetic understanding may be a resource transcending his own expectations. Much of the problem she presented for consideration in counseling involved her attitude toward authority. Inwardly though not visibly, she "shook" in talking to one of her children's teachers or to anyone else who represented authority. After this had been sympathetically discussed, but not before, she was able to say that ministers also were authority figures for her, and that she was greatly surprised, in her counseling, to be able to talk honestly and openly as she had. The modern pastor is shocked right down to the prayer book to think that some people regard him as an authority in the sense of being bowed and scraped to. Seldom is this a part of his own self-image, but many people feel that way about him. If he recognizes this as a possibility, then he will see that the expression of genuine understanding and acceptance may perform a far deeper function than is consciously intended. In such instances, it is the indispensable bridge.

This summary account of some of the clues, warnings and indicated resources that were brought home to us by the nineteen parishioners and clients not reported in the main text could go on almost indefinitely, for our detailed reflective examinations always add something new. We hope we have added some insights to the pastor's general store in this summary. We hope also that we have encouraged him to think in this same way. Any time we ask, Was there a lesson for me in trying to help that person? we are likely to get more answer than we bargained for. And even the warnings are helpful.

The Pastor and the Tests

In their function of checking on our subjective judgment about the progress, or lack of it, made by the various persons during their counseling the tests were eminently successful. Or perhaps it would be better to say that our judgments were dead wrong less often than we feared. Yet the tests were pushed as far as they would go, to see if statistically significant changes in the persons probably due to their counseling became evident.

Our two main tests tended to reinforce each other's conclusions. One test showed the change in the people at the church to be statistically significant, while the other showed it as on the verge of that status. In contrast, neither of these tests showed the changes effected collectively in the people at the counseling center as being even at the verge of statistical significance.

We do not believe that we "fudged" at the church in order to make the church scores higher than those at the center. Yet our main claim for the practical use of the pastor in this connection has been a modest one; namely, that the pastor is at least not at a disadvantage as a counselor with people who consult him. Our general interpretation of this phenomenon is that, when the pastor is counselor, he already carries generally the aura of believing in something, and when this is added to basic understanding and acceptance and to skill in counseling, he has double-barreled resources for those who have been willing to consult him at all.

214

We had anticipated that everyone at the counseling center asked to participate in the research would comply, aware of its aura of science against which none can stand. What surprised us—with the exception of our first men parishioners at the church—was how many of the people at the church agreed to participate in the research, including many who began counseling later on and could not be included in the special research project. The possibility of rendering some service to others, even while the people were themselves in conflict and trouble still unresolved, was at least as important a motive as was the contribution to knowledge by participation in science.

The Pastor and the Stages of Life

The median age of all the persons in our study was about thirty-four. For the women as a whole this figure was also thirty-four. For the women at the church it was thirty-four, and for those at the center, thirty-three. The age range was from eighteen to sixty-two, with the overwhelming majority—all but seven—falling in the thirties and early forties. Thus our study tended to concern primarily persons at a particular stage of life, the period involving entrance or approaching entrance into the middle years.

Even now there has been very little study of the middle years, or entrance into them—in contrast to the study of infants, of children, of teen-agers, of young adults, and of older people. We do have two good recent books on this subject by Smiley Blanton and Reuel L. Howe.[2] The full significance of the period of entrance to middle life is yet to be appreciated, however. It does not have dramatic physical changes like the movement from childhood through puberty to adolescence. Nor does it contain obvious responsibility changes, as those from teen-age to young adulthood with the onset of marriage and job. It does not mean any marked diminution in powers and abilities, as does the transition from middle to older years. Yet, with the absence of all these externals, it is a critical transition nevertheless.[3]

As many of the persons in our study recognized, each in his own way, life was closing in on him at this period. Earlier in this chapter, for example, we mentioned Mrs. Mary Keene, in her thirties, whose husband would not let her have children. Through a good many years of her marriage she had been content to wait. Part of the reason for her uprising now was the realization that it was, as the title of Smiley

215

Blanton's book accurately puts it, *Now or Never*.[4] With men this crisis is even less obvious on the surface than with women, and yet it exists. In basic respects we regard it as religious in nature because it deals with a fundamental but not forced shift concerning the meaning of life as expansion and growth and more of everything to an appreciation of depth even in increasing limitation.

When Starbuck and others, at the turn of our century, launched boldly into the psychology of religion, one of their primary concerns was religious conversion, which Starbuck regarded as mainly an adolescent phenomenon.[5] So in his time, and for what he described, it no doubt was. What seems now to be happening is that an increasing number and proportion of people have both the opportunity and the need for "conversion"—either the first or the second time—at the onset of the middle years. Our study speaks loudly on this point. The view of one's particular past and present—and the look ahead at the probable future from a particular point in the life journey—seem to have conspired to bring most of our people to counseling. In a restless society, it may well be that the best time to become restless enough to seek counseling is in the thirties. Whether or not that is so, this is the last time one can do it provided he wants the whole second average half of life to be better than the first. In this lies a tremendous opportunity for the pastor and for many other counselors as well.

The Pastor and Divorce

Of the seventeen women in our study known to have been married at least once, at least ten were divorced at least once. Four of these were currently not remarried, and one more completed her divorce after her counseling. That leaves five once divorced who had remarried and were still remarried.

Our study had not anticipated this proportion of divorced persons—all women in our study. We had not thought about it especially, but had assumed that the proportion of parishioners at the church consulting us would be small on divorces. Since, as has been noted before, the persons at the church were generally selected first and those at the center chosen to match on formal characteristics, the difference is significant not at the center but at the church.

Our purpose is certainly not to reconsider here the religious and ethical bases of divorce and remarriage from the Protestant point of view, important as that topic is. What we want to do is to say forcibly that any pastor really open to helping his people will be consulted by more persons who have been divorced than he would like to have statistics about. The number of and multiple causes of divorce are well known to every reader. Our first question is, Why so many divorced people in the church?

People who have been divorced, and especially women, apparently are not rejected by most churches—even, we would hazard, by those very churches whose canon laws forbid the formal acceptance of persons remarried after divorce except under carefully specified conditions. As a community church, Bryn Mawr was liberal in this regard. The fact is that there seems to be, in at least this one aspect of church practice, a great discrepancy in favor of practice in terms of accepting divorced persons into the life and activities of the church. Since most of the errors of the church come from failing to put beliefs into practice, perhaps we should just thank God for one bit of reverse English. On the other hand, it may be high time to try to let theory and practice know what each other are doing.

Our divorced persons were women. On the average, a divorce is a more catastrophic or at least total change in life plan for women than for men. Rightly or wrongly, more of a woman's self-respect tends to be tied directly to her marriage than in the case of a man. Divorced women, therefore, may indeed have, in general, a greater need to be, if not accepted, at least not rejected. Thank God many do turn to the church. Reference to our cases will show that many of the once-divorced or now-divorced women have found genuine help through the regular ministrations and activities of the church. Yet they needed more too in many cases, and hence the counseling.

Are our churches open to general ministry to divorced persons? Is our special ministry open to them to make out of their lives what they can? In general, we believe the answers to these questions are increasingly reassuring to the American churches. We believe our study underscores the necessity for us to be able to say yes to these two questions—unless we wish to exclude arbitrarily from the kingdom many able and reflective and Christian people.

217

The Pastor and the Dimensions of Context

Our original analysis of context showed it as having four dimensions: Setting, expectation, shift in relationship, and a particular relation of aims to limitations. Important as are the last two dimensions of context, we indicated that our study was not designed to study them directly. Instead, we suggested that our contribution was to be in terms of illuminating setting and expectation.

We conclude that the study, and especially the case studies, have thrown light on both the significance and the meaning of context in these two dimensions of setting and expectation. Setting means far more than church architecture. It symbolizes to the person everything the church stands for—doctrine, sacraments, preaching, prayer, and all the rest. Whether or not the setting evokes a positive, a negative, or an ambiguous response depends on his attitudes to all these things. For Esther Merz the church setting symbolized a possible basis for hope in her own life even when she was not able to see clearly ahead. For Helen Wright the church setting symbolized the kind of basic concern with which she had to come to terms even before she could deal with strictly internal problems. For Cora Verne, on the other hand, the church setting symbolized a kind of excuse or retreat. Unless these different meanings had been taken into account, much would have been lost in the counseling.

Some of our other parishioners showed still different meanings that the church as setting represented to them. For Betty Earle it was a place to invest energies even when the circumstances of life were far from being in order. For Martha Williams it was a place to turn periodically whenever any kind of personal problem arose. For Alfred Johnson it was the natural place to think of first when one recognized the need for personal help. For teen-aged Susan Graham it was a friendly place where one felt at home. For some of our parishioners the church seemed to make little connection between religion and personal problems. They thought the church a practical resource for help on personal problems but had no notion there were religious dimensions to their problems. Thus setting may mean many things. Part of the pastor's alertness to context means awareness of this variety of meanings.

We saw also a variety of expectations that different parishioners

218

brought to their counseling. Some tried to treat the pastor as a heavy father who should quickly declare himself so that they could agree with him or fight him. Betty Earle was secretly afraid to talk with him because she "quaked" in the face of authority figures. Yet as she found him to be friendly and understanding she was able to reveal this hidden feeling. Esther Merz was drawn to the pastor as representing the church about which she felt positively, and yet she rather expected he could simply "answer" her religious problems rather than have her sweat over them. Helen Wright initially expected the pastor simply to commend her over her positive religious interest and her attempt to act morally, not realizing that such commendation would have made it impossible to deal with the other feelings that lay underneath. Thus many kinds of expectations were read into the pastor by people at the church.

We were struck, however, at how little the persons at the church expected the pastor to be a miracle man. Some of the persons at the counseling center demonstrated at least as much of such a tendency; due, we believe, to the fact that science has become in many respects a greater symbol of authority than religion to many people. Our conclusions are that both pastors and other counselors have to watch for the tendency to project magical properties into them, and that the aura of science is no protection for the psychological counselor against such projections.

As we had expected, we found most of the people who consulted us at the church to be more positive than negative about what religion and church meant to them. Yet we were struck, too, by the number of such people who never mentioned religion. This might be a bad thing. Yet it might, on the other hand, suggest that the church is not, in the minds of many people, as divorced from a concern with the whole of life as has sometimes been charged. The number of people who had tragedy in their marriages, yet who were in the church and willing to consult a minister, we found encouraging.

Some of our people at the center, although they never overtly mentioned anything religious, showed themselves to be struggling precisely with the problems that have always given rise to religions. Notable among these was Margaret Reede, on whom we reported in detail. It was not solely her relation to her husband and to her own work that was at issue, but the very meaning to her of life itself. Nancy

219

Kane, who had but one interview with us at the center, and then stopped her counseling because of her husband's disapproval, said in that interview that she wished she might have been able to have her counseling at the church instead of the center. The inference is that, if the church had been behind it, perhaps she could have taken the risk of going against her husband's wishes.

Context is our term for what differentiates the pastor's counseling from that of other counselors. As we now see on analysis, this context may mean quite different things to different people even when they are for religion and the church. Yet if they seek help at the church at all, our study suggests the pastor has at least some good chance of being of help to them. We believe we have shown that the attempt to understand and to articulate to ourselves the feelings people have about the whole context in which pastoral counseling takes place, is not a nuisance but a vital instrument in the giving of help.

Appendix A

☐ FORMAL CHARACTERISTICS OF PEOPLE WHO RECEIVED
COUNSELING DURING THE TWO-YEAR PERIOD OF THE RESEARCH STUDY

The Research Group

(The figure for number of interviews includes the initial and follow-up).

		Church				Center	
Name	Age	Marital Status	Number of Interviews	Name	Age	Marital Status	Number of Interviews
Esther Merz	37	Widow [f]	22	Anne Vick	38	Married [a]	18
Helen Wright	42	Married	22	Margaret Reede	45	Married [e]	21
Cora Verne	32	Single	22	Catherine Frome	31	Married	14
Betty Earle	30	Married [b]	22	Sharon Troy	27	Single [a]	14
Alfred Johnson	33	Married	14	Bruce Charles	41	Married	12
Susan Graham	18	Single [a]	4	Laurie Day	19	Single	6
Shirley Vance	42	Married [b]	7	Ruth Farr	36	Married [b]	19
Amy Tone	35	Married [b]	21	Sarah Bloom	34	Married	19
Evelyn Brent	26	Divorced	5	Jane Young	24	Single	12
Mary Keene	30	Married [c]	16	Lucy Todd	34	Married [b]	4
Martha Williams	52	Divorced	22				
Thelma Phillips	62	Divorced	22				
Erma Austin	34	Married	6				
				Bart Lowe	41	Single	12
				Nancy Kane	33	Married	1
Median Age	34		Total Number of Interviews 205	Median Age	34		Total Number of Interviews 152

Median Number of Interviews   21 (Church), 14 (Center)

a. Married during the counseling period.
b. Previously divorced, but presently married to different spouse.
c. Separated from spouse at beginning, but reunited during counseling.
d. Separated from spouse at beginning, not reunited during counseling.
e. Divorced during the counseling period.
f. Previously divorced, presently widowed at death of recent spouse.

221

People With Whom We Counseled Who Were Not in Research

		Church					Center	
Name	Age	Marital Status	Number of Interviews		Name	Age	Marital Status	Number of Interviews

MEN:

		Church					Center	
Arthur Anderson	45	Married	2		Roger Waite	40	Single *	17
Edgar Cole	51	Married	7		Thomas Nye	23	Single	3
Philip Freeman	53	Married	16		Edward Sturn	37	Married	15
Eugene Grant	56	Married *	14		Joseph Camp	35	Married	2
Charles Hugh	47	Married *	2		Donald Black	22	Single	5
Samuel James	21	Married	8		Brady Means	20	Single	4
Evan Kent	45	Married	4					
Timothy Lake	26	Single	4					
Paul Lucas	29	Single	2					
David Robbins	40	Married *	3					
Median Age	45	Total	62		Median Age	29	Total	46
		Median	4				Median	5

WOMEN:

		Church					Center	
Marjorie Anderson (wife of Arthur)	42	Married	6		Carolyn Rudd	21	Single	22
Barbara Cole (wife of Edgar)	46	Married	10		Ardith Gwynn	26	Single	10
Sally Cole (daughter of Edgar and Barbara)	19	Single	3		Roberta Evans	36	Married	11
Alice Freeman (wife of Philip)	50	Married	4		Grace Lee	28	Married	2
Felicia Grant (wife of Eugene)	44	Married *	2		Deborah Moore	33	Single	4
Kay Hugh (wife of Charles)	45	Married *	5					
Elizabeth James (wife of Samuel)	19	Married	8					

Patricia Jackson	15	Single	10					
Andrea Porter	20	Single	2					
Dorothy Rand	31	Single	2					
Evelyn Sims	50	Divorced	2					
Beatrice Worth	29	Single	3					
Edna Graham (mother of Susan)	45	Married	2					
Median Age	43	Total	59	Median Age	28	Total	49	
		Median	3			Median	10	
Med. Age (all)	44	*Tot. (all)*	121	*Med. Age (all)*	28	*Tot.*	95	
		Med.	4			Med.	5	

ᵃ Married during the counseling period.
ᵇ Previously divorced, but presently married to different spouse.
ᶜ Separated from spouse at beginning, but reunited during counseling.
ᵈ Separated from spouse at beginning, not reunited during counseling.
ᵉ Divorced during the counseling period.
ᶠ Previously divorced, presently widowed at death of recent spouse.

We saw a total of fifty-nine persons during the two-year period for a total of 573 interviews, of which 326 were at the church and 247 at the counseling center. Of the total number of persons, forty were women—twenty-five at the church, fifteen at the center—and nineteen were men—eleven at the church, eight at the center.

We asked forty persons—twenty-four at the church, sixteen at the center—to take part in the study. The remaining nineteen were not asked for the following reasons: Four people at the church were in the city temporarily—college students on vacation; twelve people at both the church and the center asked for counseling too late in the allotted period of time for the project to be included; and three people had begun counseling before the testing program could be put into operation, hence data from these were invalidated.

Of the forty invited to participate in the project, twenty-five consented and received the initial testing prior to the beginning of actual counseling, while fifteen persons declined the invitation. Later eleven of the fifteen granted us permission to use material concerning them, with our reassurances that all such material would be disguised to protect their identity. However, since there were no electronically recorded data to which to refer and no time left after processing the material we were already getting, we could not draw on data from the nonresearch people.

MEDIAN AGE OF PEOPLE IN THE STUDY

The Median Age:

Of all persons seen in counseling 35
  1. All women 34
  2. All men 40

Of people in research:
  1. All 34
  2. All women 32
  3. Women at the church 34
  4. Women at the center 33

Of people not in research:
  1. All 36
  2. All women 32
  3. Women at the church 43
  4. Women at the center 28
  5. All men 38
  6. Men at the church 45
  7. Men at the center 29
  8. All at the church 44
  9. All at the center 28

On the whole, the group of people who did not wish to take part in our study at the church were older—median age 44—than those at the center—median age 28—and all those who participated in the research—median age 34. We may conclude that the older people were more reluctant to be involved in research than the younger of either the church or the counseling center. This was especially true of the men of the church in their forties and fifties.

For this reason, unfortunately, the research study was relatively short on case studies typical of the men seen in counseling. The age discrepancy between the people at the church and those at the center would have made matching difficult even if they had consented to be included in the study. In fact, it became readily apparent toward the end of the research period that the median age of the people we were seeing at the church was actually considerably older than that of the center as a whole, which is understandable in

224

view of the latter's location in a university community. However, this factor tended to complicate our efforts to match the people. Despite such complexities it was remarkable how closely matched in many characteristics, even including ways of approaching situations, were the pairs of people actually representing the two groups.

MARITAL STATUS

Change in marital status among all persons seen in counseling:

No change 49
Reconciliation 6
Divorced 1
Married 3

MARITAL STATUS OF WOMEN

Married		Single	Widowed	Divorced
Tone	Anderson	Graham	Merz	Brent
Vance	Cole	Verne		Williams
Earle	Freeman	Day		Phillips
Keene	Grant	Troy		Sims
Wright	Hugh	Young		
Austin	James	Cole		
Bloom	Graham	Jackson		
Farr	Evans	Porter		
Todd	Lee	Rand		
Vick		Worth		
Reede		Rudd		
Frome		Gwynn		
Kane		Moore		

Married at start 22   Previously Divorced 5
Single at start 13   Divorced during counseling ... 1
Widowed at start 1
Divorced at start 4   6

                    40

MARITAL STATUS OF MEN

Married	Single	Widowed	Divorced
Johnson	Lowe	0	0
Charles	Waite		
Anderson	Nye		
Cole	Black		
Freeman	Means		
Grant	Lake		

Married	Single
Hugh	Lucas
James	
Kent	
Robbins	
Sturn	
Camp	

Married at start 12
Single at start 7
Widowed at start 0
Divorced at start 0

────
19

Appendix B

COUNSELING SKETCHES

☐ The sketches of the personality and the counseling of the persons in the first three matched pairs are shorter than the accounts of the six persons presented in the main text but are of sufficient length to tell the story. The accounts of the remaining thirteen persons who participated in the research are merely thumbnail sketches, but they will provide the reader with the flavor of the other cases that could not, for reasons of space, be presented at length.

Betty Earle (Church)—Sharon Troy (Center)

Betty Earle. Frightened by frequently recurring nightmare-type dreams about terrifying experiences in her recent past, Betty Earle was also alarmed at having a constant "jittery feeling." She almost wept in saying, "Sometimes I feel that I'm cracking up, and I worry about it."

Always stylishly and neatly dressed, Mrs. Earle was a thirty-year-old mother of two daughters, one by each of her marriages, Pat, who was now eight years old, and Melody, three. Tall and well-proportioned, Mrs. Earle was a strawberry blond with sparkling brown eyes. She gave the general impression of a smart, sophisticated, and intelligent young woman who made friends easily.

Several years previously, she said, she had been divorced. She was concerned about how the whole experience had affected Pat, her daughter of that marriage. About her former husband she mourned, "He hurt and humiliated me, but I don't want this to affect my family now." She feared, however, that just that was happening. "I know I'm a lousy mother to Pat, but I get so provoked with her sometimes I don't know what to do."

She spoke, on the one hand, of "Pat's scars" dating from the time husband and wife lived together, and on the other hand of Pat as a

227

symbol to her of the unhappy marriage, "I'm afraid that just being around Pat reminds me of those very unpleasant times." She saw Pat as trigger to her memory and also as "the victim in the whole thing."

Trapped. Throughout the early interviews with Mrs. Earle the central theme was her responsibility to Pat and how she could meet it with benefit to Pat. In the second session she made the following statement:

MRS. EARLE: I don't see why it is that way except that maybe I have lost the love that I had for her when she was tiny and that affection that daily grows when you're with them, because I wasn't with her after she reached the age of about seventeen months. I just wasn't with her. But prior to that—ah—time before I went to work there were periods when I ignored her even as a baby. Although she was a very good baby I just ignored her when I often could have or should have taken better care of her and not felt so sorry for myself and not spent so much time on myself. I should have spent more time with her, and want to—see? Of course when I went to work it was because there was no other choice—ah—no other way.

I told you how we were living and about the life she had and what kind of a dirty, filthy hole she had to live in. And that was the thing that motivated me to leave it and go out and get work. And at least if I couldn't have a home to bring her to of my own that I could keep the way I wanted it, I'd take her to someone else's home that was decent enough for her to be in. And that's just what I did do.

Mrs. Earle was trying, in the early interviews, to come to terms with her feeling of being trapped—by the marriage and the hangovers from it, by enforced separation from Pat, by poor living conditions, by her own guilt in relation to Pat, and even by her recognition of her own attempts to justify what she had done.

Fear of Authority. After the early sessions, Mrs. Earle was able to move on to various levels of feeling within herself and examine them directly. Although much of this was contemporary and from the recent past, some of it evoked memories from her childhood too. Especially as a result of her recollections of childhood, she became aware of and articulated a particular pattern concerning her relation-

228

ships with other people. With people she regarded as peers or inferiors she felt and acted at ease. But with persons in positions of authority, "I feel all shaky and weepy."

The early recollections brought her some insight into recent happenings. After doing just what she had resolved not to do while talking to teachers at Pat's school, she had tried once more. "This time I made up my mind that I would just be calm and talk things out," she related. But the emotionality before authority was such that "as soon as I actually confronted Pat's teacher I weakened and went through the same experience all over again. I don't know what's the matter with me. I get so disgusted about it."

At the conclusion of one of the later interviews, as Mrs. Earle was in process of leaving, she spoke of ministers as authority figures. She said, "I have always been afraid to talk with ministers and thought they would be the last people with whom I could really open up and talk as I have with you. Since I have been talking with you, I think I have begun to develop some confidence in myself." She cited a recent visit to talk with one of Pat's teachers. "Oh, sure, I was shaky," she admitted, "but at least I didn't completely lose control of myself like I have in the past."

Three Sources of New Confidence. As the sessions approached their close, Mrs. Earle reported that, although she was still experiencing "ups and downs," her whole feeling tone had improved and she was even sleeping much better. Although she continued to worry at times about Pat's behavior and what she ought to do about it, she had concluded that "this is a matter that's going to require a little time."

At the twentieth and final interview she said she continued to have moments of anxiety about terminating the counseling, but she had decided not to ask to continue for the time being. Since she knew that she was free to return at any time, she went on, the termination would give her a chance to see "how I get along without coming for a while." The knowledge that she could return and the new kind of self-confidence enabling her to try it on her own were two of her three new sources of confidence. She put it in this way:

MRS. EARLE: Well, I have changed quite a bit. I have more confidence in myself and—ah—you see, before I came here I was so troubled—ah—that I would deliberately go into the past and dig up excuses or reasons or whatever you want to call them to rationalize what I'm doing now. And now that I realize that I can use my own thinking apparatus and probe a little bit—that there's no reason why I have to do that—why I have to get all this stuff involving myself out.

No, I'm happy with things the way they are now and the way I feel about it. If I run into any more problems that I know I can't handle, I'm confident that I can come back and you will help me (*laughs*). So if I ever need a crutch, you make a good one (*laughs again*). I'm not worried about cracking up any more. I was when I came here. I was very worried about it, but I'm not worried about it any more.

Throughout the period of her counseling, Mrs. Earle had been active in the life of the church, attending worship, participating in one of the women's groups, and serving as a teacher in the nursery. Apparently such activities became even more meaningful to her after the counseling. She said the church groups provide "the kind of friendly atmosphere where I can put into practice some of the insights into myself which I have gained, and I'm feeling much more secure."

Summary on Betty Earle. Our evaluation of Mrs. Earle certainly shows her as making almost steady improvement from the first to the final counseling session. When she began, she was anxious, unable to control her emotionality, self-condemnatory concerning her relations with her daughter, Pat, feeling trapped by her past, worried lest she might be cracking up. When she finished, she felt she could take hold of her life and yet not be frightened if she failed at some point, for she could get further help. She was doing better with her daughter, especially by being more patient both with daughter and with herself and thus able to see this in longer-term perspective. While acknowledging more clearly than ever her emotionality, especially before authority, she was no longer terrorized by it. Although her past was not and never could be dead, it no longer walked hourly as a specter to destroy the present. The improvement is undoubted by virtually any standards.

Granted some understanding, acceptance, and skill in the pastoral counseling, what was it that enabled Mrs. Earle to profit from these? Our judgment is that, from the beginning, Mrs. Earle had much more inner strength, both actual and potential, than she herself realized. For example, she had to go to work, but at no point was there whining about this necessity. From the start she recognized she had had some negative, as well as positive, feelings about Pat. Such a recognition is strength not weakness. After her feelings about Pat had emerged in the early sessions she was able to move to direct consideration of her own feelings and to deal forthrightly, albeit painfully, with such negative feelings as her shaking before authority figures. Although the focus of what she brought out in counseling was always the present or the recent past, she was able spontaneously to link discoveries here with feelings and events in her distant past. Troubled as she was at the start of her counseling, she nevertheless remained active in several dimensions of the life of the church. All these things manifested greater strength than Mrs. Earle knew. There was strength too in what she was *not* preoccupied with. Divorced, and with a child, she might have bemoaned poor chances on the marital market, but she had not. Putting herself in order was the best thing she could do to strengthen her present marriage, which she maintained was "so good, I don't want any of this past business to affect it."

We have asserted the presence of greater strengths in Mrs. Earle than she knew. Yet, without the counseling, she might well have continued in the state of fear she had at the start. The pastor was indeed, as she said, a "crutch," a crutch of temporary value to one who is not a permanent invalid. He was also a "bridge," especially through his being an authority figure who nevertheless manifested something of which her early experience had taught her to believe authorities devoid. This was accomplished, for the practical purposes necessary, without systematic analysis of early childhood relationships. Whatever the sources of trouble in Mrs. Earle's marriage, her own contributions to the difficulty had been rooted in just the kinds of feeling and attitude with which the counseling was able to deal contemporaneously. It is probable that the "authority-figure" dimensions of her husband were those with which she had been unable to deal. From here on she would be more alert not only to such aspects of other people but even more to such ambivalent tendencies in herself. Hence we believe the counseling built permanently for her future, whatever in detail that turns out to be.

Sharon Troy. A tall, slender, unmarried woman in her late twenties, Sharon Troy gave evidence immediately both of her sophistication and of her strong motivation for counseling. From the first session she dug in and worked hard on her concern, which was the "maddening indecision over whether or not to marry the young man I am dating." Her sophistication was shown by the way in which she originally posed the problem. There was no uncertainty about her positive feeling for the young man. But there was uncertainty about what he really represented to her. She feared that he meant to her a strong arm, especially in social situations, thus playing into her dependency needs which she was trying to get hold of. In an early session she spoke as follows:

Miss Troy: I think I mentioned in my first interview that my main reason for coming was because of my coming marriage, and I was very distraught about that at the time. I feel that I'm a very rigid, inflexible person in an awful lot of situations, and I would like to acquire more flexibility, maybe more tolerance—I don't even know if tolerance is part of it—but this is one of the reasons why I'm so attracted to the young man right now. Because he's so creative and imaginative—and through him I have done a lot of things that I wouldn't even think of doing by myself—I mean they would never have entered my mind. And yet once I'm doing them I enjoy them very much.

I don't know if I'm explaining it too well. But he has—he adds so much to my life, since we've known each other. For a long time I've disliked the idea of getting married because I don't like the role of a housewife and a mother. I thought of it as very dull, boring, and routine. And I thought that not having enough ambition or stimulation within myself—once I got married and was further handicapped by the responsibilities of a wife and a mother—I would just fall into this shapeless mass that knew no more than to hang up the wash and cook supper.

I dread this very much. And so many of the fellows that I have dated were very, very nice, and I enjoyed their company, but when I envisioned myself as being married to them I thought that such was the role that I would naturally assume. But with the young man I'm going with now—he too has noticed this

232

lack of creativeness and he's very anxious to help me in this area. Then I worry that if this is what my love is based upon, and if that is the reason I want to get married—that I wouldn't want this all by itself.

The turning point in Miss Troy's counseling came when she, spontaneously, began to realize that the very tendencies in her that pulled her two ways in relation to her boy friend were also being manifested in the counseling relationship. During the fifth session she said she was finding herself quite anxious about the counseling and feeling "very threatened by it all." She continued, "It's the realization that something seems to be expected from me. I don't know what I thought this counseling would do—sort of magically remove all my problems, I guess. I think now I am seeing it more realistically." Thus the counseling relationship itself, with its encouragement to her to assume all the initiative she could, both enabled and compelled her to try to come to terms with these conflicting forces within herself.

Progress on Passivity. About midway through her counseling Miss Troy summed up her experience in an interchange to which we have already referred. (See page 46.) She had commented on her changed expectations from the counseling, saying she felt considerably frustrated when she learned changes didn't "just happen." She had to work at it. Now, in retrospect, she recognized "things were happening," especially she was "seeing things in a new light at home."

The new light that had been coming, she continued, also embraced the indecision aspect of her passivity. Now, she noted, she was conscious of "being in control" more than she had been. She was gaining satisfaction from making decisions and acting in terms of them.

Out of the Shell. In one of the later sessions she described them as providing "much needed times for reflecting upon my lack of courage in social situations." Her "experiments," as she called them, "at coming out of my shell," had on some occasions produced amazing results, and she hoped this relative success was both genuine and permanent.

At this same period Miss Troy felt she was, for the first time, being accepted by groups that were important to her. Also she reported herself as viewing her boy friend in a different way. "We are beginning to interact more," she said, "and I think we are reaching a deeper

233

and better level in our relationship. And I'm seeing him as a person more than as an idol."

At the tenth interview Miss Troy said she believed she was about ready to terminate because "I'm getting along quite well, and I really need the time remaining to prepare for my trip overseas." She said she felt that something very positive was happening but she was not yet quite sure of its nature, and therefore she wanted to return later on for some additional sessions "to see how it goes in the meantime."

MISS TROY: I'm still riding along feeling very good, very capable and confident. I'm sort of waiting to see when I'm going to fall over (*laughs*). I wonder if this is the usual reaction—that you go through this stage of complaining about what you can't do? I can't feel that I'm cured. I don't even know what I would be cured of. But it's just that I have a different feeling than I had when I first started.

I really wasn't sure what to expect after the counseling—even at the end—because I hadn't looked forward to the end too much. I was sort of going session by session and seeing what came out.

I was talking with a girl friend yesterday who is very interested in my counseling and wants to know more about it. She was one of the first persons I spoke to saying that I needed someone to talk to, and she made the suggestion that I see one of the doctors over at the hospital. Occasionally when I see her, I have to tell her what is going on. And I really sound so enthusiastic she just sits there and sort of blinks her eyes. But I just find it good to be able to sit and talk to her about it and say the same things that I've said to you—so that I suddenly feel that I have more of a grasp of myself and am not floundering around so much.

Complexity Less Threatening. Miss Troy's new enthusiasm was evident even in the counseling sessions. But this feeling seemed to be justified by the success of her various "experimentations."

MISS TROY: And a lot of my anxiety seems to have disappeared. There are still things that I think about, but I don't become as anxious or worried about them as I did in the past. I can still go back and name them off and certainly feel that they are things to be considered and will require a lot of thought. But they don't give me this very terrified feeling—you know, that everything is just rolling in on me and if I make the step in the wrong direction about something the bottom's going to fall out.

And I find myself looking forward to getting married. The problem now is that I can't anticipate my overseas trip as much because I'm thinking, "Oh, I wish I didn't have to go away for so long." Maybe I'll come back sooner than I had planned.

The following interview came twelve days later owing to Miss Troy's packing:

MISS TROY: It's been very nice, the last week and a half. I think I really got along very well. I think I felt a little apprehensive at first—I don't know what I was apprehensive about but probably a combination of this new-found freedom and—a thought that something might come up. But nothing horrible happened and I got along very well.

I have a nagging feeling, however, that I'm also letting myself slide back by not projecting myself as much as I was before. But I can't even say that I had some urging, but I was just being made more aware of myself and my interaction with other people. Twice a week this was going on, and that was enough so that even when I wasn't seeing you I was aware of these things.

Just in the last week and a half or two weeks the edge has worn off and been dulled a bit, and I didn't realize it until today. That was a funny thing because I'd been thinking that things hadn't changed too much since I had seen you last and that I hadn't had any great anxieties and everything was going along smoothly.

And then, when I was writing this letter to a friend that I hadn't written to in a couple of months, I said I hadn't written because I was so busy with my trip plans. And that started me thinking. I said I was writing because I was sort of caught up on my trip plans. And then I was wondering whether I was really caught up, or was something taking its place?

I'm glad I thought of it because I like being—having this awareness and—and being on tiptoe. Looking at myself, looking around me, and not falling back.

235

Holding the Line. The final interview came several weeks later, just before Miss Troy's departure for Europe. She had used the intervening time to get ready. When she arrived for this twelfth session, Miss Troy plunged at once into her relationship with her sister with whom she had previously felt uncomfortable and inferior. She felt that they were, for the first time, "treating each other as equals." She reported the sister as pleased about her forthcoming marriage and said she had offered to help with the plans "but had not kind of taken over like she has done in the past." The remainder of the final session was all about Miss Troy's feelings of satisfaction over her progress.

About four months later, after her return from Europe, Miss Troy appeared for her follow-up interview, the sole time when she could manage it. Unfortunately, circumstances prevented a follow-up testing session for her. During this last interview, Miss Troy repeated her appreciation for the counseling experience, talked enthusiastically about her trip, and spoke happily about her forthcoming marriage. The pre-test and post-test findings—in Miss Troy these could not include a later follow-up period of testing—showed Miss Troy at the top of the list for significant positive changes at the close of her counseling.

Summary on Sharon Troy. The testing data showed Miss Troy as having made remarkable progress through her counseling, and our subjective impression tends to confirm this. Unlike many of the other women in this study, Miss Troy had few if any past catastrophic events to come to terms with—no divorced husband, children in trouble, dominating mother, or other similar situations. In relation to such potential events later in her life, she was, as much as anyone else we have tried to help, engaged in a kind of "preventive counseling."

At the beginning of her counseling we noted that Miss Troy had a good deal of psychological sophistication. She liked her boy friend but wondered if part of the reason for her attraction to him were unsound. In her head she apparently did sense something of the mixed motivations. Yet the test results before counseling suggest that this had not permeated. What the counseling did was to "visceralize" insights Miss Troy almost had in her head from the beginning. To change the metaphor, these could be genuinely realized only as they were domesticated.

236

Except for the needed decision to marry or not marry the boy friend, there were few pressures on Miss Troy of an external kind. This relative lightness of pressure may well have contributed to her ability to move ahead. Yet the fact generally is that persons no worse off than Miss Troy seldom seek counseling at all, even though they may be, as she proves, just the people most likely to profit from it.

By seeking counseling concerning her relationship to her boy friend, Miss Troy ran the risk of not being taken seriously—as would not have been possible if she had been contemplating divorce, were an alcoholic, or hated her child. Part of the acceptance the counselor needed to give her, therefore, involved accepting both her and her problem—because hers—as important even though she manifested no psychological equivalent of cancer, fracture, or thrombosis.

Once such acceptance was assured to Miss Troy, she began to realize the reality of her own passivity. This came to a head when, spontaneously, she saw this emerging in her part of the counseling relationship itself. That proved to be the turning point. Beneath her passivity, she saw, was a genuine desire to assume responsible initiative for her own life. She "tested out" this new-found picture of her own potentialities and in various orders of relationship found it solid and reassuring. If her passivity had been of the aggressive type it is most unlikely that any similar result could have been achieved.

Betty Earle and Sharon Troy. Not the least among a number of similarities between Mrs. Earle and Miss Troy was their high motivation for counseling. Both of them scored highest in their respective groups for change in adjustment scores from the beginning to the termination of counseling. On the Thematic Apperception Test both changed in all areas assessed by the tests, and made strongly positive overall gains.

Neither subjective evaluations nor objective tests were able to distinguish marked differences between Mrs. Earle and Miss Troy, but the latter scored the highest of both groups on all the tests.

Alfred Johnson (Church)—Bruce Charles (Center)

Alfred Johnson. Mr. Johnson was a salesman. Although he was relatively successful at his work, he was worried about being on the defensive with people. At the outset he said he also feared "a failing memory." With an embarrassed laugh he asked, "Am I losing my

237

mind? I get things in my mind that just stick there—ah—like trying to remember somebody's name. I work on it for days. I get worried when I can't remember something. Something as simple as that wears me out and makes me tense and nervous."

Frightened by Blocking. In his early thirties, Mr. Johnson was of average size and height but unusually muscular. He met people in an amiable but restrained manner. His modest and unassuming approach was generally more successful than a high-pressure manner would have been, and his recognition of this enabled him to deal successfully with what he felt to be a long-standing feeling of shyness. As an adolescent, he said, he had been withdrawn and had found it difficult to talk with people about anything of importance. He had then had, he continued, private torments which he now saw as needless.

Part of his reason in coming for counseling was his ambivalent feeling about having children. For some years, he said, he had refused to consider bringing children into the world because he recognized his own emotional instability. "I don't think I would be a fit father in this condition," he said. Yet he plainly felt guilty about denying his wife the family that she especially desired.

He told of an event that had happened when he was in high school. Lying in bed one morning, he had felt his scrotum, discovering that his testicles seemed to have disappeared. He had been terribly frightened by this situation but had not dared ask anyone about it. As a result, he said, "I worried a lot about it even after I found them there later. But I just never could talk with anyone about it."

On the Defensive. Related to his inhibition and forgetting, Mr. Johnson continued, was his tendency to react to people defensively especially if he felt they were "pushing me too much." The trouble was, however, he went on, "I can't tell whether they are or not. I guess I have a chip on my shoulder with most people. I think I could do even better selling if I could get over this."

During the seventh interview, Mr. Johnson said he felt he had gained insight into his defensiveness. He recalled an incident that had taken place with a teacher when he was in high school, which resulted in his getting a raw deal. The recollection of that painful experience, he said, had come back to him many times, showing him that he often reacted to other people as he had once to the high-school teacher. His own explanation was, "I think my whole problem could possibly stem from holding on to thoughts that I should have just cleared my mind of. I let things bother me 'way in the back of my mind, and feel a lot of resentment. But I don't let it come out. Then when it does come out it comes at the wrong time and—I guess I just kind of let my emotions loose." We felt this represented a meaningful new hold on his own life.

By the eighth interview he reported that he was "already getting along better with people." He added, "Now that I realize what I was doing—ah—I don't fly off the handle like I did." Whatever the source of these reactions, in his early life, it apparently gave him much better control over his reactions simply to have clarified them with someone and to have recognized that they were often noncontemporary in their reference.

On the Road Back. During the two additional sessions—making a total of ten—that he continued the counseling, Mr. Johnson said he was pleased to discover how much better he felt "in being released from some of my fears." He said he had decided to discontinue the counseling for a month in order to see "how things go." At the final interview he said he felt he could "get along by myself now."

After his summer vacation Mr. Johnson came to Colston simply to report, and not for counseling, that his wife was pregnant and that he was looking forward to the birth of their first child. He expressed strong feelings of gratitude to the counselor "for getting me on the road back." The counseling, he continued, had not worked miracles, "Not everything has gone smoothly. But it hasn't bothered me too much. What pleases me is I'm accomplishing much more and feel better about it."

Summary on Alfred Johnson. In his early thirties, Alfred Johnson had been so cowed by life that he was afraid to have children, intimidated by his work despite its reasonable success, and overtly concerned because of his compulsive emotionalism in dealing with people. Although the genetic roots of his difficulty were not directly touched, the briefer and less profound experience of pastoral counseling was apparently adequate to enable him to turn several corners.

Mr. Johnson had a positive feeling toward the church. He came originally to talk with Hiltner about counseling after hearing him make a speech about personal problems and their resolution. Thus

239

from the beginning of his actual counseling—with Colston—he associated the church with a counseling function.

Bruce Charles. At the time he came to the counseling center, Lieutenant Bruce Charles of the Army requested intensive counseling because he expected, in a few months, to be transferred to a distant post. Thus what he asked for was short-term but intensive counseling. It proved possible to accept him for counseling at once, and his satisfaction about that perhaps affected his decision to participate in our study. His geographical transfer came rather earlier than expected; and owing to this, he was able to have only eleven interviews before leaving Chicago. Everyone else in the study was able to select his own time for terminating counseling.

Between Two Poles. Lieutenant Charles stated initially that he felt torn between "two strong poles." One pole was his desire to have the "stimulation and adventure" of an intellectual community, while the other was "to provide as I am able now to do for my family, to play it safe, stay where I am, and make the next move with the Army."

Although he looked yearningly at the first alternative, he said he had rejected it because "at forty-one years of age it seems foolish to subject myself and especially my family to the rigors of additional preparation for what I would really like to do." The following statement, which appeared in the ninth interview, is his own best analysis of his dilemma:

LIEUTENANT CHARLES: If you really believe that you have done your best, that's the thing. I'm not real sure of—but, if you're not diddling—but I'm not real sure that it's respectable entirely about having regrets about leaving because I surely can't kick about being sent here. All I asked for was for a large city with a university. And this is one university that suits me just exactly. Precisely with everything just made to order. And if I could get what I wanted and everything, I would take all the work where you have to think something here. Darn it, it doesn't look like I'm ever going to come to grips with this thing at all. It would be awful nice if there were only machines that you could go to and put in a nickel for the little issues and put in a quarter for the big problems. And find out what really works. I don't know

240

what's right. It—ah—I think it actually makes me a little angry. I don't think I've ever known. I didn't know what I was supposed to do in college. I never did. I never knew at all clearly, for fifteen years, what it was really all about. So I never felt that I had any calling or purpose or goal but I always had a feeling that a person ought to have that. I've always wondered if other people were doing better in this regard than me, except doctors and scientists. If you knew really what was right, then all the hardships would be something that you could take. Even the risk of chance. That's something you can accept, but when you don't honestly know what is right you can't really find anything, any yardstick or anything else. Then you really don't know. At some point you have to say— well, it really doesn't make much difference.

Point of No Return. In the eleventh and final interview, when Lieutenant Charles was completely packed and ready for his long trip to his new post, he nevertheless continued to "toy with the idea" of resigning from the Army and registering in a university. Taken at face value, his statements in this last interview showed great indecision. He said he hoped that a friend of his who was a college administrator would, at this last minute, make him such a good offer that he would no longer have to see going into academic work as foolish and sacrificial to his family. No such offer came, and he made the Army move.

Certainly Lieutenant Charles' dilemma, like that of any other human being, was individual in character. Yet it seems to have been precipitated, so as to make him seek help through counseling, in part by his stage in life. A few years earlier he might have made the break, taken university work with real but yet tolerable sacrifice to his family, and had some chance of finding what seemed to him a meaningful utopia in an academic community. At forty-one, without special resources, such an option is immensely more remote. If he were decisive and energetic in his whole approach to life, such a course might not even now be impossible. But since he has rather drifted into his Army career, is not far along its ladder for his age, and presents a life history of indecisiveness, such an option is in fact out of the question for him. Even before his counseling begins, something within him tells him he has reached the point of no return. That the coun-

241

seling, especially taking place in an academic community, did not wholly resolve his dilemma is perhaps itself an indication that it stayed intimately with him and with his feelings, so far as he could come to terms with them. Had it been possible for the counseling to continue, we would have hoped to see first Lieutenant Charles's confrontation of his point of no return in more direct and realistic fashion, somewhat after the fashion of a grief reaction—true sorrow, but gradual emergence of the ability to live with what had been lost —what might have been. We would then have hoped for one of two things—either his taking the Army career seriously and finding needed additional stimuli elsewhere at the same time, or his developing enough strength of personality to move toward something else which, while it might involve temporary sacrifice, would nevertheless be tolerable.

Summary on Bruce Charles. In more senses than one, Lieutenant Charles came for "eleventh-hour" counseling. He had been stationed for some time close to a great university community where counseling had been available all along. Yet he sought counseling only when he anticipated transfer. Entering middle life, after having drifted into his present career largely for reasons of security, he faced in fact a point of no return in terms of simple or easy shift of occupation. He had been, so to speak, a "nibbler" at the edges of the academic world. Time and circumstance now converged upon him, and it seemed necessary either to eat or to eject academic life. Our counseling seems to have aided him to move in the direction of confronting the reality of his dilemma, including its irreversible aspects. Circumstance in the form of Army orders compelled its termination. What might have happened had the counseling continued we of course do not know. Under those conditions we have suggested what our hopes would have been.

At no point did Lieutenant Charles make references to his dilemma as being religious from his own point of view. Seeing him at the counseling center, Colston of course made no such interpretation to him. Yet reflection shows his problem as centering upon making one's life meaningful, dealing basically with the ethical issue of security versus fulfillment, learning to cope with the half of life in which not everything can be onward and upward, bigger and better, changing easily if you do not like what you have. If Lieutenant

242

Charles had sought counseling at the church, it is at least more probable that this perspective upon his dilemma might have come into the open. Since it did not so emerge, it was against Colston's approach in counseling to raise it arbitrarily. To do so would, if Lieutenant Charles had been pro-religion, have increased just that sense of guilt which he could not handle; and if he were antireligion, it would have given him new defenses against confronting the basic dilemma.

Alfred Johnson and Bruce Charles. Mr. Johnson had the lowest initial adjustment score of anyone at the church, consequently almost anything positive was "up" for him. He almost reached the median for the church group at the final testing point. His remarkable positive movement, however, was indicated by the follow-up score which was definitely significant of change. Lieutenant Charles's "eleventh hour" pressure, on the other hand, apparently worked a bit in reverse for him. His adjustment score at the termination point was considerably lowered and was the lowest of all the center people. The same was true on his final Thematic Apperception Test. Mr. Johnson made a few gains in critical areas on his Thematic Apperception Test and showed better overall improvement on this test.

Susan Graham (Church)—Laurie Day (Center)

Susan Graham. Eighteen-year-old Susan Graham's calm and matter-of-fact exposition of her "blow-up with my parents" revealed clearly, at the outset of the first interview, that the strong feeling behind her telephone call for a counseling appointment had already subsided. Between the call and the interview, she had a made a move she regarded as decisive. A college freshman who had been living at home, she had just moved to a dormitory room on the campus. Now, she said, things will "work out better." A bit apologetic about having requested the counseling appointment, she went on, "I don't really feel I need counseling now. This move to the campus is what I should have done in the first place."

Finding the pastor ready to accept her change of mind about counseling as understandable, Miss Graham went on to discuss what lay behind the controversy with her parents. This concerned the young man she was dating. Her parents, she said, had openly accused him of influencing Susan against them. The man's intentions toward her, she continued, were serious, and he had proposed marriage to her.

243

She said she was very fond of him and felt torn between her desire to accept his proposal and, on the other side, her desire to have her parents approve the marriage. The parents, as she saw it, felt the man was simply alienating their daughter from them, and an engagement would make this worse in their eyes.

Not wholly to Colston's surprise, since the move to the dormitory had obviously not solved the underlying problems, Miss Graham returned for two more counseling sessions. At the last session she was elated, saying she had gained the courage to tell her parents about her decision to become engaged to her young man. To her great surprise, her parents had accepted her decision. Since this enabled her to reconcile the two sides of her problem, she said, she did not feel need for further counseling at this time. She added, however, that she hoped "if something else comes up I can make another appointment" and of course was given the proper assurance.

Miss Graham did not seek further counseling. But six months after her termination, she appeared promptly in response to our request for a follow-up interview. In the meantime she had been married. The main thing she wanted to convey was that her relationship to her parents had continued to improve following her marriage.

Summary on Susan Graham. So far as our data make it possible to judge, Miss Graham's problem was the rather normal and usual one of an adolescent's need to transcend the old home ties and loyalties without alienation and bitterness. No one's personal problem is ever entirely situational in the sense that it is devoid of the biases put on it by past experience. What seemed to us most significant, retrospectively, about the counseling with Miss Graham was the relation between action and reflection in that portion of her life that was shared with us.

Here is the sequence of events. She and boy friend become close. Parents grow resentful and accuse boy friend of alienating daughter. Daughter, hotly resentful, telephones church for counseling appointment. She then decides to move to dormitory room and does so. Feeling that this action has obviated the need for counseling as first envisaged when she had made the telephone call, she nevertheless appears for counseling appointment. She finds some clarification of her two apparently conflicting desires—to marry the boy, and to have her parents approve this. She continues counseling for two more

244

sessions. On her own—i.e., without proposing a suggested course of action to the pastor and asking what he thinks—she decides to accept the proposal of marriage, confront her parents with it, and hope for the best. To her surprise, they accept her—i.e., they have changed their perspective upon her from child to adult. She marries and, at least for the first few months, all seem to live happily.

Had we not been in our unique situation, we should have been requested to perform the marriage ceremony for Susan Graham and her fiancé, at which time we should have had to consider other factors than those confronting us here. In this instance, however, nothing came to our notice showing the unsuitability of the young couple, provided one accepts marriage at eighteen as a part of normal life.

Why did Miss Graham telephone the church for her counseling appointment? She had been and continued to be active in one of the young people's groups, and her comment on this question—at the follow-up interview—suggests how important the continuity of church relationship may be at the time crisis strikes. She said, "Well, I just know people here and feel I can trust them."

One could hardly assume that two or three counseling sessions would produce sweeping personality changes. Such would be the proper assumption as far as Miss Graham's performance on the post-counseling tests was concerned. However, she indicated striking changes in her self-concept, progressively from beginning to follow-up. Undoubtedly, one major factor, which must not be overlooked, was her marriage during the counseling period. Nevertheless, it is likely that the counseling also contributed to her progress.

Laurie Day. A petite blonde with just a hint of freckles, Laurie Day was nineteen and a college student. At the first interview her sad-looking brown eyes showed unmistakable signs of weeping, and she twisted a dainty handkerchief as she talked. She had come, she said, because she had been having long periods of depression. These were disrupting her school work, over and above the feeling of misery they brought to her. She burst into tears after saying, "Although I have always been a pretty fair student, I am close to failure in some of my courses. This is just not like me at all."

Need to Be Close. Miss Day said she was especially concerned about what "my emotional state is doing to the fellow I'm dating. I can see that I am too emotionally dependent upon him. The more I

245

lean on him, the more I seem to drive him away, and this bothers me. I don't want to frighten him with my feelings, but I seem to be doing it."

When she asked herself why she behaved in that way, her own reply was, "I guess I want somebody I can be close to. I never really could open up to my mother. We've had a very funny kind of a relationship. I think she still regards me as a child, and I just don't feel free to go to her, especially since I've been here. I don't think she understands me."

Miss Day continued for five counseling sessions, the content of which was virtually all of the type illustrated above. She then telephoned to say that she had decided not to continue the counseling. The reason given was that she had become involved in some extra-curricular school activities. Several months later Colston telephoned Miss Day to ask if she would be willing to take the final tests for the purposes of our research. She agreed, and an appointment was made, but she did not appear. Through other sources it was learned that she had, at least for the remainder of that accademic year, left school and returned to her parents' home.

Summary on Laurie Day. Although no evidence came to light in the five counseling sessions that would suggest Miss Day's "depression" to be of psychotic proportions, she nevertheless had a deeper conflict than did Susan Graham. As the excerpts in her own words show, she used the counseling sessions largely for "cathartic" purposes. In the counselor she did find someone ready to listen. Having felt inhibited about talking to her mother, and then having found herself opening up explosively to her boy friend, the talk to the counselor was apparently like a steady and controlled escape of her inner steam.

In the counseling sessions, however, the catharsis had no sequel. She did not begin, in a new way, to take hold of her inner conflict. From our general knowledge of psychodynamics we suspected that her depression masked feelings of unacknowledged hostility and that she was not merely seeking closeness and intimacy. None of her discussion ever moved in such a direction, and we felt it would have been disastrous to make such suggestions. Precisely why she arrested the counseling after the fifth interview is uncertain. Our best guess is that certain psychological material, as for instance the possibility of unrecognized hostility, had been, through the understanding manifested in counseling, brought near the surface and, if she had continued, she would have had to take a different kind of look at herself. Not psychically strong enough to take such a look at this stage, she discontinued. This reaction, if our hypothesis is correct, suggests one respect in which genuine understanding may carry with it threat and judgment from the point of view of the person being helped.

Whether Miss Day's return to her parents' home turned out to be a giving in or a merely strategic retreat, of course we do not know, but whether at home, with her boy friend, or at college, she is probably in for a great deal more inner turmoil than Susan Graham.

Shirley Vance (Church)—Ruth Farr (Center)

Shirley Vance. A stout but attractive housewife in her forties, Mrs. Vance's bulldoglike characteristics were evident even in her talking through clenched teeth. Remarried to a man some years her senior, she was disturbed over the way he treated her children and herself, his staying away from home without explanation, and his refusal to regard any of this as worthy of discussion. Throughout her six counseling sessions Mrs. Vance concentrated single-mindedly upon the problem as she saw it—i.e., how to look at her husband. By the close of the sessions she reported that "things are smoothing out a little." Her tests showed her as making a little progress.

Whatever her husband's vagaries and their initial cause, our interpretation is that Mrs. Vance's tenacity—even about discussing the situation—increased his determination to keep distance between himself and his family. After Mrs. Vance decided that she would try to "let him alone," the chances are that her husband experienced this as a decrease in pressure. With her bulldog qualities, then, Mrs. Vance concentrates on temporarily letting her husband alone. She makes some real, but not bulldoggish, requests of him and is surprised by their congenial reception. We were not able to help her to examine the tenacity itself, but were able to help her to utilize it constructively instead of otherwise. A corner was turned, which is likely to be continuingly helpful in the life situation.

Ruth Farr. A Roman Catholic who had been divorced and was now married to a Protestant, Mrs. Farr had first become concerned over her eight-year-old daughter who was receiving therapy at the

247

counseling center. Her divorce had complicated relationships with her own church, and Mrs. Farr had simply let those ride. Recently, however, she had begun talking with Roman Catholic authorities to clarify her status. Her daughter was attending parochial school.

At first Mrs. Farr saw herself as "over-sensitive," but then as having a "kind of chip on my shoulder most of the time." Once brought out, these feelings were dealt with rather directly during the remainder of the counseling, which extended for nineteen interviews. Before the counseling was over, she said she felt there had been great gains in her relationship to her husband as well as her daughter and in facing up to the reality of her situation with regard to her church. Her test scores showed considerable change.

Our explanation of Mrs. Farr is that, all along, she had had a good deal of genuine inner strength despite her many problems. When her daughter became difficult she swallowed her pride and sought effective help. Then she did the same for herself and had to swallow more pride in discovering how aggressive was the chip on her shoulder. Although her relationship with her church was bound to be other than she would desire, she nevertheless pursued it and clarified her status. All these are marks of strength, upon which the counseling relied. Yet the strength alone, without the counseling, would have been insufficient.

Amy Tone (Church)—Sarah Bloom (Center)

Amy Tone. In her middle thirties, small, dark-haired, and attractive, Mrs. Tone called her problem "getting myself into messes." Divorced and now remarried, she said she had a "terrific antipathy" to the two daughters by her first marriage, and yet "I love my children too." Having once held a responsible and interesting job, Mrs. Tone now missed its satisfactions. "Men get all the breaks," she said. A woman's world has no "adventure" in it. Even when wrestling hardest with her problems, Mrs. Tone never lost her sparkling wit and spontaneous humor.

After her twenty-one interviews, Mrs. Tone felt she was improved but not cured. She said she now found moments when she was "actually enjoying my children." Her test scores showed her as making small overall gains throughout, suggesting the accuracy of her self-assessment. Since the sessions showed that Mrs. Tone had many unresolved problems dating from early relationship to her parents, further improvement at a deeper level would probably have required extended psychotherapy. Yet the counseling brought her genuine gains. Two of her biggest assets were the ability to see the ludicrous side of things and her honest acknowledgment of her negative feelings especially concerning her children.

Sarah Bloom. Mrs. Bloom, also in her mid-thirties, was married and the mother of two children. She co-operated with our research throughout her nineteen interviews, but later requested that no information be reported about her except the test results. Her wish has of course been respected. This much may be said, that it was not ingratitude for the help she felt she had received in counseling but rather the unusual character of her life situation that made her believe it could not be so disguised as to be unrecognizable. Mrs. Bloom's test results showed her gaining during the counseling in motivation but dropping in adjustment, which we interpret positively—that, at the end, she was more dissatisfied with herself and more determined to do something about it than before. By the time of the follow-up testing, she showed continued gains.

Evelyn Brent (Church)—Jane Young (Center)

Evelyn Brent. A tall, slender blond in her late twenties, Mrs. Brent was divorced, earned her living by work in an office, and had a seven-year-old boy who was a "terrific problem." She came for counseling on the urging of a friend and spoke timidly and softly. What she requested was advice on how to "handle" her son. Despite all the counselor's efforts, Mrs. Brent was unable to talk directly about herself. A typical statement was, "It's not me that I'm concerned about." She terminated after five interviews. Her test scores showed no change.

Outwardly timid and well controlled, Mrs. Brent's underlying character was very different. She came to counseling wanting gimmicks. If it had been possible to help her see the relationship to her son as her problem, some limited progress might have been possible, but she was unable to go even this far. All her life Mrs. Brent had presented a mousy exterior and probably had utilized this apparent compliance as a way of getting other people to do what she wanted. This attitude was reinforced by moral righteousness—"It's not me I'm concerned about"—and she could thus avoid considering the

249

deep contradiction within herself. Unless the pastor is aware of the underlying forces people like Mrs. Brent can make him violate his own principles by making him feel professionally guilty.

Jane Young. A young schoolteacher in her mid-twenties, Miss Young presented a sophisticated exterior as she talked about the impasse she had reached in her relationship with a young man who shared her interest in science and in teaching. He was Jewish; she, Roman Catholic. She felt his reaction against her faith was too strong. During the counseling, which continued for twelve sessions, she indicated various phases of an in-and-out relationship with David. Eventually David took himself off the market by his relationship to another girl, but Miss Young did not internally give him up.

Miss Young felt the counseling had helped her, but all the test results went the other way. Her scores were high at the beginning and declined markedly. Our interpretation is that Miss Young was holding herself together by great concentration on surface matters, while underneath there was a strong movement in the direction of apathy and resignation. The tests suggest a flattening out of her affect. Getting the young man seemed the symbolic basis of her self-respect, and as the chance of this declined her interior hopelessness grew. Our counseling with her failed, we believe, because this trend made her less, rather than more, able to deal with the complexities of her own feelings. Ambiguity became less tolerable to her.

Mary Keene (Church)—Lucy Todd (Center)

Mary Keene. A petite woman in the early thirties, Mrs. Keene spent nearly all the time of fourteen interviews complaining about her husband. He refused to let her have children, he changed his mind about getting counseling for himself, his behavior was infantile, he acted as if he were unmarried, and he would have no common interests with his wife. Her refrain was, "I'm so sick of it all."

In the period before her final interview Mrs. Keene's anger toward her husband reached "white heat"; she hit him with her fist; his nose bled all night; and as a result she reported, "I was surprised to discover how much real feeling I had for him." This made her realize, she said, that "I'm just going to have to learn to live with this." Mrs. Keene's test scores showed some movement in a positive direction.

It seemed likely to us that Mrs. Keene's husband had many infantile traits. The evidence, however, pointed to Mrs. Keene's having many similar tendencies. Some of her dependency and passivity had drawn her to this man, whereas she would have had nothing in common with a self-reliant man. Her conclusion that "Somebody's got to stop it" and that she would accept her husband as he was, was certainly realism unless she were able to conquer her own passivity and dependency. Her solution will offend idealists, but the ways of winning peace from tragedy are often less than perfect.

Lucy Todd. In her thirties and mother of a son and a daughter, Mrs. Todd was the sole Negro in our study. Divorced and recently remarried, she entered upon counseling at the center because her son was having "play therapy" there. Yet actual counseling never began. Everything she said was careful, objective, and external. Despite all the counselor's efforts, Mrs. Todd showed strong resistance to opening up at all. After four interviews she terminated counseling.

Our regret over the failure to help Mrs. Todd was not made less by what the tests suggested to the psychologist—even though not shown clearly in scores—that she was a person of high intelligence, unusual sensitivity, and keen perceptions. Our conclusion is that her extreme objectivizing, which is just the opposite of the cultural stereotype of the Negro, had something to do with using her strength to react against the stereotype. Had we recognized this as a possibility at the time, we might have been able to win her confidence enough to lower her resistance to opening up.

Martha Williams (Church)

A tall and pleasant woman of fifty-two, Mrs. Williams had been divorced and was the mother of two teen-agers. She had sought counseling from ministers of the church on various occasions including the time of her divorce, and her present concern involved her relationships with the fifteen-year-old son. She was ready to consider her attitudes toward the boy up to a certain point, although no great light dawned upon her at any time during the counseling. After reflecting upon her sessions, she would go home, try a different tack with her son, meditate upon its effects, and discuss those in counseling. This brought some actual improvement in relationship to the boy. Our guess was that this happened because the new methods suggested to the son that his mother was not so rigid as he had thought.

251

The tests showed no basic positive changes in Mrs. Williams after her counseling. Yet there was some actual improvement in relations with her son. Our interpretation is that Mrs. Williams made certain moves to overcome some of her rigidity—trying new tacks with her boy—and that even the effort had some effect, but that she never was able really to move far enough beyond it to ask what the teen-agers are trying to work out. She seems to us a rather classic example of what Freud referred to as "unconscious guilt feelings." The pastor who failed to recognize this could easily overestimate the progress that counseling with such persons can achieve in limited time.

Thelma Phillips (Church)

A divorced grandmother in her early sixties, Mrs. Phillips came for counseling because she was concerned about being "cut off" from her daughter and grandchildren. The situation was all the harder to understand, she said, because she had always put the interest of her family above her own. "I know I'm partly to blame," she said, "but surely not to deserve this treatment."

As the counseling proceeded Mrs. Phillips came slowly and spontaneously, although imperfectly, to recognize that what she had done for her family was to get attention and recognition from them in the present and to make them feel obligated to her for the future. She came partly to see her apparent altruism as a means of domination. These new understandings from the counseling were of help in her life situation and brought some measure of acceptance from her daughter. The tests showed Mrs. Phillips as making some progress, although she had slipped back a bit at the time of the follow-up testing.

What Mrs. Phillips got was the tools, so to speak, for getting out of her particular kind of difficulty. That she put them to use only in part is no doubt due both to her age and to the long-standing character pattern involved. But she does suggest at the very least that the benefits of counseling may accrue to persons in older years as well as younger.

Erma Austin (Church)

Thirty-four-year-old Mrs. Austin, giving the impression of self-assurance and sensitivity, came for counseling because she was

252

"puzzled" about her ten-year-old daughter, whose school achievement was much less than her tested abilities and who seemed to be "in a fog." She said, "I didn't come for counseling myself. It's my daughter I'm worried about." Colston offered to try to make arrangements for the daughter to be helped at the counseling center; Mrs. Austin agreed; and arrangements were made, but Mrs. Austin then did not follow through. In spite of the counselor's attempt to get Mrs. Austin to deal with herself and her relationship to her daughter, she would not do so and terminated after the sixth interview.

Our interpretation is that Mrs. Austin had an unusually strong dose of the middle-class attitude that regards any seeking of personal help as weakness. She had swallowed some pride to talk about her daughter; she could not swallow more to think about herself or to get direct help for the girl. Her self-assured exterior, beneath which lay the possibility of complicity and guilt concerning her daughter, was her own, but it was made possible and reinforced by this common middle-class attitude of our culture.

Bart Lowe (Center)

A bachelor of forty-one, Mr. Lowe was a shy "peace-maker." Living frugally, he spent his life on working for peace, doing volunteer work for peace organizations, writing a book on "Great Battles of History" to understand the problems of peace, and similar activities. He came for counseling because he felt his "personal inadequacies" stood in the way of making his efforts effective. His comments showed his daily life as preoccupied with small details, as wasting time, as failing to "produce" anything. During the counseling Mr. Lowe did, in a minor way, become more decisive about some things—actually discussing his manuscript with a publisher, learning to play the recorder, having dinner with a girl. The test results showed his self-concept as expanding at the close of counseling, although in other respects he was unchanged. After his twelve interviews a change in his life situation moved him to another part of the country.

Mr. Lowe was the male equivalent of the old-maid stereotype, and his manuscript was a bit like her "sampler." Living frugally without a regular job, so he can pursue intellectual interests, he then wastes the time saved. Persons like this are generally regarded with a mixture of pity and contempt. The main thing counseling may do for Mr.

253

Lowe is to take him seriously. In effect, no one else does so. Because they do not, however, the "loss" of being thought pitiable is partly offset by the "gain" of not having to produce. If taken seriously, such a person has some chance of coming to terms with his lack of productivity. For Mr. Lowe time has marched on and his chances may be small, but they are not nonexistent.

Nancy Kane (Center)

An attractive brunette in her early thirties, Mrs. Kane sought counseling but felt, rightly or wrongly, that she had to conceal this fact from her husband. Having small children, she had to have a baby sitter when she went out, and this added to her apprehensiveness over being found out. She took the tests and had one counseling interview in which she said, "I'm just trapped, I guess." She added, "I had made up my mind I was going to 'sneak out' and get counseling for myself anyway, but I find I just can't do it." She did not return after the initial interview.

References

Foreword

☐ 1. The two ground-breaking books destined to set the tone for later work were John G. McKenzie, *Souls in the Making* (New York: The Macmillan Company, 1929) and Charles T. Holman, *The Cure of Souls* (Chicago: University of Chicago Press, 1932). It is possible that Karl R. Stolz, *Pastoral Psychology* (Nashville: Cokesbury Press, 1932) belongs in this group. Two radical implications of the rising interest were soon in print: Richard C. Cabot and Russell L. Dicks, *The Art of Ministering to the Sick* (New York: The Macmillan Company, 1936), and Anton T. Boisen, *The Exploration of the Inner World* (New York: Harper & Brothers, 1937). Cabot and Dicks began to relate principles to concrete case reports in their search for better pastoral methods. Boisen studied the relation of some forms of religious experience to some forms of mental disorder, driving the obligations of pastoral care into new dimensions of depth. Among the more recent American authors who have been influential are, for example: Carroll A. Wise, *Pastoral Counseling: Its Theory and Practice* (New York: Harper & Brothers, 1951); John Sutherland Bonnell, *Pastoral Psychiatry* (New York: Harper & Brothers, 1938); Wayne E. Oates, *The Christian Pastor* (Philadelphia: The Westminster Press, 1951); and Paul E. Johnson, *Psychology of Pastoral Care* (Nashville: Abingdon Press, 1953). These authors have also published other works bearing on the subject. An attempt to present a brief history of this movement was made in the final section of Charles F. Kemp, *Physicians of the Soul* (New York: The Macmillan Company, 1947). Since much of the best writing has come since 1947, however, his account is only preliminary.

Chapter 1: THE PASTOR AS COUNSELOR

☐ 1. In the order of publication, these four books are: *Pastoral Counseling*, 1949; *The Counselor in Counseling*, 1952; *Preface to Pastoral Theology*, 1958; and *The Christian Shepherd*, 1959. All are published by Abingdon Press.

2. *Op. cit.*, p. 7.

3. *Ibid.*, pp. 125 ff.

4. The most comprehensive recent information about clinical pastoral education is available in the reports of several national conferences on this subject held during the 1950's, some of which are still available from John M. Billinsky, Andover Newton Theological School, Newton Centre 59, Mass.

5. Hiltner, *Pastoral Counseling*, pp. 227 ff. presents samples.

6. An excellent introduction to these studies is contained in *Psychotherapy and Personality Change*, eds. Carl R. Rogers and Rosalind F. Dymond (Chicago: University of Chicago Press, 1954). The reports of studies completed more recently are several and have been published in the psychological journals. The specialist reader may find them most easily by consulting *Psychological Abstracts*, published by the

American Psychological Association, or through the Counseling Center, The University of Chicago, Chicago 37, Ill.

7. The findings of this pilot study were not published. Information about it, however, may be secured from the Department of Pastoral Services, National Council of Churches of Christ in the U. S. A., 475 Riverside Drive, New York 27, N. Y.

8. Concerning this time-limited study at the counseling center, a summary of its research design and some early conclusions drawn from data collected up to the time of writing may be found in John M. Shlien, "Time-Limited Psychotherapy," *Journal of Counseling Psychology*, IV, 4 (1957), 318-21. Segment I of that study provided the model for the counseling center aspect of our research design.

Chapter 2: THE PROBLEM OF CONTEXT

◻ 1. We have not been able to trace the first use of the term "pastoral counseling" in its present meaning, but Holman and Stolz did much to put it into general circulation. Yesterday, today, and forever the British regard it as barbarous to spell "counseling" with but one "l." We do not know who is responsible for this practice, but we like it.

2. *Pastoral Counseling*, pp. 34 ff.

3. Recognition of this point was most clear cut, among the early modern works, in Holman, *op. cit.*

4. On this point we are especially indebted to Donald E. Super, *The Dynamics of Vocational Adjustment* (New York: Harper & Brothers, 1942).

5. An excellent discussion of this in the fields of medicine, psychology, social work, the ministry, education, marriage, and vocation may be found in *Counseling and Psychotherapy* (New York: New York Academy of Sciences, 1955). This is the report of a conference involving several professions, each reporting on how it proceeds in counseling. Parts of the report were reproduced in *Pastoral Psychology* magazine (March, 1956). Hiltner presented a more detailed discussion of the question in "Tension and Mutual Support among the Helping Professions," *The Social Service Review*, XXXI, 4 (December, 1957).

6. One of the best brief statements of what differentiates the pastor from other helpers is by the late Otis R. Rice, and appears in *Alcohol, Science and Society* (New Haven: Quarterly Journal of Studies on Alcohol, 1945), Ch. 28. Other good general discussions are by Russell L. Dicks, *Pastoral Work and Personal Counseling* (New York: The Macmillan Company, 1944), and by Wayne E. Oates, *op. cit.*

7. In many respects the most classic and widely read expression of this view in Protestantism is that of Richard Baxter, *The Reformed Pastor*, first published in 1656 (London: The Epworth Press, 1950).

8. See report of the group headed by Perry in the report issued by the New York Academy of Sciences, cited in note 5.

9. Good discussions of this question may be found in Wayne E. Oates, *The Bible in Pastoral Care* (Philadelphia: The Westminster Press, 1953), and in Lewis J. Sherrill, *The Gift of Power* (New York: The Macmillan Company, 1955).

10. Hiltner has outlined the place of these resources in his *Pastoral Counseling*, pp. 187 ff.

Chapter 3: CONTEXT AND METHOD

◻ 1. Louis Linn and Leo W. Schwarz, *Psychiatry and Religious Experience* (New York: Random House, 1958). The authors are for "religious counseling," which "in both its general principles and its specific practices . . . is different from all other counseling." (P. 116.) The attempt to spell out the "moral and spiritual" resources and role, however, that characterize the clergyman remains ambiguous. The

256

authors wisely warn, as do we, against the clergyman's doing psychotherapy or otherwise imitating some other profession. It is not true, however, as Linn and Schwarz seem to suggest, that if you can put your finger on it it does not belong to the clergyman or that if it is "irrational" (p. 88) it belongs to the psychiatrist. The intention of these authors is excellent, to have the clergyman be himself, to represent what he should represent, and not to be envious of other professions. The execution is, in our judgment, at all points ambiguous and, at some, dangerously misleading.

2. *Die Lehre von der Seelsorge* (Zurich: Evangelische Verlag, 1947 and 1957). Soon to be published in the U. S. A. by John Knox Press.

3. This principle was set forth as the preferred basis of general psychology by Donald Snygg and Arthur W. Combs, *Individual Behavior: A New Frame of Reference for Psychology* (New York: Harper & Brothers, 1949). It has become best known in counseling through Carl R. Rogers's lucid attempts to show that some change of attitude on the part of most counselors is necessary if they are not to depreciate "the difficulty of perceiving through the client's eyes", *Client-Centered Therapy*, (Boston: Houghton Mifflin Company, 1951), p. 32. In its more general meaning, however, this principle is chiefly derivative from Sigmund Freud, who came upon it first, naturally enough, in the special form that is relevant to psychoanalysis. "I now let the patient himself choose the subject of the day's work, and in that way I start out from whatever surface his unconscious happens to be presenting at the moment." Freud, *Collected Papers* (London: The Hogarth Press, 1950), III, 19. Anything remotely resembling a list of questions, or a merely logical movement from one topic to another, became impossible in Freud's view. "On this plan everything that has to do with the clearing-up of a particular symptom emerges piecemeal, woven into various contexts, and distributed over widely separated periods of time." (*Ibid.*) When this principle is generalized beyond the specific therapy of psychoanalysis, it becomes quite similar to what Rogers noted.

4. As a matter of fact, this term is used sparingly in Rogers's published writings. One attempt to prevent the idea from reverting to a mere technique is shown in the use of the phrase, "reflection of attitudes," in *Client-Centered Therapy* (see note 3).

5. Nashville: Abingdon Press, 1952.

6. For the nontechnical reader, the best exposition of the nature, utility, accuracy, and limitations of the tests that may have therapeutic significance is to be found in Molly Harrower, *Appraising Personality* (New York: W. W. Norton and Company, 1952).

7. Several excellent pamphlets for the clergy dealing with such matters as danger signals are published by the National Association for Mental Health and are usually available from local mental health societies.

8. *Pastoral Counseling*, pp. 187 ff.

9. Nashville: Abingdon Press, 1958.

Chapter 4: REPRESENTATIVE CASES

☐ 1. *The Idea of the Holy* (London: Oxford University Press, 1923). Called in German *Das Heilige*, and published several years previously.

2. See, for example, Soren Kierkegaard, *The Concept of Dread* (Princeton, N. J.: Princeton University Press, 1944).

Chapter 7: TEST RESULTS

☐ 1. To what degree do age and sex as such influence the outcome of counseling? A contribution to answering this question has been made by Desmond Cartwright, in "Success in Psychotherapy as a Function of Certain Actuarial Variables," *Journal of Consulting Psychology* (1955), XIX, 5, 357-63. He wrote, "Counselor ratings of success in client-centered psychotherapy for 78 clients were examined in relation to variables of sex, age, student vs. non-student status, and length of therapy. It was found that neither sex nor age were significantly related to degree of rated success."

2. Although it does not discuss the TAT, we suggest that the nontechnical reader interested in further light on the projective tests consult Harrower, *op. cit.* Material on the TAT is presented in more technical fashion in Henry A. Murray, *Explorations in Personality* (New York: Oxford University Press, 1938). The most authoritative account is found in the manual prepared for professional use of the TAT, by Henry A. Murray, *The Thematic Apperception Test Manual* (Cambridge, Mass.: Harvard University Press, 1943).

3. See Rogers and Dymond, *op. cit.*

4. *Ibid.*, Ch. 5.

5. William Stephenson, *The Study of Behavior: Q-Technique and Its Methodology* (Chicago: University of Chicago Press, 1953).

6. New York: Harper & Brothers, 1950. The tests we used were abridged from their use in the Adorno study, and special scoring methods were devised by Desmond Cartwright.

7. The full set of items may be found in Rogers and Dymond, *op. cit.*, p. 79.

8. In order to determine whether or not they had statistical significance all the test results were subjected to statistical treatment. Technically, the level of confidence for statistical significance was regarded as .05. For the benefit of technical readers we present the formula of the one-tailed test used to determine the value of t. When X is the mean average of scores on tests taken before counseling began, Z is the mean average of scores on tests taken at the end of counseling, N is the number of persons involved, and x is the representation of the numerical value of change between the precounseling and post-counseling test scores, then the formula is:

$$ t = \frac{Z - X}{\sqrt{\dfrac{\sum x^2 - \sum (x)^2 \div N}{N(N-1)}}} $$

Chapter 8: CONTEXT AND THE PASTOR

☐ 1. For a pastoral treatment of this see Melvin D. Hugen, *The Church's Ministry to the Older Unmarried* (Grand Rapids, Mich.: William B. Eerdmans Publishing Company, 1959).

2. Blanton, *Now or Never* (Englewood Cliffs, N. J.: Prentice-Hall, Inc., 1959), and Howe, *The Creative Years* (Greenwich, Conn.: The Seabury Press, 1959).

3. Carl G. Jung was the first to make this plain, for example, in *Modern Man in Search of a Soul* (New York: Harcourt, Brace & Company, 1933), Ch. V.

4. *Op. cit.*

5. *The Psychology of Religion* (New York: Charles Scribner's Sons, 1899).

Index